Classical Literature, Translations, &c.

THE WORLD OF HOMER. By ANDREW LANG. 8vo, 6s. 6d. net.

TALES OF TROY AND GREECE. By ANDREW LANG. Crown 8vo, 4s. 6d. net.

HOMER'S ODYSSEY. Done into English Verse. By WILLIAM MORRIS. Crown 8vo, 5s. net.

THE GROWTH OF THE HOMERIC POEMS. By G. WILKINS. 8vo, 6s.

HANDBOOK OF HOMERIC STUDY. By HENRY BROWNE, S.J., M.A. With 22 Plates. Crown 8vo, 6s. net.

HELLENICA. A Collection of Essays on Greek Poetry, Philosophy, History, and Religion. Edited by EVELYN ABBOTT, M.A., LL.D. Crown 8vo, 7s. 6d.

THE EUMENIDES OF ÆSCHYLUS. With Metrical English Translation. By J. F. DAVIES. 8vo, 7s.

THE ARCHARNIANS OF ARISTOPHANES. Translated into English Verse. By R. Y. TYRRELL. Crown 8vo, 1s.

SOPHOCLES. Translated into English Verse. By ROBERT WHITELAW, M.A., Assistant Master in Rugby School. Crown 8vo, 8s. 6d.

RELIGION IN GREEK LITERATURE. By the Rev. LEWIS CAMPBELL, M.A., LL.D. 8vo, 15s.

SELECT EPIGRAMS FROM THE GREEK ANTHOLOGY. Edited, with Revised Text, Translation, Introduction, and Notes, by J. W. MACKAIL, M.A., LL.D. 8vo, 14s. net.

POCKET EDITION, 2 vols. (Greek Text, 1 vol.) (English Translation, 1 vol.), fcap. 8vo, gilt top, each 2s. net; leather, 3s. net.

LECTURES ON GREEK POETRY. By J. W. MACKAIL, M.A., LL.D. 8vo, 9s. 6d. net.

CHARICLES; or, Illustrations of the Private Life of the Ancient Greeks. By W. A. BECKER. Translated by the Rev. F. METCALFE, B.D. With Notes and Excursuses. With 26 Illustrations. Crown 8vo, 3s. 6d.

LONGMANS, GREEN AND CO.
LONDON, NEW YORK, BOMBAY, AND CALCUTTA

Classical Literature, Translations, &c.

DUBLIN TRANSLATIONS INTO GREEK AND LATIN VERSE. Edited by R. Y. TYRRELL. 8vo, 6s.

THE PHARSALIA OF LUCAN. Translated into Blank Verse by Sir EDWARD RIDLEY, sometime Fellow of All Souls College, Oxford, one of the Judges of the High Court of Justice. 8vo, 14s.

CICERO'S CORRESPONDENCE. By R. Y. TYRRELL. Vols. I., II., III., 8vo, each 12s. Vol. IV., 15s. Vol. V., 14s. Vol. VI., 12s. Vol. VII., Index, 7s. 6d.

GALLUS; or, Roman Scenes in the Time of Augustus. By W. A. BECKER. Translated by the Rev. F. METCALFE, B.D. With Notes and Excursuses. With 26 Illustrations. Crown 8vo, 3s. 6d.

A DICTIONARY OF ROMAN AND GREEK ANTIQUITIES. By A. RICH, B.A. With 2000 Illustrations. Crown 8vo, 6s. net.

VIRGIL.

> **THE POEMS OF VIRGIL.** Translated into English Prose. By JOHN CONINGTON. Crown 8vo, gilt top, 6s.
>
> **THE ÆNEID OF VIRGIL.** Translated into English Verse. By JOHN CONINGTON. Crown 8vo, 2s. 6d. net.
>
> **THE ÆNEIDS OF VIRGIL.** Done into English Verse. By WILLIAM MORRIS. Crown 8vo, 5s. net.
>
> **THE ÆNEID OF VIRGIL,** freely translated into English Blank Verse. By W. J. THORNHILL. Crown 8vo, 7s. 6d.
>
> **THE ÆNEID OF VIRGIL.** Translated into English Verse. By JAMES RHOADES. Crown 8vo.
>> Books I.–VI., 2s. net; Books VII.–XII., 2s. net; complete in One Volume, 3s. 6d. net.
>
> **THE ECLOGUES AND GEORGICS OF VIRGIL.** Translated from the Latin into English Prose. By J. W. MACKAIL, Fellow of Balliol College, Oxford. Square 16mo, 5s.

SOME PASSAGES IN THE EARLY HISTORY OF CLASSICAL LEARNING IN IRELAND. An Address delivered at the Inaugural Meeting of the Trinity College Classical Society. By the Right Hon. Mr. JUSTICE MADDEN, M.A., Hon. LL.D., Vice-Chancellor of the University of Dublin. Crown 8vo, 2s. 6d. net.

LONGMANS, GREEN AND CO.
LONDON, NEW YORK, BOMBAY, AND CALCUTTA

LECTURES ON POETRY

BY THE SAME AUTHOR

LECTURES ON GREEK POETRY. 8vo, 9s. 6d. net.

SELECT EPIGRAMS FROM THE GREEK ANTHOLOGY. Edited by J. W. MACKAIL, with Revised Text, Translation, Introduction, and Notes. 8vo, 14s. net.

Pocket Edition. 2 vols., sold separately. Greek Text and English Translation. Fcap. 8vo, cloth, each 2s. net; leather, 3s. net.

THE SPRINGS OF HELICON: A Study in the Progress of English Poetry from Chaucer to Milton. Crown 8vo, 4s. 6d. net.

THE ECLOGUES AND GEORGICS OF VIRGIL. Translated into English Prose by J. W. MACKAIL. 16mo, 5s.

THE LIFE OF WILLIAM MORRIS. With 2 Portraits and 8 other Illustrations by E. H. NEW, &c. 2 vols., 8vo, 10s. net.

Pocket Edition, 2 vols., cloth, 4s. net; leather, 6s. net.

WILLIAM MORRIS: an Address delivered in the Town Hall, Birmingham, 28th October 1910. 8vo, paper covers, 1s. net.

LONGMANS, GREEN AND CO.
LONDON, NEW YORK, BOMBAY, AND CALCUTTA

LECTURES ON POETRY

BY

J. W. MACKAIL

LL.D. EDINBURGH AND ST. ANDREWS
FORMERLY FELLOW OF BALLIOL COLLEGE AND PROFESSOR OF
POETRY IN THE UNIVERSITY OF OXFORD

NEW IMPRESSION

LONGMANS, GREEN AND CO.
39 PATERNOSTER ROW, LONDON
NEW YORK, BOMBAY, AND CALCUTTA
1914

All rights reserved

TO

MARGARET

CONTENTS

	PAGE
INTRODUCTION	ix
THE DEFINITION OF POETRY	1
POETRY AND LIFE	23
VIRGIL AND VIRGILIANISM	48
THE AENEID	72
ARABIAN LYRIC POETRY	93
ARABIAN EPIC AND ROMANTIC POETRY	123
THE DIVINE COMEDY	154
SHAKESPEARE'S SONNETS	179
THE NOTE OF SHAKESPEARE'S ROMANCES	208
THE POETRY OF OXFORD	231
IMAGINATION	259
KEATS	281
THE PROGRESS OF POETRY	309

INTRODUCTION

THE main substance of the following pages consists of public lectures given to the University of Oxford in the years 1907 to 1911. Together with two volumes previously published, *The Springs of Helicon* (1909) and *Lectures on Greek Poetry* (1910), this volume contains all the lectures given by me from the Chair of Poetry, except a few which were given on particular occasions or were of more local and transitory interest.

The paper on the Divine Comedy was read to the Oxford Dante Society; and that on the Aeneid incorporates the substance of two addresses given to the Classical Associations of the University College of South Wales and the Victoria University of Manchester. The greater part of the lecture on Virgil and Virgilianism has already been printed in the *Classical Review* for May 1908.

The Professorship of Poetry is an institution possessed by Oxford alone among the two hundred and fifty Universities of the modern world. It is a Chair which allows its successive occupants an infinite variation of scope, even were it not the case that the import of poetry and the substance of poetical criticism are themselves subject, from age to age, to processes of change and continuous growth. The guiding idea pursued by me during my tenure of the Chair was

INTRODUCTION

that of the progress of poetry regarded as a vital and organic art: my object was to give, so far as I could, an interpretation of poetry, to trace its pattern, in some such way as poetry itself presents an interpretation and pattern of life.

In the volume of *Lectures on Greek Poetry* I attempted to trace the progress of poetry in the Hellenic civilisation, from the Homeric epics beyond which records are wanting down to the absorption of Greece in a new world. At the end of that cycle, the central life of European poetry passed to Italy, to the civilisation created and imposed on the West by Rome.

English poetry is not merely the successor of Greece and Italy in the line of torchbearers, but at all the critical moments of its development has drawn fresh life from Greek and Italian sources. In *The Springs of Helicon* I touched on the progress of poetry in England between Chaucer and Milton, from the time when the goal first shone before it until the time when the consummation was attained. This progress was in pursuance of native growth, but growth and progress were alike affected by the influx into English poetry of earlier and distant springs. In that volume of lectures I attempted to indicate how decisive was the effect of the Italian classics of the fourteenth century on Chaucer, and how under that influence Chaucer launched English poetry on its main current: how largely the development of poetry in the age associated with the name of Spenser was due to the impact of the full Italian Renaissance, conveying as it did not only the impulse of its own great poetry, but the revitalisation of Rome and the rediscovery of Greece: how at last, in Milton, English poetry came into complete touch and gained organic affinity with the whole body of both the Greek and the Italian classics.

The contents of this volume range over a wider area. They all bear on the interpretation of poetry in one or other of its aspects, in one or other of its endless embodiments. Their object will have been attained wherever they send back a reader to the poetry which is their subject with any fresh or quickened interest. Their unity, so far as I may have been able to impress any unity on them, is that of a single central doctrine; that poetry, like life, is one thing, but that this one thing is perpetually transmuting and re-creating itself in the progress of history. Essentially a continuous substance or energy, poetry is historically a connected movement, a series of successive integrated manifestations. Each poet, from Homer or the predecessors of Homer to our own day, has been, to some degree and at some point, the voice of the movement and energy of poetry: in him, poetry has for the moment became visible, audible, incarnate; and his extant poems are the record left of that partial and transitory incarnation.

These lectures take up the study of poetry here and there, at certain points, or in relation to the work of certain poets. Everywhere the point taken up appears as the centre of a vast organism which radiates from it in all directions. All poetry involves all other poetry; for all poetry is the interpretation of life: but life is one thing; and the interpretation, the appreciation, of any poet or poem implies the potential interpretation and appreciation of poetry itself as a substance or energy coextensive with life.

More than a hundred and fifty years ago, Gray, the finest scholar and poet of his age, laid down in his famous *Ode on the Progress of Poesy* what still remain the main lines, the guiding ideas, of poetical criticism. That Ode is not less remarkable for its just thought and profound insight than for its perfection of phrasing and movement. In it he set forth, under the imaginative light which only poetry itself can throw upon poetry, the doctrine of the power and function of poetry in itself, and of its progress in the life of mankind. It remains true still that poetry, in Gray's classic words, is the controller of sullen care and frantic passion; that it is the companion in youth of desire and love; that it is the power which in later years dispels, or solaces where it cannot dispel, the ills of life—labour, penury, pain, disease, sorrow, death itself; that it is the inspiration, from youth to age and in all times and lands, of the noblest human motives and ardours, of glory, of generous shame, of freedom and the unconquerable mind.

No less permanently true is the envisagement which he gives of the secular movement of poetry in her central progress from age to age and from race to race. But we see that movement now with immensely increased knowledge; we see it with an insight deepened, an outlook widened by generations of research and rediscovery, by new methods, by organised study, by the enrichment added to our inheritance through a century and a half of fresh poetical creation.

INTRODUCTION xiii

The progress of poetry, with its vast power and its exalted function, is immortal. The great poets are the immortals in the fullest sense in which we may speak of anything human as exempt from the common law of mortality. The laws of poetry are at the same time the conditions of life.

> "Onde convenne legge per fren porre,
> Convenne rege aver, che discernesse
> Della vera cittade almen la torre :
> Le leggi son ; ma chi pon mano ad esse ?"

The true city is now, as it always has been, discernible only in the distance, by glimpses. But in the fully socialised commonwealth which, as a dream or vision, mankind begin to have before their eyes, there may be a future for poetry larger, richer, more triumphant than its greatest achievements in the past have reached. Poetry will become the nobler interpretation of an ampler life. That vision is in the future. But to some at least, here and now, it is a vision and no dream.

LECTURES ON POETRY

THE DEFINITION OF POETRY

IT is a maxim of civil law that definitions are hazardous. Whoever first asked the question, What is poetry? and waited for an answer, stimulated thought and provoked discussion, but has perhaps not earned much gratitude. For the definition of poetry has ever since been, as it still is, the *ignis fatuus* of criticism. A thousand definitions have been offered, all varying from one another, sometimes to the extent of not having a single element in common. Some have been given by those whose views demand close attention and deep respect: many have been brilliant, enlightening, suggestive; all are unsatisfying. In no part of the field of letters have the Baconian idols exercised greater sway, particularly the idols of the cave and of the theatre. Definitions of poetry are nearly all infected by some fallacy due to a received system or an individual predilection. They escape from these dangers, if they do escape, only to fall victims to the idols of the market-place. For the influence exercised over men by words is greatest, and most difficult alike to estimate or to disentangle, when words themselves, the art of language, are the subject-matter as well as the medium of the enquiry.

Such attempted definitions, varying infinitely as

they do, fall into many different groupings according to the point of view from which they are regarded, no less than according to the position they occupy in the historical evolution of criticism, the progress and development of the human mind with regard to poetry. We may, for example, divide them into two classes accordingly as those who have framed and offered them are or are not themselves poets. A poet's definition of poetry cannot be quite negligible; for he knows, in a more intimate way than others, what it is that he is talking about. Poetry, whatever account he may be able to give of it, is to him at all events something actual and vital. The presence of this vital understanding, rather an instinct as it would seem than an acquired faculty, is always subject to doubt in critics who are not poets. These may have logic and lucidity, they may be acute, observant and sensitive; but they only look in at the windows, they are not children of the house. Yet, on the other hand, the children born in the house often take it all for granted. Their knowledge is latent and inarticulate; their very familiarity has the effect of ignorance. They have never been away from it enough to know what it is really like. Still less does their experience inform them how it was planned and built, or how, through many conscious changes as well as under the continuous touch of time, it became the thing with which they are so familiar. And even if they do know, it is their business to produce poetry, not to explain or define it. "I will not reason or compare," says Blake; "my business is to create." They may be quite unable to give an intelligent or intelligible account of what they do habitually and instinctively.

Or we may distinguish, in theory if not in fact, two other kinds of definition: those arrived at by a deductive method and based upon metaphysical postulates, and those induced from large reading among the poets, and from that familiarity which has made the appreciation of poetry into a sort of acquired aptitude or secondary instinct. In the former kind, as always happens when the deductive method is applied to organic functions and vital processes, there is the risk of some essential element being unconsciously added or dropped in the train of reasoning. In the latter, such an element may be ignored, forgotten, or never brought into its real connexion with the other elements, although it affects these others, gives them their colour, or determines their movement and relations. A definition of poetry in the terms of a philosophical system may be unimpeachable in theory, yet just miss the quality that makes poetry an organic creative art. A definition of poetry which is gathered from observation of the art may be only empirical, may be nothing more than a loose generalisation: at the best it will hardly be more than an imperfect, if vivid, impression.

Or again, we may distinguish definitions of poetry, as we may distinguish the whole attitude of mind towards poetry of which the definitions are the distilled expression, accordingly as they are mechanical or vital. "By poetry," wrote Macaulay in his famous essay on Milton, "we mean the art of employing words in such a manner as to produce an illusion on the imagination." It would be waste of time to analyse that definition. One is tempted to call it an instance of the art of employing words in such a manner as to produce an illusion of meaning. Macaulay had a genuine love of poetry. Yet he thinks of it, or at least he speaks of it, as something mechanical and external, something that acts on a receptive and passive faculty, which he calls the imagination. Only four years earlier, Shelley in his *Defence of Poetry* had defined poetry as the expression of the imagination, as that which lifts the veil from the hidden beauty of the world. To the one type of mind poetry is the mechanism of an illusion; to the other it is the vital energy of a revelation. The definitions of poetry which they frame are accordingly in essential contradiction.

Again, there is a whole class of definitions of poetry which are not philosophical but rhetorical, and the object of which is not to state facts or even to draw generalisations, but to win persuasion, and to create an attitude of mind favourable or unfavourable to poetry. According to the aim in view, these may be definitions of eulogy or definitions of detraction. Their object and effect is to create a prejudice for or against poetry. "One of the Fathers," says Bacon, "calleth Poesy *Vinum Dæmonum*": the definition is at all events succinct, but it is uncritical: it is given, as Bacon says, "in great indignation." Thus too Nash, in a sentence where the words seem to tumble over one another in excitement, wrote, "Nor is poetry an art whereof there is no use in a man's whole life but to describe discontented thoughts and youthful desires." Of as little technical value are the many splendid tributes which have in all ages been paid to poetry by its lovers under the guise of a definition. "Poetry," writes Wordsworth, "is the breath and finer spirit of all knowledge; it is the impassioned expression which is in the countenance of all science." "Poetry," writes Shelley, "is the record of the best and happiest moments of the happiest and best minds." "Poetry," writes Arnold, "is nothing less than the most perfect speech of man, that in which he comes nearest to being able to utter the truth." These and like sayings are stimulating, interesting, and illuminating: but they define nothing.

Or you may remember how the two things, the eulogy and the detraction, are flashed together by Aurora Leigh, in a passage most characteristic of Mrs. Browning's generous, passionate, chaotic mind.

> "You write so of the poets and not laugh?
> Those virtuous liars, dreamers after dark,
> Exaggerators of the sun and moon?—
> I write so of the only truth-tellers,
> The only speakers of essential truth,
> The only teachers who instruct mankind
> To find man's veritable stature out."

Even when definitions of poetry are not mere rhetorical flights or imaginative descriptions, even when they approach poetry with the intention of saying the real truth about it, and telling what it is, they do so normally and almost inevitably by singling out one side or one element of it, and defining that. It may be singled out either as the most obvious of the many elements which go to make up the full content of poetry, and therefore, as it may be argued, the most characteristic: or as the least obvious of them, and therefore, as it may be and has been argued, the deepest and most central. In any case it is the thing on which special stress is laid for a special purpose; and the special purpose in view determines the choice. Under this head fall many of the most brilliant things that have been said about poetry, the sayings that are most arresting in their brevity and most pregnant in their implication. One might fill a sort of jewel-cabinet with these lustrous fragments. I will quote a few, not more remarkable in some cases from their own weight and point than from the time at which they were said and the persons who said them. "Poetry is the best words in the best order": this is the saying not of a prosaic mind, of one who slighted poetry and wished to put it down into its proper place, but of the mystic and romantic Coleridge, the poet whose genius may almost be said to have created a new world for poetry. "Poetry is invention": this is the conclusion, not of any imaginative artist or leader of a new movement, but of the massive common-sense of Johnson. "Poetry is articulate music": we owe this definition, which sounds so modern and so romantic, to the master of the classicist school, a poet no doubt of high rank and immense influence, but one who has his highest title to fame and his most permanent value as a prose writer and critic; for the words are those of Dryden. One more and I have done. "Poetry is a speaking picture": these are the words not of any modern, not of any rhetorician: they are those of Simonides, the master of the matured Greek lyric, and the earliest, as one may call him, of the supreme poets of Athens. When one thinks over and thinks out these definitions—so far as they may be called definitions—in relation to the personality and the poetical quality of the men who framed them, they open up in all directions a limitless field of thought.

Such are only a few of the classes into which definitions of poetry, or what purport to be definitions of poetry, may be variously distributed. Most of the definitions which have been offered do not belong to one single type, but partake of several. We shall seldom find in them either the rhetorical or the scholastic, the mystical or the mechanical element, fully disengaged and standing by itself without admixture. Very generally too we shall find that, not in one type only but in most if not in all, another element has to be taken into account, and this time a deflecting or vitiating element. For the greater part of all these definitions are in their origin polemical: they assert a doctrine rather than disengage an essence. They are dogmatic; and even if a dogma is true, here and now and relatively to its place in a scheme, it is by its very nature not the whole truth. Such definitions express a view of poetry which is the reaction from some other view, and which so far as it is a reaction is necessarily off the truth itself, on the other side. What wonder then if after considering and rejecting definition after definition we end in a sort of bewilderment? if we find ourselves landed either in philosophic doubt or in unphilosophic dogmatism, in either case concluding the whole thing to be undefinable?

Undefinable in a sense it is, but not in the sense implied by either of these conclusions. For either of these conclusions is based on an essential fallacy. On the one hand it is a fallacy to suppose that an art can be defined in terms of science, or that a vital and functional process can be defined in terms of mechanism. On the other hand it is a fallacy to suppose that the impossibility of such definitions means the impossibility of any definition at all. In any case, before we begin trying to define, we must have some notion of what the thing is that we would define. And it is here that in the matter of poetry confusion begins.

The sources of confusion, like the resulting confusions themselves, are many. But the principal one is this: that in defining poetry, as more generally in speaking or thinking about poetry, two different and incommensurate things are mixed up with one another, namely, poetry as a function of life, a vital, creative, and progressive energy, and poetry as an art or technique. Poetry is both the one and the other; but the

8 THE DEFINITION OF POETRY

two are formally distinguishable, and the distinction is at the root of all clear thinking about poetry. The object of the following pages is to separate the formal or technical element in poetry from the other elements which go to make up its essence, and to try to get at a clear notion of that one element. Poetry in this sense is a concrete art, its material being language.

Let us then for the moment dismiss all the definitions of poetry, the good and the bad alike, which attempt to define it in its full meaning. For these are not really definitions of poetry, but things said about it, or about its effects or its objects; through them at best we see it, in Wordsworth's fine phrase, "not otherwise than through a tender haze or a luminous mist." In many of them the mist is indeed wonderfully luminous, but it is a mist none the less. Within it, things melt into one another and have no certain outline. "I have said," Wordsworth writes in the Preface to the Lyrical Ballads, "that poetry is the spontaneous overflow of powerful feelings." We turn back to verify the reference; and we find that what he had said was that "all good poetry is the spontaneous overflow of powerful feelings"—a very different thing. That is not a definition of poetry; it is a statement as to its origin, which at the same time, in the more carefully limited form of words, is made a criterion of its quality. "Poetry," says Mr. W. B. Yeats, himself a poet whose technical mastery of the art is indisputable, "is an endeavour to condense out of the flying vapours of the world an image of human perfection." It is true and beautifully said; it cannot be called a definition, but it seems at least to give us a glimpse in clear outline of the thing itself which is to be defined. To some of these and the like sayings we may have occasion to return: meanwhile let us set them aside, and con-

THE DEFINITION OF POETRY

sider poetry as an art, in its formal and technical definition.

It is singular, and not without an odd sort of relevance, that the very etymology of the word poetry, apparently so simple, is remote and obscure. It is generally and very naturally supposed to be a word formed by the addition to the word *poet* of the old French and English suffix which is one of the commonest in both languages. We have it in a thousand common English words like dairy, buttery, pantry, laundry. But in fact it seems that this is a merely accidental coincidence. The Latin word *poetria* in the sense of poetry is found in scholia on Horace's Epistles written as early as the seventh century and extant in MSS. of the tenth. Its use may be traced down from there to Dante. In the *Convito* (ii. 14), and also in the *Vita Nuova* (c. 25, *Siccome dice Orazio nel principio della Poetria*) he calls the *De Arte Poetica* of Horace by this name. How or when the Latin word originated, what if any relation it has to the other Latin word *poetria* meaning a poetess, is a problem still unsolved and apparently insoluble.

On its technical or formal side, which is what we are now considering, poetry may be taken for all practical purposes as in antithesis to prose. The relevance of the antithesis from another point of view may of course be, and often has been, disputed or denied. That is an old doctrine, though it was only in comparatively modern times that it was insisted upon strongly or had any wide predominance. "One may be a Poet without versing, and a versifier without poetry. Verse is but an ornament and no cause to poetry, sith there have been many most excellent poets that never versified": thus it runs as laid down in the orthodox Elizabethan text-book. The contrast between "poetic

10   THE DEFINITION OF POETRY

prose" and "prosaic poetry" is stated in these express terms in the middle of the eighteenth century. More modern instances might be quoted by the hundred. But they all only serve to emphasise the broad recognised distinction; in all of them there is a more or less conscious rhetorical artifice. What they imply is either a fallacy or a mere figure of speech. Advantage is taken of the fact that the exact boundary between the two things is not easily defined and leaves a strip of debateable frontier, in order to suggest that they are not two things; or stress is laid on some particular quality which they have in common to the extent of ignoring other qualities, equally essential, which they do not have in common; or oftener still, language is used in a loose metaphorical way, just as one might (and occasionally does) speak of a piece of architecture, or the movements of a dancer, or an apple pie, as poetry.

This then need not trouble us. But the distinction between prose and poetry on which the technical definition of poetry has to be based is not the same as the distinction between prose and verse. It is so nearly the same that the terms poetry and verse might often be used indifferently; but there is a difference, which though subtle is yet important, and the neglect of which leads certainly to confusion. It is worth while to look into the matter a little more closely. Prose, *prosa oratio*, straightforward or continuous language, is, as the etymology of the word implies, the complement or antithesis to language which is discontinuous, which does not move straight forward. But this latter kind of language includes more than verse, if the word verse be taken in its ordinary meaning as equivalent to metre or a series of metrical units. To quote Wordsworth's Preface to the Lyrical Ballads

THE DEFINITION OF POETRY

again: "I here use the word poetry," he says, "as opposed to the word prose, and synonymous with metrical composition: but the only strict antithesis to prose is metre; nor is this in truth a strict antithesis." It is on the last clause of this sentence, on the words "nor is this in truth a strict antithesis," that special stress is to be laid. Its truth is obvious if we consider that we must needs use the word metre either to express something which is a quality of some poetry only, not of all, or to express something which is a quality not only of good poetry but of good prose. We must exclude here such language, whether it purports to be prose or verse, as has no artistic quality: for we are here considering not mere language, but language as a fine art. The fine art of which language is the vehicle or means of expression, as in the other arts the vehicle is colour or form or sound, is literature. The art of language includes both prose and poetry: both in this sense are composition, both have structural and artistic quality; both have laws of composition, and apply to language a technique which is no less subtle and elaborate in prose than it is in poetry; but the kind of composition, the quality of technique, is different in the two. Johnson, in the middle of the eighteenth century, defines poetry on its technical side as "metrical composition": this is the definition alluded to by Wordsworth. It bears the mark of Johnson's plain good sense and rough justice; it is pretty near the mark. A century earlier, Edward Phillips, quoting perhaps, or possibly just misquoting, words that had been beaten into him by Milton, had said that poetry is writing "consisting of rhythm or verses." This is still nearer the mark: so near that it seems too good to be Phillips' own. I am not sure that it is possible to better this definition

THE DEFINITION OF POETRY

materially: only the words used in it are, like all the terms with which we are dealing, not wholly free from ambiguity or rather from something falling short of exact certainty of meaning. This certainty we may at least attempt to give by going back a little and approaching the problem from a slightly different direction.

All art implies composition: to the art which uses language as its vehicle, the term composition is specially and as it were primarily appropriated; and the definition which we are now seeking is that of poetry as a species of composition distinct from other species of composition all coming within the wider scope of the application of art to language, or what we call by a single comprehensive word, literature.

The essence of poetry technically, of poetry as an art working in language, is not that it is rhythmical. All elevated or impassioned language is that; at all events all elevated or impassioned language which possesses the amount of structure, of conscious artistic purpose, that is implied in its being literature at all. Nor is it the essence of poetry technically that it is metrical; for unless we stretch the meaning of the term much beyond ordinary usage, metre is not a necessary, though it is a normal and habitual predicate of poetry. What then is it?

The essence of poetry technically is that it is patterned language. This is its specific, central, and indispensable quality as a fine art. Pattern, in its technical use as applied to the arts, is distinct from composition generally. It is composition which has in it what is technically called a "repeat." The artistic power of the pattern-designer is shown in the way he deals with the problem of his repeat: the problem

THE DEFINITION OF POETRY

being, stated baldly, to make the rhythm of his repeat felt in such a way that the pattern which is based on and consists of a repeated unit may at the same time not fall asunder in separate units, but move and spread in a continuous and larger composition over the whole surface which is covered by the pattern.

In poetry this repeat is what is known by the name of verse. Verse opposed to prose is, in fact as well as in etymology, returning or repeating language, opposed to language which moves on without any such return or repeat. In this sense the definition given by Phillips is exact, if instead of saying that poetry consists of "rhythm or verses" we say that it consists of "rhythm in verses." In verses which are merely mechanical there is not the rhythm; in rhythm which is not in verses there is not the quality that constitutes pattern. Neither apart from the other is technically poetry. A pattern which merely consists of mechanical repetition, without the repetition being caught up into a larger rhythm, is a pattern in the mechanical, but not in the artistic sense; it fails of being art because it lacks composition. A composition which has not pattern is art and may be art of a very high kind, but it is not the specific art with which we are dealing. In the art of composition applied to language, verse which consists of a series of detached units is not poetry, because the verse is not caught up into a larger rhythm; and rhythm which is not based on the repeat of verse is not poetry, because it has not the specific quality of pattern.

In language which comes within this technical definition, the verse, the return and repeat of pattern, may be of many kinds. Some are more patent, where the repeat is more obvious and as it were more detachable. Others are more subtle, where the repeat is more implicit and more organic. The feeling for poetry (we are still speaking of poetry in its technical sense) very largely consists of the feeling for rhythm in pattern, and for pattern in rhythm. With the born designer this feeling is instinctive; with all designers it is felt most in the actual process; it grows with exercise; up to the culmination of the artist's power the senses go on feeling it more swiftly and certainly, the hand executes more and more of what the senses feel. *Poeta nascitur et fit.* But when the artist tries to explain what he is doing, or why and how he does it, he is often quite at a loss; he tries to give a reasoned explanation, and it is inadequate, it is perhaps unintelligible; it lays itself open to the easy task of destructive criticism. Or he falls back upon images and metaphors, in the attempt to give some vivid and concrete expression of what he feels but is unable or unwilling to define. These last are illustrations rather than definitions: among them however are included many of the most searching and illuminating things that have been said about poetry. In the double attempt the artist often falls into obvious inconsistencies, due to the emphasis being thrown on one or another aspect of the complex matter with which he is dealing. It is through the grouping and synthesis of these partial and formally inconsistent views that we arrive at a larger and more comprehensive view. Thus, to take one instance out of many, Shelley in his *Defence of Poetry*, when he is putting emphasis on the quality of poetry as a means of imaginative expression, lays down the sweeping doctrine that "the distinction between poets and prose writers is a vulgar error." Yet, just a little before, when he was regarding the subject from another side, he had said, with perfect truth but obvious inconsistency, that "the language of poets has ever affected a certain uniform and harmonious recurrence of sound, without which it were not poetry." Uniform recurrence not only is not a quality of prose, but is a quality which vitiates prose, makes it cease to be prose in an artistic sense. Wherever it is allowed to occur through negligence or accident, it results in what is technically bad prose. A little later in the same treatise, Shelley combines the two aspects of the thing. "The functions of the poetic faculty," he says, "are twofold; by one it creates new materials of knowledge and power and pleasure; by the other, it engenders in the mind a desire to reproduce and arrange them according to a certain rhythm and order."

The repeating and yet continuous pattern in language which makes it technically poetry is subject to the general laws of composition and also to certain special laws of its own. These special laws vary from language to language, from country to country, and from time to time; they allow of many types. These are often far apart from one another; and it is only by paying attention to the general test of pattern that we can readily bring them under a single definition. So likewise the repeat in the pattern may be simpler or more complex, may be patent on the surface or implicit in the structure. A general rule may indeed be laid down, that the repeat must not be so accented as to destroy the continuity, nor the movement so continuous that there is no repeat left. It is clear that a very wide field is left between these limits. On the one hand there is the kind of poetry where the recurrence does not amount to what is generally called verse, is not measurable in definite lengths of stresses or quantities or accents, and yet is there sufficiently to be felt. In such cases it may be difficult to draw a precise boundary between poetry and impassioned prose: in the Book of Job, to take a familiar instance, or in other parts of what are called the poetical books of the English Old Testament: for in such cases we are on the borderland where poetry and prose tend to coalesce or are not yet fully differentiated in function; where poetry has not worked out its full nature, in the Aristotelian phrase, or else where prose attempts to clothe itself in the garments and exercise the functions of poetry. On the other hand there is the kind of poetry where the verse has not only become definite metre—whether that metre be expressed in terms of quantity or accent or stress—but has let metre dominate over continuous rhythm of structure and has treated the specific requirements of metre as though they covered the whole technical requirements of poetical composition.

Milton's attack on rhymed verse in the preface to the second issue of *Paradise Lost* is directed towards emphasising this latter defect. That famous pronouncement is often misquoted or misinterpreted. Milton did not, as is often supposed, wish to abolish rhymed verse. What he did was to point out, with exact truth, the dangers or inconveniences to which rhymed poetry is subject; and even so, he limits his strictures carefully to large works, which require a correspondingly large freedom of pattern, "rime being," as he says, "no necessary adjunct of poem or good verse, in longer works especially," where its tendency is to make poets "express many things otherwise, and for the most part worse, than else they would have expressed them." But he goes on to lay equal stress on the like defect in rhymeless metres which allow the

unit of pattern to dominate the larger rhythm. The
" musical delight " of poetry, according to his doctrine,
" consists in apt numbers, fit quantity of syllables, and
the sense variously drawn out from one verse into
another." In the complex fabric of patterned language
which is poetry, each artist, according to the particular
tendency and affinity of his genius, lays stress on one
or another element. He may even deny the authenticity
or relevance of elements to which exaggerated importance is attached by popular usage. But such a denial
must be taken in relation to the circumstances, and to
the particular point on which he is at the time insisting.

Let me recapitulate the substance of the matter
in the briefest possible words. Poetry, while in its
essence it is a function of life, and as indefinable
as life itself except through imagination expressing
itself in symbols and metaphors, is formally and
technically patterned language : the technical essence
of pattern is repeat : and where there is no repeat,
there is technically no poetry. The art of the pattern-
designer lies in the choice of the unit of repeat and
thereafter in the way he uses it as the basis of structural composition obeying the larger laws of rhythm
and growth : and so it is with the art or technique of
the poet.

If we keep firmly by this definition (or if we prefer
not to call it a definition, by this central clue) we shall
not be much troubled by the dust of controversy that
has risen round such phrases as " prose poetry " ; for we
shall realise that all such phrases arise in a confusion,
and it is natural therefore that fresh confusion should
arise out of them. As composition, as a fine art, prose
has its own nature and virtue, and they are different
from those of poetry : if forced beyond these in order
to be brought within some loose definition of poetry

it only departs from its own nature and loses its own excellence, without acquiring the specific nature and specific excellence of poetry.

This definition of poetry as a formal art must be judged on its own merits, and as it appears to give, or to fail in giving, a sufficiently logical and precise account of the facts. But there is a test to which we are able to submit it. If it fails to meet this test, there is something wrong with it. If it satisfies this test, there is at least a presumption that it is sound. I will now proceed, very briefly, to indicate the test and apply it, or at least suggest its application.

Much of the confusion which has arisen with regard to the nature and definition of poetry has arisen, as we have seen, from failure to draw any clear distinction between two things which are different. One of these is the formal quality of poetry as an art; the other is its essential or vital quality in relation to life —whether we speak of poetry in this regard as the interpretation of life, or as the imaginative expression of life, or in more general terms as a function of life. But these two things, though formally distinguishable, are not actually separable. There is no such thing as art in the abstract. Concrete poetry consists of form and substance; and just as there is no substance apart from form, so there is no form apart from substance. It follows that in the thing poetry, form and substance must have a mutual and intimate relation. We may express this relation, according to the general terms in which we choose to put our system of thought, by saying that form embodies itself in a certain substance, or that substance takes shape under certain forms, or that between form and substance there exists a certain pre-established harmony. In any case, what is true formally of the

THE DEFINITION OF POETRY

form must also be true substantially of the substance —of the thing in which the form has its visible embodiment and concrete existence. The work of art must have a relation to life analogous to the relation between the form of art and the material in which it works. Poetry is a particular form of art working in the material of language, and we have defined it as patterned language. If the technical art of poetry consists in making patterns out of language, the substantial and vital function of poetry will be analogous; it will be to make patterns out of life.

And this is the case. This is what poetry has been doing from its earliest days and is doing still. This is what it will always continue to do, and what ensures its progress and its immortality. So long as the instinct to make patterns out of life endures, so long as language is the means of giving shape to human thoughts and emotions and aspirations, so long will the making of poetry be a necessity, because through poetry alone can that instinct be satisfied. The poetry of the past is our inheritance, and it is priceless; but it is not enough. The poetry of each age must reinterpret and reincarnate life anew. Not the art which we inherit, but the art which we create, is our own art, the expression of our own life. Let me quote once more from Shelley.

"The language of poets," he says, "is vitally metaphorical; that is, it marks the before unapprehended relations of things, and perpetuates their apprehension, until the words which represent them become, through time, signs for portions or classes of thoughts instead of pictures of integral thoughts; and then, if no new poets should arise to create afresh the associations which have thus been disorganised, language will be dead to all the nobler purposes of human intercourse."

Thus we find that in periods when the vital creative energy of poetry has been at its lowest, the effective energy, the effective appreciation, of existing poetry has also dwindled. The classics have survived; but they have lost their vital force, their vitalising influence, in the torpor of classicism. To the extent that poetry ceases to be a living art, to that extent the work of the older poets ceases to be living poetry and becomes like the contents of a museum. It is preserved, catalogued, annotated; but it remains living art only to the measure in which living artists keep in touch with it, reincarnate it, find in it kinship with their own instincts and impulse for their own inspiration, and can say in its presence, *Anch' io sono poeta*.

If we pass in review the most notable things that poets or great thinkers have said of poetry, we shall find running through them and giving them substantial coherence this notion of the function of poetry being to make patterns out of life. Sometimes it is distinctly expressed, more often suggested or implied. This is what is implied in Sidney's quaint words when he says in the *Apology for Poetry*, still harking back, you will notice, on the old confusion of technique with substance: "It is not riming and versing that maketh a poet, but fayning notable images of vertues, vices, or what else, which must be the right describing note to know a poet by." This is what underlies the vivid Platonic metaphor of a seventeenth-century author when he speaks of poetry as being " the dreams of them that are awake." This is the central thought in the striking words of Shelley, "A poem is the very image of life expressed in its eternal truth," and again, " Poetry is a mirror which makes beautiful that which is distorted "—which brings out the pattern in life, that is to say; a pattern that is there, though it is confused, broken, or hidden until poetry disengages it. The same thought is expressed with great beauty by Carlyle in his *Lectures on Heroes*, and it is worth while setting the words beside Shelley's and noticing how nearly two minds so different as theirs approached one another. "It is a man's sincerity and depth of vision," says Carlyle, "that makes him a poet. See deep enough, and you see musically; the heart of Nature being everywhere music, if you can only reach it." We come still closer to the point, even down to the exact phrasing, in a celebrated sentence of Milton's: "A true poem, that is, a composition and pattern of the best and honourablest things." It is the last words of this sentence on which Milton is for the moment laying stress: the words "composition" and "pattern" fall from him as it were incidentally. But they are all the more significant for that: for in them we have Milton speaking as it were off his guard, not laying down any law or formulating any theory, still less confuting any other view, but saying quite simply and instinctively what lay at the foundation of his own thought and guided his own practice. It would be tedious to multiply quotations further; and I have singled out these few *ad narrandum non ad probandum*. It is not the office of a Professor of Poetry, as I conceive it, to lay down laws about poetry, or to argue about poetry, but to present poetry, and so far as he can, to present it as it really is. His privilege is to do for poetry something faintly analogous, on its lower plane, to what poetry itself does for life.

Let me then recur to two passages which I have already quoted in part, and quote them once more in full: for they are among the most considered and authentic utterances that poets have given about their own art; and they will bear repeating; for they must be thought out and thought over before they will yield their full significance.

"Poetry," said Shelley, "lifts the veil from the hidden beauty of the world, and makes familiar objects be as if they were not familiar."

"All art," says Mr. Yeats, "is in the last analysis an endeavour to condense as out of the flying vapours of the world an image of human perfection, and for its own and not for the art's sake."

To lift the veil from the hidden beauty of poetry and make familiar poems be as if they were not familiar is the highest aim and function of poetical criticism or exposition. For our own and not for the art's sake, I have endeavoured here to condense, out of the flying vapours of definitions, an image of poetry.

POETRY AND LIFE

In leaving Homer and Chaucer we pass away from the Middle Ages. These two poets, both so full of the unexhausted joy of life, both so steeped in what seems to us the radiance of morning, represent the final splendours of a day that was drawing near its close. Unlike in profound essentials as are the poetry of the Iliad and Odyssey on the one hand, the poetry of *Troilus* and the *Knight's Tale* on the other, they are alike in being the finished product of a mediæval art which perished in creating them. Once in the East, once again after more than two thousand years in the West, a mediæval period came to its final fruition in the two countries which lie on the extreme verges of the European world. When the darkness that follows these two great sunset splendours lifts we find ourselves in the pallor of a new dawn; here in modern England, there in a Hellenic world which, however we may speak or think of it as ancient, is in its whole quality as distinctively and as essentially modern.

The Iliad and the Odyssey are the treasure saved from the submerged world of pre-Hellenic Greece. Beyond what can be divined from the poems themselves, we know little or nothing of their poetic predecessors, and almost as little of their immediate poetic successors. Traces of pre-Homeric poetry are in the Iliad at all events extant, however much they may be elusive and however often debateable. Traces of post-Homeric poetry are to be found in accretions which have attached themselves to the authentic Iliad, and also, it may be, in the conclusion of the authentic and unfinished Odyssey. The later poetry of the Cycle has perished. Its fragments lie in a dim twilight, among the beginnings of the Greek lyric. With Chaucer the case is entirely different. We know nearly everything that we want to know. We know the earlier native and foreign poetry that preceded him, the soil out of which his poetry grew, the political and social environment; we have abundant examples of the contemporary arts other than poetry. We know too what came after him, the poetry of the Chaucerian school which reached up to and overlapped the renaissance of poetry in England in the sixteenth century. Of this post-Chaucerian poetry we possess large masses. But it is in quality as secondary as were the lost Cyclic epics; it represents decadence, not progress, for the progress of poetry had diverged from it. In both cases the new birth of poetry comes after a long engulfing interval, and begins afresh in a changed world.

But before passing on, as poetry itself passed on, to those fresh developments, something still remains to be considered. All art is a function of life; and the matter which we now must pause upon is one with which poetry, as a function of life, is deeply concerned. The Homeric poems present us with the picture of a world; a world embodied in art at a high tension, vivid, various, convincing. So do the poems of Chaucer in a lesser degree. His world is as various and fresh as Homer's, if not so large or noble; more coloured and crowded, but conceived at a lower imaginative heat. But neither of them is the whole world. I have had occasion, when dealing with Homer and Chaucer, to speak in passing of another world that lay alongside of or beneath theirs, and that suggests another aspect of the function of poetry. The world of Hesiod and of Langland is not one of high passions or romantic achievements; it has little enchantment and little joy; it is the under side of that pattern of life, whether epic or romantic, through which the central current of poetry had been moving.

Whatever our opinion may be as to the poetical value of the *Works and Days* and the whole of what is called, by a brief and useful term, Hesiodic as opposed to Homeric poetry, we must remember that it occupied a very important place in the development of the Greek genius for poetry, and in later Greek literary judgment. The coupling of Homer and Hesiod was a thing fully established as early as the middle of the sixth century B.C. It is assumed as a matter of course by Xenophanes, and is thereafter habitual. Virgil's ambition to be the Roman Hesiod was quite unaffected, and does not seem to have caused any surprise, or even any comment. For us, as we read the timid, halting work of the Boeotian school, with its lack of constructive power, its narrow range of imagination, its inexpert use of the Homeric court-language, it seems strange that *Ascraeum carmen* should be the title given by its author to a work which is the highest technical achievement of Latin poetry. Clearly the Hesiodic poetry was nothing inconsiderable to the classical mind. Nor were the place and influence of Langland inconsiderable in his own time or in the age which immediately followed. There are forty-three extant MSS. of *Piers Plowman* in its different versions as against sixteen only of Chaucer's greatest poem; nearly as many, in fact, as there are of the *Canterbury Tales* with their obvious appeal to a large and to a somewhat mixed public.

But Langland's poem had not a long life, as length of life in such matters is to be computed. It lay outside of the main stream of poetry, and did not become a classic. Partly this is due to the overwhelming triumph of the exotic forms of verse. After Chaucer, this was a decided matter. In the first printed edition of *Piers Plowman* (1550) there had to be a preface to explain the metre. After a second edition a few years later, the poem was never reprinted until the nineteenth century; it had dropped out of poetical currency. This was not all a matter of obsolete language and metre; it is one very largely of inner poetical quality. Neither of course would it be true to say that Chaucer himself remained a vital influence over later English poetry through its full extent. Homer and Hesiod were a part of Greek life; they dominated it to an extent to which no English poet, not even Shakespeare, has dominated English life. They were—and this is even more true of Hesiod than of Homer—the Greek schoolbooks, the Greek Bible. Neither Chaucer nor Langland was ever that.

Hesiod, the body of poetry passing under that name, is the antithesis or complement to Homer. It is the poetry of the *minutus populus;* of what Langland, and we after him, call the commons. It is the voice of the democracy which was implicit in the static mediæval system, and which was destined, when it became self-conscious and dynamic, to annul that system, to create a New Doctrine, to launch the world upon a changed orbit.

The versified textbook of theology known as the *Generation of the Gods* need not detain us as poetry. Whatever poetry it has is derivative, and of no substantive value. In the *Works and Days*, on the other hand, we see and feel a new poetry in the making. The poetical art is moving towards a new subject, a new audience, a new aspect of life. It applies itself to what may be called in a sense real things, in a sense different from that in which we can speak of the Homeric world as real. Its subject is the life and labour of the people. Discarding both the epic and the romantic treatment, it sets itself to deal with conduct, which, in Arnold's phrase, is three-fourths of life, and with the poor, who, in no mere phrase, are three-fourths of the human race. It leaves the bright sunlight of the epic; it leaves the shadowed halls and gardens of romance: it passes from these into a grey world, lying obscure in a doubtful dusk which is also a dawn. It turns the methods and language of poetry, hesitatingly and awkwardly, to a new use; it wavers between adapting old and creating new forms of expression. The Homeric life lies all broad in the daylight; in sharp contrast to this is Hesiod's remarkable expression, "The Gods have made the life of mankind hidden." With the collapse of the epic structure or pattern of life there came the beginnings of a new movement of poetry, one that goes out into the wilderness, that seeks to reconstruct some sort of shelter from the ruins of a Palace of Art.

> "So when four years were wholly finished
> She threw her royal robes away.
> " Make me a cottage in the vale,' she said,
> Where I may mourn and pray.'"

In Hesiod is the beginning of the instinct of the commonalty after something that, even if poor, shall be its own. It is the same instinct which, later, created the personal poem, the lyric, and with the lyric, made what we mean by Greece. For while the Greek genius created the state, it also created the individual. The growth and the interaction of these two forces are what, throughout Greek history, gives Hellenic life its enthralling and immortal interest. The full synthesis of the two, once nearly realised in the brief central splendour of Athens, was not, as it still is not, of this world. Greece was shattered in the attempt to do what, on a larger scale, with greater experience and greater resources, mankind are still attempting to do now, and still without success.

In this life and labour of the people, the κλέα ἀνδρῶν, the deeds of kings and heroes, count for nothing. Fleetfoot Aeacides and Argive Helen have faded away into a phantom White Island beyond the unfriendly sea. The world of ladies dead and lovely knights— ἀνδρῶν ἡρώων θεῖον γένος, "the god-like hero-brood," αἱ πάρος ἦσαν εὐπλοκαμῖδες ’Αχαιαί, "Achæan women lovely-tressed of old"—has become a chronicle of wasted time, a tale of little meaning. The motives of the Iliad and Odyssey have ceased to exist. The great motive force in life is λῖμος, hunger, the bodily hunger for bread, and with it, the growth of a hunger for understanding what life really means. To the farmer of Ascra, as at or about the same time in another country to the herdsman of Tekoa, "the days come that I will send a famine into the land, not a famine of bread nor a thirst for water, but of hearing the words of the Lord." They wander from sea to sea, they run to and fro to seek that word, and do not find it. The physical unrest of the Greek migrations and colonisations reflects a corresponding ferment in things of the mind. Poetry is turning to what are felt to be in a new way real things; for the things with which it had dealt hitherto are losing reality. It has exchanged the opulence of autumn, full-foliaged and rich-fruited, for the pinched faint greenness of what is hardly yet spring—

> "For all the miles and miles of unsprung wheat,
> And for the Spring waiting beyond the portal,
> And for the future of its own young art:"

grey under the east wind, leafless, only with here and there a point of vivid colour, a waft of piercing scent. Inchoate, uncertain, immature, it yet has stirring in it the principle of life. But its hope is still overburdened by its sense of the misery of the world.

Thus, the author of the *Works and Days* sums up what is to him the whole upshot of the Iliad and Odyssey, when he says that the Son of Cronos now and again destroys a broad army or a walled city, or takes vengeance on ships at sea. Thus, too, he draws the picture of Justice sitting helpless by the side of Zeus, and complaining to him of the injustice of men. The mediæval or Homeric world had a gap in its completeness; at that gap it is breaking down.

But between these two great changes, with their striking and fertile analogies, there is one profound difference. In Homer the way of looking at life is instinctive rather than reasoned. The Homeric theory of the world—so far as it can be said to exist—is implicit and vague. In mediæval Europe, on the other hand, it was explicit, and worked out to the utmost detail; in the feudal system, in the *Summa Theologiae*, in Dante's *Divine Comedy*. *Piers Plowman* is the last effort made by poetry in England to think seriously about that world before the thing itself vanished. It embodies, for the last time, that organised coherent system of politics and theology which to the mediæval mind gave a complete account of the whole of human life.

Langland himself has no forecast of the modern world. The so-called prophecy of the dissolution of the religious houses by the Tudor monarchy is only one of those many passages in poetry which have been distorted into prophecy after the event, like the Fourth Eclogue in Virgil. But as in Hesiod, the new spirit which was to create the modern world, before which the whole structure of mediæval poetry and of mediæval life was destined to melt away, is working inarticulately within him. The life of the court, the ordinances of chivalry, the romantic side of feudalism, he only sees from a distance and without sympathy, as a villager might look on at a tournament, or glance, as he passed by on his daily work, through the open doorway of a lord's castle. What interests him as a poet, what for him has become the substance of poetry, is the life and labour of the people; of the landowners in their manor-houses, of the merchants and shopkeepers, of the labourers who make up nine-tenths of the population, of the floating mass of landless men, outlaws, beggars, and thieves. His vision of the world is as precise and distinct as that portrayed on the shield of Achilles. But this new world is full of agonies, of the cry of the poor, of the stirrings of a far-off democracy. The "mirror of middle-earth," into which he looks in his vision, is a "land of longing," set between the two unseen worlds.

> "I saw the sun and the sea
> and the sand after:
> And where that birds and beasts
> by their mates they yeden:
> Wild worms in woods
> and wonderful fowls,
> With flecked feathers
> and of fele colours.
> And sithen I looked upon the sea
> and so forth upon the stars:
> I saw flowers in the fryth
> and their fair colours,
> And how among the green grass
> grew so many hues."[1]

[1] This and the other quotations from *Piers Plowman* are from the **B** text, with the spelling modernised on the principle indicated at the end of the Introduction to *The Springs of Helicon*.

The world lies outspread before him, bright, clear, changeable and yet constant.

> "Lo! birds and beasts
>   that no bliss ne knoweth
> And wild worms in woods
>   through winters thou them grievest,
> And after thou sendest them summer
>   that is their sovereign joy,
> And bliss to all that been
>   both wild and tame."

But in human life, evil preponderates; and its preponderance is against nature, is a thing against which humanity instinctively revolts.

> "Bliss and bale
>   both I saw at once;
> And how men tooken meed
>   and mercy refused."

"Much mirth is among rich, as in meat and clothing," Langland says. For the upper classes life had become refined and luxurious beyond all former experience, and was made even more so by contrast with the increasing poverty of the poor. Feudalism was hardening into tyranny; lawlessness had spread in the track of the French wars, and the Black Death shaken the foundations of all customary morality. There is a description in the poem of a feast in a rich house on a winter's night, towards Christmas, with music and minstrelsy under the light of the great twisted wax tapers, which recalls the Phæacian palace of the Odyssey. But meanwhile, Langland breaks out,

> "The careful may cry
>   and carpen at the gate
> Both ahungered and athirst,
>   and for chill quake;
> Is none to nymen him near
>   his annoy to amend,

> But huen on him as an hound
> and hoten him go thence:
> Ne were mercy in mean men
> more than in rich,
> Mendinants meatless
> might go to bed.
> And beggars about Midsummer
> breadless they sup:
> And yet is winter for them worse,
> for wet shod they gang
> Athirst sore and ahungered,
> and foul y-rebuked
> And arated of rich men
> that ruth is to hear."

The life of the labourer was hard and joyless:—

> "Ere I have bread of meal
> oft might I sweat,
> And ere the commune have corn enough,
> many a cold morning."

His housing was (as it is now) scandalous:—

> "If his house be unhilled
> and rain on his bed,
> He seeketh and seeketh
> till he sleep dry;
> And smoke and smoulder
> smiteth in his eyen,
> Till he be blear-eyed or blind
> and hoarse in the throat."

And to make matters worse, he was (as he is now) hopelessly entangled by the petty usurer: "evermore needy, and seldom dieth he out of debt."

The revolution was on its way. As yet, however, the old religion on which the whole mediæval system was based reigned in almost unimpaired power and charm. Langland is deeply moved by the civilised life and splendid art of the great religious communities.

His poetry kindles, he becomes almost romantic, when he turns to these, when he speaks of the superb architecture, the huge glazed windows of the churches, the covered cloisters, the white walls all painted and portrayed, the bells of brass or of bright silver, the gospels and psalters with their leaves of burnished gold, the volumes of "Plato the poet," of "Ypocras and Virgil" that filled their libraries, the skill of hand and love of nature that made their gardens and orchards a fit surrounding for their beautiful buildings. More deeply still is he moved by what underlay that life and art, the beauty of holiness, the mysterious angelical grace of the Catholic religion: the consolation that lay in the offices of the Church and its appointed minister:

("For he shall answer for thee
at the high Doom")

the uplifting brought to people for whom this world was wretched enough by that great mediæval art where music, architecture, and painting, no less than poetry, converged through all the avenues of beauty upon an almost visible heavenly world.

"Woolward and wet shod
went I forth after,
Till I waxed weary of the world
and willed eft to sleep:
Of girls and of *Gloria Laus*
greatly me dreamed,
And how Osanna by organy
olde folk sungen."

But the cry of the poor was no longer to be stilled by spiritual narcotics. The ferment of the modern spirit, within a few years after the date of Langland's poem, had spread so alarmingly in England that the Church, in self-defence, instituted the burning of heretics alive.

The claims of labour are becoming identified with the claims of life.

> "Joy, that never joy had,
> of rightful judge he asketh."

The right to have joy is indefeasible, unless life is to be, in the proper sense of the word, hell. For the poor,

> "That all their life have lived
> in languor and in default,
> But God sent them sometime
> some manner joy
> Either here or elsewhere,
> Kind would it never.
> Angels that in hell now been
> hadden joy sometime."

Either here or elsewhere it must be; but the claim is now definitely made that it shall be here and not elsewhere:—

> "For all are we Christ's creatures
> and of his coffers rich,
> And brethren as of one blood
> as well beggars as earls."

To "have ruth of the poor" has become the first and great commandment. Those who ignore or neglect that duty are swept away out of the fellowship of Christ in a passage of splendid invective:—

> "But ye liven truly
> and eke love the poor,
> And such good as God sent
> truly parten,
> Ye have no more merit
> in mass nor in hours
> Than Malkin of her maidenhood
> that no man desireth."

In such passages as this Langland's verse kindles to a white heat: there is no question about their being noble poetry: and poetry that might seem to be of a higher quality than Chaucer's as dealing with more real things. Here is all the high moral passion that Chaucer lacks; and it is not merely the moral passion of the preacher, but the imaginative passion of the poet. All art is an endeavour to condense an image of human perfection. Is not then, it may be asked, this image of human perfection a truer one than any that has taken shape in epic or romance, in tales of the feats of princes before windy Troy, or of the whispering of lovers in moonlit gardens? Is not the poetry which fixes this image a higher poetry, a superior art? And if the answer be no, is not art an illusion? and have we not come to the point where, with Plato, we shall expel the poets from our commonwealth?

The answer is no: and art is not an illusion. Poetry moves through this world as in it but not of it. It deals with real things, for only in real things can be found the image which it desires. But they are not real things in the technical philosophic sense of that term, any more than they are real things in the crude popular sense. Either of these may be, and have been, called illusions; be that as it may, neither are the real things of poetry. No theory of life, no drapery or stage presentment of life, but life itself, is the poetic reality.

If we consider what is the reason of the admitted fact that *Troilus* is greater poetry than *Piers Plowman*, that the Iliad is greater poetry than *Troilus*, the most obvious answer is that Chaucer was a greater poet than Langland, and Homer than Chaucer. But this answer only restates the question. The poet and the poetry cannot be separated; each only exists in virtue of the other, or, we might say, as a function of the other. What is real for poetry, what is real to the poet, has not, as such, either tangible or metaphysical reality. It is that in which and through which both these other kinds of reality exist, life itself.

Hence it is not possible to define poetry except in terms of life: just as, conversely, it is not possible to define life except in terms of poetry. The poet, at a given moment, in a given aspect, fixes life, makes it imaginatively visible. Round that point, for that moment, the whole universe groups itself, takes rhythm and completeness. This is what the poets themselves, in metaphor and allegory, or in the "little flash" of a sublimed lyric, have touched, and have expressed so far as it is expressible. It is put most succinctly by Blake.

> "To see a world in a grain of sand
> And heaven in a wild flower,
> Hold infinity in the palm of your hand
> And eternity in an hour."

For a more sustained attempt to express the same thought we may turn to Browning, the one among all modern poets who realises most intensely and most clearly that poetry is what gives form to life, and life the substance of poetry. The passage where he expresses his doctrine most clearly and fully is the concluding part of the Epilogue to *Dramatis Personae*.

> "Witless alike of will and way divine,
> How heaven's high with earth's low should intertwine!
> Friends, I have seen through your eyes: now use mine!
>
> Take the least man of all mankind, as I;
> Look at his head and heart, find how and why
> He differs from his fellows utterly:

> Then, like me, watch when nature by degrees
> Grows alive round him, as in Arctic seas
> (They said of old) the instinctive water flees
>
> Toward some elected point of central rock,
> As though for its sake only roamed the flock
> Of waves about the waste: awhile they mock
>
> The mimic monarch of the whirlpool, king
> O' the current for a minute: then they wring
> Up by the roots and oversweep the thing,
>
> And hasten off to play again elsewhere
> The same part, choose another peak as bare,
> They find and flatter, feast and finish there."

The particular point, the particular moment, is the centre of reality only in virtue of being the focus, or if we prefer to call it so, the radiating point, of life as the poet then and there realises it. Apart from its formal or technical quality, poetry is greater, not as it purports to deal with a greater subject, but as it gathers and absorbs into itself more of life, more of what Browning at the end of this poem calls "my universe that feels and knows," the sum of self-conscious existence. When we speak of the Iliad as greater poetry than *Troilus and Creseide*, or of *Troilus and Creseide* as greater poetry than *Piers Plowman*, we do not mean, or at least we ought not to mean, that the Wrath of Achilles is more a subject for high poetry than the story of an unhappy love, or the story of an unhappy love more a subject for high poetry than the life and labour of the people. No subject is in itself, we may say, even though the statement may wear an appearance of paradox, more poetical or less poetical than another; for no subject is poetical at all, except in so far as poetry touches and kindles it. A subject does not inspire poetry: it is poetry that inspires a subject.

An unpoetical subject means a subject which has not become poetical because poetry, the shaping spirit, has not in fact condensed out of it an image of perfection.

Life itself, the whole vitally organised universe, is, as the philosophers teach and as experience tells, in constant flux. It is, in the vivid phrase of Lucretius, *natura rerum*, "the being born of things." And poetry, which is a function of life, is similarly in constant flux or progress. It touches now one point of the whole, now another. Where it touches, it creates. That which it touches becomes a real thing; and not only so, but it becomes, there and then, the centre and essence of reality. This is what is expressed by Browning's image of the rock in Arctic seas. Only there is this difference: the peak which the spirit of poetry has once touched and lit is not "finished"; the concrete work of art, the embodied imagination of life, survive; and through imaginative sympathy, may live on, may live again and again, for other minds in other ages. They may seem to fade, to die, to be forgotten. But there are not instances wanting to show that a poet for long forgotten or slighted may come again to be prized and remembered.

The history of poetry is full of such ironies and reversals. Homer passed through a period of submergence; so did Dante. The case of Shakespeare's Sonnets is a familiar instance. That the Sonnets should ever, to any generation of men, have been dead poetry might well astonish us, if it were not that at the present day an acute and able scholar has sought to show, with an imposing array of arguments, that they never were living poetry at all. Every eye has its limit of vision, and far within that limit, actually in the central field, has its blind point: it is only as the parallax shifts, with the progress of poetry or with the progress of life, that certain things become visible. Of many poets, long after they had seemed forgotten or dead, we may say in the words of the wise Centaur,

> "Siete voi accorti
> Che quel di retro move ciò ch' ei tocca?
> Così non soglion far i piè de' morti."

The eclipsed light resumes its luminousness, the suspended force renews its potency. Of no poetry that has once been alive, that has once moved what it touched in the souls of men, can we say with certainty that it will not do so again: that it will never again be a centre from which the threads of life radiate. Least of all can we base any such doctrine on what we consider the inadequacy, the unimportance, the irrelevance to life, of its subject. For all things imply all other things; and the system of things has no centre other than that of which some one, at some moment, can say, "It is here."

Poetry may receive an adventitious, and, in a strict use of words, a non-poetical value from the largeness of its subject, as largeness is judged by ordinary measurements. Just so a poem may derive a secondary but quite real importance from its length. Greek criticism, with its cool good-sense, noted size, $\mu\acute{\epsilon}\gamma\epsilon\theta$ος, as a quality which counted towards the value or importance of a work of art; not so much theoretically or with any direct relation to the essence of art, as practically and in view of the normal capacity of the human eye or mind for receiving an impression and retaining it. That is a matter not so much of art as of experience. If elevated to a criterion of art it is rejected by instinct as much as by reflection. It becomes, so far as it is accepted, gravely misleading, and has been responsible for many aberrations of criticism, when criticism, as it always tends to do, has founded itself on current generalisations and elevated them into regulating laws. As an instance, let me quote from a writing which for long exercised great influence over English thought, Addison's essay on Milton in the *Spectator*, which was said to have established, or almost to have created, Milton's fame as a poet among his own countrymen. He is speaking of the largeness of the subject of the *Paradise Lost*, which gives it, he says, an importance greater than that of the Iliad or the Aeneid.

"The anger of Achilles was of such consequence, that it embroiled the kings of Greece, destroyed the heroes of Asia, and engaged all the gods in factions. The settlement of Aeneas in Italy produced the Caesars, and gave birth to the Roman empire. Milton's subject was still greater than either of the former; it does not determine the fate of single persons or of nations, but of a whole species."

"A Roman," Addison goes on, "could not but rejoice in the escapes, successes, and victories of Aeneas, and be grieved at any defeats, or disappointments, that befell him; as a Greek must have had the same regard for Achilles. Milton's poem is admirable in this respect, since it is impossible for any of its readers, whatever nation, country, or people he may belong to, not to be related to the persons who are the principal actors in it. We have an actual interest in everything they do, and no less than our utmost happiness is concerned, and lies at stake in their behaviour."

As formal criticism this is obsolete. In quoting it I may possibly seem merely to be setting up a man of straw for the pleasure of knocking him down again.

But there is a reason for quoting it and for laying emphasis on it. It is this; that while the criticism is obsolete, the misapprehension of poetry which it implies will never be obsolete. Now it is just this misapprehension of itself, and of life as functionally related to itself, that poetry has perpetually to come into fresh existence in order to correct. So long as the misapprehension of poetry exists, the progress of poetry is secured.

At the centre of all poetry, just because it is poetry and in so far as it is poetry, is what is central and elemental. The relative largeness or smallness of its subject-matter is, to use the luminous metaphor of Plato, the same text written in larger or smaller letters. It may be written in the script of epic or romance, of lyric or of drama. It may deal with feats of kings and destinies of nations, with the life of those who wear soft raiment and are in kings' houses or with the obscure labour and sorrow of the people. The thing round which it takes shape may be so slight as a dead sparrow or a flower in the crannied wall: whatever it be, Addison's words apply in the full weight of their literal meaning: " We have an actual interest in it, and no less than our utmost happiness is concerned."

Poetry ranges in its progress over all the immense scale of existence. The image of perfection which it condenses from the flying vapours of the world fades, dissolves, is re-condensed, over and over again. It never continues in one stay. Movement is the condition of its being.

Hence it is that poetry, like life, is always beginning afresh. In all the embodiments of itself through which it passes it is mixed with matter. To that matter it gives life; by its incorporation in that matter it makes its own life visible and sensible. But the matter tends to encroach upon the vital spirit which informs it; poetry becomes encumbered by its own creations. It has to shake itself free from them, to volatilise for a new condensation. What is called —and not unjustly—the full development of any body or age of poetry is the sign that poetry is preparing to pass elsewhere, to pass away from what it has created and resume its function of creating.

This holds true not of mediæval poetry only, but of all poetry. It is equally true of Sophocles and Euripides, or in more modern times and in our own language, of Tennyson and Browning. The great innovation of the Athenian dramatists (to quote the familiar sentence of Grote) consisted in the rhetorical, the dialectical, and the ethical spirit which they breathed into their poetry. That stage in the progress of poetry means, once again, that poetry is preparing for a new embodiment. The rhetoric, the dialectic and the ethics soon clog the poetry. They were not the essence of the poetry, but only its transitory vesture. The vesture wears out, it ceases to fit; the live body of poetry outgrows it, slips it off, casts it away. Poetry finds that it has no further use for rhetoric and dialectic, or even for ethics. The image of human perfection is not permanently in these. The realities of life lie deeper, and are simpler.

"In the eyes of the Gods
War-laden galleys, and armies on white roads,
And unforgotten names, and the cold stars
That have built all are dust on a moth's wing.
These are their lures, but they have set their heart
On tears and laughter."

Or again, what makes the Aeneid (that I may take an instance now from Latin poetry) is not the greatness of its subject, great as that is: as Heyne describes it in the fine preface from which it is a delight to quote, *Magna et ardua consilia, excelsi et magnifici animorum sensus, virtus ultra vulgarem mortalitatis modulum, salus civium et imperii maiestas.* These are not what make the Aeneid: they are what make a *Pharsalia* or a *Thebaid.* What makes the Aeneid is the divine Virgilian pity. These are the lures of the high Muses, but they have set their hearts on tears and laughter. To Virgil they gave the "tears of things."

Let us take, as another instance, the poetry of Horace—a poet who for the purpose of testing theories or generalisations about poetry is of unique value, because he gives us, as one might say, poetry stripped to the bone. It is not the enlarged matter, the high argument of his political and moral odes that gives him his quality as a poet: indeed it is only his exquisite workmanship that redeems these from being, as all lyrics based on their model have since been, mannered and dull. He makes that universal appeal against which time and change and fashion seem powerless, because the Odes deal with the central realities of life—the little things. By the piled logs when Soracte is white, under the ilex that shadows the spring in the summer heat, yes, even in the suburban back-garden with its clipped vine, he sees the whole pageant of the world pass as though at a great distance. Unconcerned with the life and labour of the people—*neglegens ne qua populus laboret*—he is almost as little concerned with the large subject-matter of epic or romance, with high actions, and deep passions, and wide adventures. *Cetera fluminus ritu feruntur;* in the quiet life, with its bounded scope, its narrow range of thought and feeling, he found and fixed that on which the gods, and men too, have set their heart: tears and laughter, *debita lacrima, lentus risus*—note the scrupulous felicity of the epithets, those weighed and measured epithets in the use of which Horace is so consummate a master, —the " quiet laughter," the " due tears " of that narrow bounded space which is most central and most real in life.

Thus it is that the progress of poetry involves, in a certain sense, a continual reversion to its first elements. It develops and expands under the hand of successive poets, gathering into itself more and more of the whole complex fabric of life, conquering province after province. With the development of technique things that once were difficult for it to express become comparatively easy. It masters the art of expression; it meets the requirements of a closer truth to nature; it becomes more and more realistic: and then, one day, men find that with all its achieved realism it has lost touch of reality.

The first result of this discovery is dismay and disillusion; the cry goes up that poetry is exhausted. According to their temperament, people raise this cry with feelings that range from exultation to despair. To one view, the progress of human thought has got beyond poetry and is putting it away as a childish thing. To another, the world has entered upon an age too late, and the Muses have left earth. Both views are profoundly wrong. It is not that poetry is exhausted: it is that poetry has exhausted one particular form of expression, one particular embodiment of perishable matter. It has used up that, done what can be done with it, and turns to look elsewhere for a new body to fill with its own unexhausted, imperishable life.

That phrase of an age too late is familiar. As it was first used by Milton (if he was the first to use it, which

I do not know: the meaning, if not the exact wording, was of course no novelty, then or in Virgil's time or in a time as far back again beyond Virgil) it had a special and obvious relevance. At the age of over fifty, blind, poor, amid the wreck of all his own earlier hopes and the triumph of his enemies, it was natural that he should fall into a mood of despondence. We may not all remember that the exact phrase is used again, whether by coincidence or design, by Wordsworth in 1798, the *annus mirabilis* from which modern poetry began its splendid progress. "The world's a sleepy world, and 'tis, I fear, an age too late," he wrote then, just when the sleep was being broken and the new day had begun. And in the very next verse of the same poem comes that wonderful confession of faith in which poetry itself becomes reincarnate:

> "Long have I loved what I behold,
> The night that calms, the day that cheers:
> The common growth of mother-earth
> Suffices me—her tears, her mirth,
> Her humblest mirth and tears."

With these words poetry has gone back to life; or rather, we might say, life has come back to poetry.

Neither poetry nor history repeats itself. With both, the movement of revolution is also a movement of advance; and when the wheel has come full circle, it has reached a different point from that at which the circle began. Of that large orbit on which the epicycles are described we know little; we have not its formula and cannot, except by divination, predict its course. We call it, whatever be the implication attached to the word, by the name of progress. It has a periodic element; the periodic element in it is indeed obvious, and often appeals strikingly to the imagination. We can speak quite rationally of the lessons of history, although they are lessons the relevance of which is generally perceived only after the event. Just so we can speak of the lessons of poetry, can learn them and in some degree teach them. We can trace successive cycles of poetical development, and use the analogies of one to throw light upon another.

The analogies between the two bodies of poetry with which I have been particularly dealing are in a high degree suggestive and fertile. An interesting point on which I have barely touched is that in both cases the "popular" poetry, the poetry produced by the people for the people, is more archaic and hieratic than the poetry of the court. It reminds one of the saying that nothing is so conservative as a democracy. New departures, while they are in a sense the product of a progressive consciousness diffused through a whole race or nation, are in fact initiated by a single person, or a few persons, who are different from the mass of people, and with whom the mass of people are out of sympathy. Genius is individual, while taste is a matter of diffused habit; and every new development of poetry is at first as unpopular with the general public as it is with the expert critic. To gain its ground, the new poetry may have for a time to clothe itself in the garments of a language which has been so long familiar that it is on the point of becoming obsolete. Its forms remain conservative, while its spirit is revolutionary. The most splendid renascences have taken the form of going back to a past, when they were really creating a future.

Homer and Chaucer are alike in this, that they both represent static worlds, "middle ages." Langland, in the way which I have attempted to indicate, gives the complement of the Chaucerian world, as Hesiod does of the Homeric. They deal with what Homer and Chaucer left out. In that part of life left out, that unaccounted-for residuum, there lay, as in the unexplained errors in the calculations of astronomy, the promise and potency of fresh advances among unimagined worlds. The advance was not through Hesiod in Greece, nor through Langland here. It was through the gap in the Homeric and Chaucerian poetry which the existence of Hesiod and Langland implies. Nor did it take the form of filling up that gap. The progress of Greek poetry did not take the direction of regaining the romance which in Homer is suppressed. The progress of English poetry did not take the direction of regaining that touch with the pathos of existence, the life and labour of the people, which Chaucer had ignored. It was a new birth. In both cases a long interval elapses, obscure in history in the one case, obscure in literature in the other. Then comes in both cases the Renascence, the new world: there Hellas and the Greek lyric, here England of the sixteenth century and the predecessors of Shakespeare, rising to embody in modern poetry the many-sidedness, the mobility, the thrusting and expanding movement of modern life.

VIRGIL AND VIRGILIANISM

VARIOUS collections of minor Latin poetry, extant in MSS. dating from the eighth to the eleventh century, have been put together by modern editors into the volumes which are briefly and conveniently called the Latin Anthology. They contain a considerable number of pieces attributed at one time or another, and with or without reason, to Virgil's hand. At the one end of the scale is the *Culex*, where the external evidence for Virgilian authorship is exceptionally strong. At the other end are pieces where the Virgilian attribution is obviously a mere piece of ignorance or stupidity; the best known instance being the *Pervigilium Veneris*, where the first word of the title was misread by a blundering transcriber into the words *Per Vergilium*. It will be sufficient here to confine our attention to the pieces printed in Professor Ellis' volume, *Appendix Vergiliana sive Carmina minora Vergilio adtributa*. The contents of this volume are as follows: the *Culex*, the *Ciris*, the *Moretum*, the *Dirae*, the *Copa*, the *Catalepton*, the *Est et Non*, the *Vir Bonus*, and the *Maecenas*. Of the last three, the *Est et Non* and the *Vir Bonus* are in the manner, and may be confidently assigned to the period, of the fourth-century revival in which Ausonius is the principal figure; while the elegy on the death of Maecenas, whether it is a piece actually written on the occasion, or an academic exercise on that theme composed at a somewhat later date, has in either case no connexion with a poet who predeceased

Maecenas by eleven years. The others fall into two groups.

The first of the two groups consists of three poems, the *Culex*, *Ciris*, and *Moretum*, which stand by themselves. They were all, we may say with full assurance, written within Virgil's lifetime; and for the ascription to Virgil himself there is strong tradition in the case of the *Culex* and *Ciris*, and a greater or less amount of *prima facie* plausibility in the case of all three. On any theory of their authorship they throw much valuable light on the development of Latin poetry in the Virgilian age, and on the poetical methods and tendencies which contributed towards Virgil's own poetry.

The second group is at once slighter and more miscellaneous in its contents. The *Dirae* consists of two hexameter pastorals, in the manner, and attributable to about the date, of Virgil's Eclogues. In the hands of some transcriber they had been run together as a single poem, but are distinguished as two, the *Dirae* and the *Lydia*, by modern editors since Friedrich Jacobs. The bright little elegiac piece called the *Copa* belongs to about the same date. It is the work of a real poet: but the touch and handling are totally unlike Virgil's. Next on the list come three pieces prefixed to the *Catalepton*. They are inscriptions for a garden-statue, each in a different metre. All belong to the school of Catullus, whose language and manner they follow closely and with no small measure of grace and charm. The *Catalepton* proper is a collection of fourteen pieces, omitting the two numbered 13A and 14A, which are epigrams of no literary value and of obviously late date. Eight of them are in elegiac verse, and the rest in iambics or scazons. There are only three among the fourteen of which it can be said confidently that they are not early works of Virgil; there is only one of which it can be said confidently that it is: and the confidence in its case rests on no internal certainty, but on the express testimony of Quintilian.

Such, described as succinctly as possible, are the contents of the *Appendix Vergiliana*. In regarding them from the point of view which I wish to take, that of a study of Virgilianism in the age of Virgil, they group themselves rather differently. For this purpose the Juvenilia may be left pretty much out of account. Whether occasional pieces or merely school exercises, they are of little use towards our understanding of Virgil: they do not tell us anything about the development of his genius, and the surroundings in which it developed, that we do not already know. One exception may be made to this general statement. They enforce the recognition to be given to the influence of Catullus on the generation which succeeded or outlived him, on the movement in poetry which was proceeding at Rome midway between the Ciceronian and the Augustan age, say from the death of Catullus in 54 to the appearance of the Georgics in 30 B.C. They enable us therefore to appreciate rather more fully than we could appreciate without them how much it meant, to himself and the world, when Virgil by the publication of the Eclogues cancelled the existing tradition and announced a new poetry to a new age.

Dismissing these minor pieces then with this single note of recognition, we find that we have to deal with five poems which fall into two groups. The earlier of the two groups stands in intimate relation to the Virgil of the Bucolics; the later, in a relation possibly less intimate—as to this I shall have something to say later—but in any case marked and important, to the Virgil of the Georgics. The one group consists of the

Ciris, Dirae, and *Lydia*; the other, of the *Culex* and *Moretum.*

If any argument were needed to show how baseless is the notion of a hostility between poetry and science, one might be found in the immense gain that has come in the last generation to appreciation and understanding of the poets from the introduction of scientific method into the study of poetry. It is only this which has enabled us to realise, in any full way, how poetry is a function of life. It is only this which has enabled us to realise at all, how the progress of poetry is not something discontinuous, accidental, and unaccountable. Our very notions of poetic creation have silently and profoundly changed. We no longer think of poetry as something half mechanical and half magical. The mechanism and the magic are both there, both as wonderful as ever; but they are being realised now as the mechanism of life and the magic of life.

One result of this changed attitude is that the poet does not present himself to us as an isolated personality or the poem as an isolated fact. Both are attached organically to their environment by a thousand filaments. All poetry is the projection on a visible plane of a vast and exceedingly complex mass of poetical tendencies and potentialities. It is a living organism with powers of absorption, assimilation, reconstitution. The originality of a poet or of a poem does not mean that he makes it, or that it makes itself in some unaccountable way, out of nothing. The greatest poets may derive the most from predecessors or even from their contemporaries. The greatest poems— and this is the case with Virgil's poems to an eminent degree—may be the fullest of what are called borrowings, if they do not receive the blunter name of thefts.

Before the organic quality of poetry was illuminated by modern science, this fact, which is unquestionable, had to be apologised for and explained away. "His known wealth was so great," said Johnson of Cowley, "that he might borrow without loss of his credit." We know now that in dealing with the vital energy of poetry the case cannot be put fully in these mechanical terms. The poet does not borrow, he absorbs and assimilates; what passes into his imagination reissues as his own, because it has become part of himself. The boundaries of personality are, in this as in other matters, elusive, and can only be fixed by certain conventions. But the central fact of personality is as vital as it is indisputable.

It is in this light that we must regard Virgil if we are to understand his position in poetry. For at least ten years before the publication of the Eclogues he had been studying his art intensely. But it is equally important to remember that he had not done so in isolation. He was one of a school or circle— so close were the relations among them that we may perhaps call them a brotherhood—to whom poetry had taken a new meaning and who felt in it new possibilities. Something of the same sort happened in Elizabethan England with the group of young poets and students which included Sidney and Spenser. In both cases, as if to make the parallel more complete, the most brilliant and accomplished member of the group was swept away from poetry into public life, and died young. Sidney, more fortunate than Cornelius Gallus, was struck down on the field of battle, and died before the coldness with which he was regarded by his sovereign had matured into disgrace. The heartless words in which Elizabeth is said to have commented on his death are such as one may fancy Augustus using of Gallus if he had perished gloriously while still viceroy of Egypt. But in both cases the decisive step in poetry was taken by the student, not by the courtier. The Eclogues, like Spenser's *Shepherds Calendar*, were issued and accepted as the manifesto of the new poetry. Their shy, diffident, reserved author found himself the leader of a movement, the gate-vein of the heart's blood (to use the vivid phrase applied by Browning to the poet who, nearly thirteen centuries later, attempted a like task anew), which was to fill the exhausted channels of poetry. Virgil became, at once and once for all, the mouthpiece of that larger movement which, as we now look back upon it in the result, we may best describe by the name of Virgilianism.

In spite of all the obvious weaknesses of the Eclogues, they obtained an easy, immediate, and almost universal conquest alike of popular fame and of critical admiration. There were two reasons for this. One was what I have just mentioned, the fact that they bore the standard of the new poetry. Latin poetry was in a critical position. The extraordinary personal genius of Catullus had given an adventitious lustre to the hard, scholarly Alexandrianism of the school to which he technically belonged. It seemed to hold the field. But it was leading poetry up a blind alley. From this the new poetry opened an outlet; and the enthusiasm evoked by the Eclogues was very largely due to a sense of relief. Still tentative, uncertain, imperfect, full of faults of workmanship, the new poetry had shaken off the fetters of an exhausting convention; its feet still stumbled, its eyes did not see clear, but it was alive. It bore the hope and promise of the future.

But there was another reason. We are too apt

to fancy, in an age intoxicated with discoveries, and staggering under its new armament of critical methods, that we can understand and interpret the poets better than their contemporaries could—better even than they could themselves. Do the Eclogues mean more to us now than they did to their first readers? Can they mean half as much? They come to us indeed charged with a thousand associations which have gathered round them in the course of nearly twenty centuries. But these associations, while they enrich, also obscure. We can never have a first impression of them, as a thing hitherto unknown, a new voice, the dawn of a new day. To some at least of their earliest readers—perhaps to many—they represented not merely a movement but a literal creation. They were not only Virgilianism, but Virgil himself; something wholly new, wholly alone, in tenderness and sweetness, in vibrating pathos of language, in that melancholy majesty which was to expand later into what we know. The criticism passed on them by scholars may have been, as it still tends to be, formal and shallow; it was not however on the critics, but on the lovers of poetry, that they told in their full effect as poetry. The new poet, no less than the new poetry, became a passion, an adoration.

Virgilianism spoke through Virgil in the Eclogues. But it also spoke through other voices. Gallus, Varius, Macer, Cinna, the poet only known under the unidentified pseudonym of Codrus, perhaps others of whom all certain trace is lost, were likewise its exponents, though each of them added some personal note of his own. Even did we possess all the poetry produced by the circle, we should find it hard to distinguish sharply between the work of one and that of another, or to distinguish that in any one of them which was the product of the movement, and almost impersonal, from that which was individual. The methods and language of the new poetry were not yet crystallised. As they became fixed, Virgil's work came to differ more and more from that of his brother-poets of the school, not because it was more original in the sense of deriving less from others, but because of two qualities in which he left the others far behind. One of these was the constructive and architectural power which was part of his own gift from nature, and which he slowly developed through unceasing study. The other was his power of fusing his material by the greater intensity of his own genius. In this latter quality he was pre-eminent from the first.

The output of the Virgilian circle, other than the Eclogues, was certainly large in these years; but the three poems which we are now considering are the only substantial fragments which survive. Their authorship has been long a puzzle, and the wildest conjectures have been made with regard to it. No one in modern times has seriously argued that they are by Virgil himself; it is their relation to Virgil that is the problem. It will be convenient to take the *Ciris* first.

What leaps to the eyes in reading the *Ciris* is its saturation throughout with Virgilian phrases. A passage of three lines occurs, with one slight verbal change, in the sixth Eclogue. A passage of four lines occurs, with no change at all, in the first Georgic. But these are only the two most glaring instances of what is the case throughout. Go through the *Ciris* carefully, marking all the lines and half lines and phrases which occur, with or without some slight variation, in the Eclogues, in the Georgics, and in the earlier books of the Aeneid, and you will find at the end that your *Ciris* is a mass of pencil-marks. The most obvious conclusion to draw would naturally be that the *Ciris* is a post-Virgilian poem, and that Virgil's poems have been ruthlessly laid under contribution for it, as they were, hundreds of years afterwards, by the cento-makers of the decadence, and by the Latin poets of the Renaissance. But this explanation will not bear scrutiny. For on the one hand the *Ciris* is not merely a set of verses cleverly strung together: it is not an exercise in a dead language, nor a fabric of verse mechanically compiled. It is a living and a complete work of art, with a genius of its own, an unmistakeable personal note of style and manner. And on the other hand the internal evidence of language and versification fixes it demonstrably within the period we are now considering, the twenty years or thereabout after the death of Catullus. That being its date, it follows from its pervading and inwrought Virgilianisms that it is a product of the Virgilian circle. This fact, together with certain very distinguished poetical qualities of its own, makes it a document of great importance in the history of poetry.

Only in recent years have the delicate and rigorous processes of modern analysis been applied to the *Ciris;* only in recent years indeed could that have been possible, for such analysis is the creation of modern science—or rather perhaps we should say, is a creation of that development of the human mind from which modern science itself has been created. Professor Skutsch of Breslau, one of the ablest of modern Latin scholars, has approached the problem in his two treatises entitled *Aus Vergils Frühzeit*, published in 1901 and 1906. If any fault is to be found with these two volumes, it is that they show here and there, in particular criticisms, a somewhat imperfect realisation of the way in which a poet works and the way in which poetry comes into existence. No one who is not himself a poet quite knows this; and few scholars, even if they be scholars of real judgment and insight, are wholly free from a tendency to analyse poetry as if it were an inorganic substance. *Dann hat er die Teile in seiner Hand; Fehlt leider nur das geistige Band:* the old gibe of Mephistopheles is still true of scholars in the country of Faust—and in other countries as well. But subject to this reservation— and it is a reservation only, not a detraction—Professor Skutsch has produced a work of masterly constructive criticism. He has not only seen and stated the problem; though that would have been much, for it had hardly been done at all adequately or lucidly before. He has done much more; he has given a solution of it which may be accepted as in the main right; and in doing so he has made the most important contribution of modern times towards the appreciation of Virgil as an artist, and of Virgilianism as art.

The solution, as he states it, is that the *Ciris* was written by Gallus, at the time when Gallus and Virgil were both young poets living in the closest intimacy. That intimacy has always been matter of common knowledge; one need not go beyond the Eclogues themselves for evidence. The association was probably quite as close as that of Spenser and Sidney in 1579, or even as that of Wordsworth and Coleridge in 1798. But the true inference, as it bears both upon the *Ciris* and on those lines in the sixth and tenth Eclogues which, according to the Servian commentary, were taken from poems by Gallus, now lost, was until recently missed. It may be taken as now established that, so far as the *Ciris* is the work of Gallus, the phrases and passages which are common to it and to the Georgics or the Aeneid were taken by Virgil from the *Ciris*, and not taken by the author of the *Ciris* from the Aeneid and the Georgics.

There is nothing surprising in this. Nor is it perhaps surprising that some German critics should find in it an opportunity for taking a turn at their national pastime of Virgil-baiting. Virgil was hotly assailed with the charge of plagiarism by his own contemporaries; but it never seems to have troubled him much. He knew his art. He knew that the thing that matters is not where a poet gets his material, but what he does with it. Whether from Homer, or from Apollonius, or from Theocritus, or from Euphorion and Parthenius; whether from Ennius or from Lucretius and Varro of Atax, or from his own friends and fellow-students, he took, largely and unsparingly, whatever he found in them that served his purpose. What he took, he made his own by the mere act of taking it. Homer —by Homer I mean the poet who gave us our Iliad— had done the same thing long before. Both argosies are freighted with the treasure of many sunken ships.

But there is an important point to be added. "So far," I said just now, "as the *Ciris* is the work of Gallus." That it is the work of Gallus, to something of the same extent as the Eclogues are the work of Virgil, we cannot I think on view of the whole evidence reasonably doubt. But the two young poets were not only linked by a close friendship, and inspired by common aims and enthusiasms. They worked at their art together. Their poetry in those years sprang up between them, in the interaction and mutual influence of their two minds. To what extent this was so in any particular poem or passage we cannot tell. But the fact, with all it involves, is indisputable.

We do not know what of Sidney there is in the *Shepherds Calendar*. Coleridge in later years gave a statement of what he had contributed to Wordsworth's pieces, and Wordsworth to his, in the *Lyrical Ballads*. We may accept that statement as correct, or not, according to the view we are disposed to take of the accuracy of Coleridge's memory or of the degree of his regard for truth. But the poems came into being through the interpenetration of genius between the two: their authors were the Wordsworth who was influenced by Coleridge, and the Coleridge who was influenced by Wordsworth. Such, or of such a kind, was the relation between Virgil and Gallus. And this would be true even if it were the case that the sensuous, brilliant, erratic Gallus was as far below Coleridge in essential poetic genius as the brooding solitary Virgil was above Wordsworth.

When therefore Servius tells us that certain lines in the tenth Eclogue were taken over (*translata*) from Gallus; or when we come ourselves to the conclusion that certain other lines common to the *Ciris* and the Georgics must have appeared in the *Ciris* first, because it was written before the Georgics; or when Professor Skutsch, entering on a much more debateable ground, argues that certain other lines or phrases common to the *Ciris* and the Eclogues are Gallus' and not Virgil's, because to his mind, and according to his canons of criticism, they come more naturally and more relevantly in the *Ciris*—in all these cases it is necessary to emphasise the very subtle nature of joint poetical authorship and mutual poetical influence. " Great contemporaries," said a famous critic long ago, " whet and cultivate each other; and mutual borrowing and commerce makes the common riches of learning." This is true of poetry as well as of other branches of the literary art. Gallus was a borrower, if we must use the word, as well as Virgil: the *Ciris* is full of borrowings, and it is more likely than not that among them are borrowings from Virgil. What Virgil may have lent he had the right to resume, as what he borrowed he had the right to keep. Both were his own.

Yet with all its Virgilianism, the quality of the poetry in the *Ciris* is different from that of the poetry in the Eclogues. It has a distinct individual touch. The line of development taken by its author is not the same as Virgil's, though as yet the two have diverged from one another but little. We may trace, I think, in the *Ciris* a genius that had developed faster than Virgil's, that was more quick and alert. It is the common case of early brilliance which shoots ahead, but soon comes to its limit. Virgil, we know, composed slowly and with difficulty: the author of the *Ciris* seems to write with ease, and to have a great natural gift of imitating the style of his predecessors. The *Ciris* begins with four lines which are pure Catullus. Of the opening line,

"Etsi me vario iactatum laudis amore,

one might be tempted to say, *Aut Valerius aut diabolus*. Then follow a dozen lines more which are as pure Lucretius; not only full of Lucretian phrases, but accurately reproducing the Lucretian colour and movement. The first forty-seven lines are indeed throughout a brilliant exercise or variation in a synthesis of these two styles. Then, in lines forty-eight to fifty-three, the new style shows itself for the first time.

" Impia prodigiis ut quondam exterrita mollis
Scylla novos avium sublimis in aere coetus
Viderit, et tenui conscendens aethera penna

Caeruleis sua tecta supervolitaverit alis :
Hanc pro purpureo poenam scelerata capillo
Pro patria solvens excisa [et] funditus urbe."

That new style is Virgil's. Eclogues, Georgics, the earlier part of the Aeneid: we have them all in these six lines. It is as though Virgil himself had sat down by Gallus and guided his pen, or as though Gallus had suddenly felt and begun to reproduce Virgil's own melody and phrasing. So it goes on, in the same rapid brilliant movement, with the same enriched style and language which seem crossed and mingled, as in a web of shot silk, to produce a new fabric with a sheen and lustre of its own. It would be fascinating to follow this through the poem line by line: let me just quote one instance in which the two elements, the older and the newer, lie side by side most unmistakeably. (ll. 349–352.)

"Postera lux ubi prima diem mortalibus almum
†Extulit et gelida taedam† quatiebat ab Oeta
Quem pavidae alternis fugitant optantque puellae,
Hesperium vitant, optant ardescere Eoum."

The MSS. are corrupt and the reading uncertain in the second of these four lines: and what I have printed above has no authority. But for the rest, the first line of the four is in the exact phrasing and rhythm of the Aeneid; the third and fourth are in the exact phrasing and rhythm of the marriage-hymn of Catullus.

Virgil tells us that he had already begun to sing of kings and battles when he wrote the Eclogues. The Aeneid was the work not only of the eleven years after the publication of the Georgics, but of his whole lifetime; and the number of instances in which the *Ciris* recalls or anticipates the Aeneid lends support to the view, which is in itself highly probable, that much of what afterwards became the Aeneid was written in these early years, in the ardour of youth and under the stimulus of close friendship and emulation among that circle of young poets. All through the Aeneid, here and there, a trained ear and eye can still retrace the lines and cadences of that youthful composition, though it was afterwards brooded over, remoulded and retouched year after year, and left still imperfect at his death in Virgil's own fastidious and merciless judgment.

When we turn from the *Ciris* to the two pastorals, the *Dirae* and *Lydia*, we find ourselves still in the same circle of poetry, but reading the work of a third poet. Who he was cannot be even plausibly conjectured. The Sicilian landscape in the two poems seems not wholly conventional; nor have they that delicate but distinct romantic touch which the *Ciris* shares with the Eclogues, and which it is tempting, though fanciful and of doubtful relevance, to connect with a Northern and Celtic element in the blood of both Gallus and Virgil. They suggest the Latin of the South; there is a flavour in them which is analogous to that of the volcanic wines of the *Terra di Lavoro*. A little hard, a little heavy, they are more on the ordinary lines of Roman poetry, and show its characteristic defects. They have a quality of style and substance which is peculiarly Roman but likewise peculiarly un-Virgilian. The influence of Virgilianism is strong in them, but it has not penetrated to the centre.

A note in their style, which is also Roman, is the tendency to be sententious, and the tendency to state things clearly and leave little to suggestion or implication. "Virgil," says Dryden, and it is one of his many exquisite criticisms, "had the gift of expressing

VIRGIL AND VIRGILIANISM 63

much in little, and sometimes in silence." That gift was personal to himself; he did not share it with his school. This other poet will not be content to end, in the final apostrophe to Lydia, on the cadence of *semper amabo*. He must needs add another line to make all sure:

"Gaudia semper enim tua me meminisse licebit."

So too in the *Dirae*—

"Piscetur nostris in finibus advena arator,"

he says, and then cannot forbear from going on:

"Advena civili qui semper crimine crevit."

"The last and greatest art" is lacking here. Dryden's criticism recurs: "as he knew what to say, so he knows also when to leave off, a continence which is practised by few writers." This failure of continence, it may be noted in passing, is also characteristic of the *Culex*. We find it there in passages which reproduce the exact phrasing of this passage:

"—impia lotos,
Impia, quae socios Ithaci maerentis abegit,"

or,

"—feror avia carpens,
Avia Cimmerios inter distantia lucos:"

or

"—Ditis sine iudice sedes,
Iudice, qui vitae post mortem vindicat acta."

If the *Culex* is from Virgil's own hand, we see here what those first drafts of Virgil's were like which he distilled and concentrated later, and which he kept so jealously from the public eye.

Yet this poet was no mere versifier. He is at his best when he is perfectly simple; sometimes he is almost Greek in his faculty of putting into a phrase of plain prose that faint inner glow, that just perceptible musical cadence, which make it poetry. This is most striking in the *Lydia*, the second of the two pieces.

> "Non ulla puella
> Doctior in terris fuit aut formosior"—

it is like a phrase from a Greek lyric for pellucid colour. Or again:

> "Luna, tuus tecum est: cur non est et mea mecum?
> Luna, dolor nosti quid sit: miserere dolentis."

There is the touch of Theocritus here in the way that the popular ballad-verse is taken up and woven into the structure of a poem. It is not such an easy thing to do. Theocritus could do it, but that was because Theocritus was not only a poet but a Greek poet: for a quality of the finest Greek poetry, from Homer to the late Anthologists, is its power of taking common language and transforming it into poetry by an all but imperceptible touch. Virgil could do it, but not always; he attempted it in the last four lines of the fourth Eclogue with very dubious success.

Nor is that all. One can hear in this couplet, pulsing under the foreign vesture of the quantitative hexameter, the native poetical form of Italy, the accentual rhyming trochaic. Listen, and it will emerge.

> "Luna, tuus est ut tecum,
> Cur non est et mea mecum?
> Luna, quid sit dolor sentis,
> Miserere tu dolentis."

The subterranean current of the native metres was, long afterwards, to come to the surface again. Even in the central classical period it was never wholly lost; and here it is.

This poet had, too, a sensitiveness beyond the common run of Latin poets for the aspects and processes of nature. In this quality Virgil stands alone; but in Virgil it is from the first mixed up with the rapt, almost mystical spirit in which he regards the external world. There is none of this here; but there is a notable power of seizing and expressing natural phenomena, especially visible tones or colours, with a delicate precision. This may be seen for instance where he speaks of the rain smoking on the hills, *fumantes montibus imbres:* or of the first appearance of the stars at evening faint in a clear green sky: *sidera per viridem redeunt cum pallida mundum.*

The poems we have been considering are all that is left to us to supplement the Eclogues themselves in trying to reconstitute and appreciate the earlier growth and movement of Virgilianism in the Virgilian circle. When we pass from them to the *Culex* and *Moretum* we pass from the period of the Eclogues to that of the Georgics. In the ten years between 40 and 30 B.C. the group of new poets had grown or drifted apart. Virgil had developed his unique personal genius, and already stood alone, in unquestioned and solitary eminence. Gallus had been absorbed into public life, and perhaps had already exhausted his precocious and brilliant gift of poetry. Of the work of Macer, Varius, Cinna, and the rest, we know little or nothing. So far as the progress of poetry showed itself in them, we may conjecture that it took developments analogous, up to the limit of their powers in each case, to the development which took place in Virgil himself. But

Virgilianism, in the significant sense of the term, is now no longer a common poetical impulse, a joint poetical movement, of which Virgil is the recognised mouthpiece, the chosen standard-bearer. It has become the movement and impulse produced by Virgil, and communicating itself from his poetry to that of other poets, who are now not his colleagues, but his imitators or his followers. It is already well started on its way towards becoming an external model, an academic standard. The Virgilians have become a school, of which Virgil is the master. The result is that the *Vergiliana* belonging to these later years throw but little in the way of side-light on Virgil's own poetry. The problems of authorship which they involve are difficult, subtle, and interesting, but they have not the same suggestive and fascinating quality.

The poems in question are the *Culex* and the *Moretum*: and the question with regard to them is whether one or both are, in part or in whole, Virgil's own work.

That Virgil must have written a good deal, besides the Georgics as they were given by him to the world, during the ten years after the publication of the Eclogues, would be obvious even if there were not express and authentic testimony to the fact. His whole life was given up to poetry. He wrote much, brooded over it long and wrought on it endlessly, altered it, expunged it, destroyed it mercilessly. The Eclogues, a volume of little over eight hundred lines, were all that he published as the result of ten or twelve years of work and study. In the ten years which followed he was working as incessantly, and with expanding power, greater sureness of hand, more mastery over his art. He was content that what he had to show for those ten years should be the Georgics. Even after that, the Aeneid as he left it at his death is the final distillation of immense labour and of fresh experiments and developments which were going on up to the end of his life. By his will he left express instructions that nothing of his should be published beyond what he had published himself. It required imperial command, or at least a strong expression of opinion by the Emperor, to except the Aeneid itself from this ordinance. But the ordinance was carried out as regards all the rest of his unpublished poetry. Much of this we must suppose to have been destroyed. With what was not so destroyed one or both of two things may have happened. Some of it was, we know for certain, extant in copies which were beyond the control of his executors. Some of it was, in all probability, not destroyed by them, although they did not publish it. It is obviously possible that any of his poetry which fell under this latter class may have crept into private and later into public circulation. But if any of it had reached us, it would reach us in an unauthorised and dubious text, and would be very liable to confusion and interpolation. These considerations must be carefully borne in mind when we enter on the question of authorship as it applies to the *Culex* and the *Moretum*.

Both poems are alike in this, that on formal analysis they show nothing which makes it impossible, or even improbable, that they should have been written by Virgil. Their grammatical, verbal, and metrical technique is the same as his. This is, however, only negative evidence; we may attach greater or less weight to it, but it decides nothing. Beyond it, the factors which have to be weighed and balanced towards forming a conclusion are, curiously enough, almost exactly reversed for the two poems. Briefly, the case may be put thus. The external evidence for the Virgilian authorship of the *Culex* is so good, that but for certain internal or poetical considerations it would be accepted without question, or only doubted by professional athetisers. The internal evidence for the Virgilian authorship of the *Moretum* is so good that it would require but little external support: but there is no external evidence for it at all. For the ascription of a poem to Virgil in a collection which does not date back beyond the fifth century, and which also included under Virgil's name pieces that bear the mark of the fourth century on their face, is not evidence enough to hang a dog upon.

As regards the *Culex*, we have the express testimony of Martial and Suetonius, and twice over, of Statius, that a poem of Virgil's under this name was extant. In a matter of this sort, Statius, who was not only a scholar and poet but a profound student and literal worshipper of Virgil, could hardly be mistaken. That the poem known to Statius was a different one from the poem which we possess there is not the slightest ground for supposing. Attempts have been made to argue that it both was and was not, by a hypothesis of large interpolations in our poem made on a basis of Virgil's poem. But they are futile. The texture of the *Culex* as we have it is uniform. Two theories alone seem possible: either that it was written by a contemporary of Virgil who had caught the Virgilian technique to perfection, that it became confused with a poem on the same subject which Virgil had written but which he or his executors had destroyed, and that the confusion was so complete as to impose on the whole body of Virgilian scholars of the Silver Age: or, that it is Virgil's work. The former theory seems a desperate paradox. But the latter involves a paradox apparently almost as great, and from the point of view of poetry more interesting. For it means this: that Virgil, at a time when he had matured his technique, could write a poem as long as a book of the Georgics with great care and finish, and yet leave out of it the specific personal note of the Virgilian genius. Is such a thing possible, and if so, how? The question opens up a larger one: that of the whole method and process, or body of methods and processes, by which the concrete work of art called a poem comes into being.

In poetry, as in painting or in any other art, each great artist has his own method. Within certain large limits, fixed by the nature of the material, these methods vary much from one another. The artist himself cannot, if he would, always give an account of them; they are partly conscious, but in large measure sub-conscious or instinctive. Of Virgil's methods we know something from fairly authentic tradition, and can gather a good deal more from study of the poems themselves. In the Life by Donatus there are two statements made which are of great interest in this connexion, and which we need not hesitate to accept as substantially true: first, that before beginning to compose the Aeneid, Virgil set it out in prose (*prosa prius oratione firmatam componere instituit*) and worked on various parts of this prose framework or sketch according as the fancy took him at one time or another: secondly, that in the actual composition, he wrote down passages which were merely meant to fill a gap temporarily, and to be rewritten later: shores, *tibicines*, he called them, which were to keep up the structure until the solid pillars were ready to take their place. From these statements, in the light thrown on them by careful study of those portions of the Aeneid which have clearly not received the final touches, we may gather that at certain stages in its progress, an episode or even a whole poem may have been in a sense complete, while it still had to be worked over from beginning to end in order to give it its final colour, life, and tone. "Though I alter not the draught," Dryden said of one of his own masterpieces, "I must touch the same features over again, and change the dead colouring of the whole." The metaphor is taken from painting: and this is the practice of some painters. A picture over which months of work have been spent is brought to a stage in which it is highly finished, but dead: and then (for the artist knew what he meant, and up to what he was working, from the first) two or three days' work all over it, by such slight touches as to be individually almost imperceptible, transfigures it and makes it alive. It is not impossible that the *Culex* is a work of Virgil's which had reached that stage, and which he then laid aside, either knowing that he could put the vitalising, Virgilianising touches to it when he chose, or because it was written as an exercise and he had no further use for it.

If this general theory may be hazarded to explain the problem of the *Culex*, it would exactly fit the facts as regards the *Moretum*. This little highly-finished cabinet-piece is said to be pretty closely modelled on a Greek idyl with the same subject by Parthenius of Nicaea. Parthenius was an accomplished scholar and poet. Gallus was his patron and pupil, and he was in intimate relations with the Virgilian circle: Virgil himself together with the rest of them no doubt owed much to his instruction and criticism. But the *Moretum*, to whatever extent it may have followed a Greek original, is itself a work of finished and individual art. It may remind us of some early piece by Raffaele, in which the composition and colouring of a painting by Perugino are closely followed, but transformed to new beauty by the genius of the pupil. It has a Raffaelesque suavity and grace. No one else among the pupils of Parthenius, so far as is known, could have done work of such luminous silvery colour, such order of composition and purity of line.

That the little piece, if it be authentic, should be omitted from the lists given in the Life by Donatus and in the Servian commentary is curious, but not at all unaccountable. It was probably among Virgil's unpublished works, and its existence even may have been known only to a few friends. That it was not wholly lost may be a chance due to the preservation in private hands of a single copy. Even published poems had then a very precarious life when they were not regularly reproduced for the market. It was easier to suppress them than to ensure their preservation. The original ending of the fourth Georgic had been published for four or five years before it was recalled and cancelled. Many copies of it must have existed. Yet it has vanished utterly, and not left a line or a trace. Virgil chose to be represented to future ages only by his approved and finished work. He was not allowed to exclude the Aeneid from his gift to Rome and to the world: with that exception, he has had his desire.

THE AENEID

The Aeneid is eminently, and perhaps more than any other single work of the Graeco-Latin world, a classic in the full sense that can be attached to that word. This statement is not meant either to put Virgil in some way into competition with other Latin authors, or to put the Latin classics in some way into competition with the classics of Greece. In such matters there is no question of competition.

This is well understood as regards any rivalry between Greek and Latin; it is indeed implied throughout when we speak, as we all traditionally and quite rightly do, of Greek and Latin authors conjointly under the common name of the Classics. Greece and Rome represent two forces, two different streams of tendency and bodies of achievement which are nevertheless indissoluble, which flow together, intermingle and reinforce each other to fill the sources from which succeeding ages have drawn. But of the two, Rome is the closer to us, the more directly in the line of ascent. Modern life owes its highest ideals, directly or indirectly, to the inspiration of Greece; it owes its whole structure and existence to the creation of Rome. And so also with the two languages; for while Greek is a language of unequalled beauty, flexibility, and strangeness, Latin is, to us and to all the inheritors of the Latin civilisation, a second mother tongue.

Of that Latin literature through which the life and

thought of Rome and the Latin race most fully expressed themselves, and have continued most fully to impress the world, the Aeneid is the central point. We may put aside any question as to the relative value of prose and poetry in the world of letters, as we may put aside any question as to the relative poetical merits of Virgil and the other Latin poets, Lucretius for instance, or Catullus, or Horace. As a mere matter of fact and history, Virgil has been, from his own day until now, the voice, the interpreter, the chosen recorder and exponent of Rome—of the Latin race, the Latin empire, the Latin civilisation. *Virgile,* said the great French critic, and the sentence, though familiar, is still well worth repeating, *depuis l'heure où il parut a été le poete de la Latinité toute entière.* Virgil has been from the hour of his appearance the poet of the whole of Latinity, of the Latin world: not merely of those countries and ages, which have been fully Roman and possessed, as one might say, the full Roman citizenship, but also of that far wider circle over which the *Latinitas*, the secondary citizenship of the intellectual and spiritual Rome, has extended itself. He sums up and in a way includes or at least implies all the rest. It is almost impossible to imagine what a difference it would make to the whole of Latin literature if Virgil had disappeared from it. All that comes before him leads, in one way or another, up to him: all that comes after him is profoundly affected by him, holds of him, draws from him, to a greater or less degree, but always visibly, and for the most part deeply, its inspiration, its ideas, much of its very language. That this is true of the later Latin poets is a familiar commonplace; but post-Augustan Latin prose likewise is saturated with Virgilianism; you will find this direct Virgilian influence in authors so widely remote from one another, to name three typical instances, as Tacitus, the last of the classics, Apuleius, the first of the mediævalists, Augustine, the greatest of the Christians. The literature of the pagan decadence, of the Christian Middle Ages, and of the emancipated Renaissance all draws from Virgil as one of its main sources, just as the constructive work of those successive ages, their life and civilisation, all draw from Rome. To sum the matter up in a single sentence; so far as language embodies life, so far as men's written words are the soul and action of mankind made incarnate, so far, in no mere metaphor but as actual fact, Virgil was Rome.

He became so at once, even within his own lifetime. Horace was the laureate of the Augustan age, if one may use the term of laureate in a wide sense without pressing its meaning too far: he was the court poet, and in his official odes the greatness of Rome, of the Roman character and the Roman civilisation, found memorable expression. But Virgil was much more than laureate; he was the voice of Rome and of the whole Italian race; in him they instinctively and all but universally recognised, not only their poet but their prophet and interpreter. Some seventy or eighty years after his death, a brilliant and accomplished man of letters had occasion to mention him and Horace in the same sentence. It is in that sentence that he gives us that singularly fine and luminous phrase with regard to Horace which has passed into universal currency—*curiosa felicitas*. The two words even now sum up the genius of Horace more exactly than a whole volume of critical appreciation. But for Virgil he has no such brilliant phrase; what he says of him is even briefer, only one word, but a word of just insight and profound meaning: *Romanus Vergilius*, Roman Virgil.

The art, the achievement, the purpose and effect of Virgil culminate and are summed up in the Aeneid; what I desire to do now is to consider the circumstances in which the Aeneid was created, and to consider its quality as a work of art, and as an expression and interpretation of life. Within the limits of a single lecture it is of course impossible to deal, even in outline, with the whole subject. I will merely indicate briefly some of the more important things to be borne in mind, and some of the lines upon which a fuller study may be pursued, as time and circumstances may permit. What follows is to be taken as suggestive rather than informing, and its object will be fully met if it sends back any reader to the Aeneid itself with some amount of quickened interest in the study from one or another point of view.

A movement has been spreading in recent years among our schools and colleges, towards the reading of the Aeneid as a whole. That it should be so read, that it must be so read if it is to be either understood or appreciated, is a proposition so self-evident that it requires no argument to support it. The Aeneid is a single and complete work of art, which is meant to produce, and does produce, a single and complete effect. Certainly it is only by reading it as a whole and letting it produce its total effect upon the mind that we can see it for what it is: only then can we begin to grasp its full significance, to feel its actual quality: only then can we realise the way in which it gathers up, so to say, all the threads of interest which run through the Graeco-Latin world at its fullest development. The Aeneid as a whole, in its total accumulated import, embodies and makes visible the Latin genius on all its sides; in its own native growth, and as affected by Greek influence and again interpreting Greece to a larger world, and once more, as itself affecting for succeeding ages their whole thought and art and view of life. No one knows Latin in any real sense who does not know the Aeneid; and it may be said conversely that any one who really knows the Aeneid knows Latin. What one can call a real knowledge of the Aeneid of course implies long study, and a scholarship both wide and deep. But the beginnings of it can be made by all who have advanced beyond the merely elementary stage of learning Latin: and they can be carried on, to such an extent as each student may find possible, and in such directions as he finds most specially interesting, with constant pleasure and profit, because with perpetually increasing appreciation.

The composition of the Aeneid was begun by Virgil at the age of forty, after he had finished and published the Georgics. It went on through the rest of his life; when he died at the age of fifty-one he left the MS. of it almost complete, though it still lacked the final revision. Three years' more work, he thought, was still necessary to bring it to completion, or such completion as was within his power. So sensitive was he towards his own ideals in poetry, so merciless towards imperfect work of his own however good it might be, that his last instructions to his executors were to destroy the manuscript. This was not done; it was carefully and competently revised; a choice was made between the alternative drafts which were found of some passages, and other passages were struck out which were clearly imperfect, or as to which there was evidence that he had himself meant to omit them; but no retouchings or additions were made. The poem as thus revised was published; the rejected material was suppressed, and except for one passage of four lines, has wholly disappeared.

While the Aeneid thus represents the systematic and incessant work of eleven years, it represents a good deal more than this; for Virgil wrought into it the work of a whole lifetime. Epic poetry had been his earliest ambition; he had begun, in his own words, "to sing of kings and battles" long before he wrote the Eclogues; and in the Aeneid we can find here and there traces of quite early work. We can find passages which though worked over, remodelled, and partly rewritten later, still bear clear signs of youthful composition in substance as well as in style and diction: just as elsewhere we meet with episodes which seem to incorporate separate shorter poems, *epyllia* or short epic pieces, that may have been composed in their original form before he had set the scheme of the Aeneid definitely out. Such for instances are the epic idyls, as they may be called, of Nisus and Euryalus, of Hercules at Pallanteum, and of the life and death of Camilla. These and others were absorbed into and became parts of the larger design after he had resolved to concentrate himself wholly on the Aeneid and include in it all that he meant to give to the world.

It was this resolution which determined the form and substance of the Aeneid: it was this which on the one hand made it the richest, the most fully charged, of all Latin poems, perhaps even of all poems that ever have been written, and which on the other hand caused it to remain up to the last something expanding, widening, even in a sense tentative and incomplete in the whole design as well as in the execution of its parts. Throughout we can see and feel the substance of the poem changing and growing under Virgil's hand. We can trace in it successive moods, successive interests. The motive idea is throughout complex, but in varying measures of complexity; one can hardly speak of a single dominant motive in the whole poem, though in portions of it one or another motive asserts itself beyond the rest. Still less however can one disentangle in it separate layers of poetry. During all the years in which Virgil brooded over it and wrought upon it, he kept his material, with but few exceptions, in fusion, not crystallised and hardened into a final shape. It was continually taking from his hands not only enlargements of plan but increasing depths of substance from an increasing store of knowledge, sympathy, imagination, vision. To such a process there could really be no end, except the end which came of the swift fever at Brundisium in the autumn of 19 B.C.

But while it is impossible in the Aeneid to divide Virgil's work into layers where all is interwoven and to a greater or less degree fused; while it is impossible to speak of enlargements or accretions where the expansion is vitally imaginative and the growth organic, it is yet possible in various directions to trace that growth; and such a study is not only possible but in the highest degree interesting and fertile. We can do so in two ways more particularly; on the one hand formally, by study of his diction, rhythm, and phrasing; and on the other hand structurally, by considering the various objects which he had to combine, or among which he had to choose, and the various models which lay before him for guidance or stimulus or suggestion.

It is on this latter side, the larger, more human and more widely interesting of the two, that I shall proceed to offer a few notes and suggestions, rather by way of indicating lines of enquiry and points of view than of following out any one of these in detail.

The poetry of kings and battles towards which Virgil had bent his early ambition represents the simpler form of the epic. It might take the form of celebrating a half imaginary heroic age, and some great action or episode in it, as had been done by the creator of the Iliad. Or it might follow the example of later poets and of Virgil's own great Latin predecessor, and take the annalistic scope of a historical epic, to which unity was given by national sentiment, and in which the central thread of interest, the hero of the poem as one might almost say, was the nation itself, imagined as having a life and story of its own extending over successive ages of mortal men. This, according to the possibilities of a ruder art and a more undeveloped language, had been the achievement of Ennius; and Ennius' *Annales* were in Virgil's own youth established as the national poem and schoolbook of Rome, much as the Iliad had been the national poem and schoolbook of Greece. Or once more, it might take a form which was, for obvious reasons, in high favour, that of the celebration of the events, struggles and triumphs of the poet's own age. This was what was actually done by Varius, the friend and poetical colleague of Virgil, and joint-editor of the Aeneid after Virgil's death; it was what Horace, with his customary tact and good sense, declined to attempt at the suggestion of Augustus; it was pressed upon Virgil himself repeatedly by the Emperor, in a way which he found it difficult wholly to ignore. In the actual Aeneid we can see all these three kinds of scope and subject mingling to produce a poem which, from one point of view, was called the Latin Iliad; which from another point of view was named, as a sort of second title, *Gesta Populi Romani*, "the deeds of the Roman people"; and which, from yet another point of view, was expressly dedicated to the glory of Augustus and was meant to fulfil the promise held out in the Georgics, where the *reges et proelia* of the sixth Eclogue had become specifically the *pugnae Caesaris* which he then undertook to celebrate.

The fusing of three motives which are in their nature so disparate was a task which taxed the genius of Virgil to its utmost. He felt it himself to be almost impossible; he had periods of discouragement in which he was inclined to renounce the attempt as hopeless, even as senseless: " I seem to myself," are his own striking words, " to have been almost mad when I undertook it,"—*paene vitio mentis tantum opus ingressus esse videor*. But it had by that time mastered him; even if he could have let it go, it would not have let him go. It absorbed into itself all his other interests, all his other schemes in poetry; and as his life went on, each fresh motive, each new study and acquirement, all the results of his vast learning and profound thought were used up for what had become his single outlet in expression and creation, the one and all-including work of his life.

Modern scholars have accustomed themselves to speak of an original Iliad, out of which an Iliad (the Iliad of Homer) was produced by successive expansions, remodellings, and additions. In the sense in which this view is poetically tenable, we may speak also of an original Aeneid; and it is useful to do so, if we take care to remember that the original Iliad and the original Aeneid are both abstractions, and never existed in any intelligible sense as actual poems. Abstractly and constructionally, we may think of the Aeneid as having grown up round or out of an original Italian Aeneid, just as we may think of the Iliad as having grown up round or out of an original Achilleid; and it is not absurd to conjecture that such an Italian Aeneid represents something like Virgil's earliest project; that it was what he dreamed of and had in his mind before he wrote the Eclogues, and what he never wholly abandoned—as we never do wholly abandon our young dreams—however much the scheme became enlarged and transmuted. This conjectured original, the *Ur-Aeneis* or core of the actual Aeneid, is represented roughly by Books VII. to XII. The epic of kings and battles which these six books contain has a substantive unity and is constructed upon a definite epic scheme. That scheme is one well chosen and of ample scope. Stated in summary, its subject is the arrival of Aeneas and his Trojans in Latium, and their establishment there, after varying but finally successful battles and negotiations; the incorporation of the two races which ensues, with the resulting enrichment of blood, capacity, and tradition, laying the foundations upon which Rome was created and the imperial Roman race came into being.

Mr. Warde Fowler, in his admirable volume, *Social Life at Rome in the Age of Cicero,* has brought out more clearly than ever had been done before, how the national and Roman character of this subject is the dominant motive in one beautiful episode; which indeed in this fresh illumination becomes less an episode than a keynote. The scene in Book VIII. where Aeneas sails up the Tiber and lands on the spot which was to be the site of Rome has always been recognised as one of those in which Virgil reaches his highest point of romantic beauty. The vivid pictorial treatment is raised to inspiration by an impalpable sense of natural magic. But it is only now that we can fully realise all that it implies. The little town nestled among the three hills which rise round the hollow of the Forum bore to Virgil the same or much the same imaginative associations as it bears again to us now, after the centuries have been re-illumined. That long hollow with cattle grazing on it in the westering sunlight—the *Campo Vaccino* then, as it became again long afterwards and remained until a time still within living memory—was to become the centre of the world:

> "Armenta videbant
> Romanoque Foro et lautis mugire Carinis."

Virgil brings it before us in a clear and charming picture; and he makes it as clear that from it his imagination passes over the whole course of history. Here was to be founded the settlement which was to be Rome; the Latin frontier-fortress against Etruria and the populous North, with the mid-Italian peoples clustered on hill and plain behind it, and with its waterway down to Ostia, "the sea-gates" fronting towards Sicily and Africa. Here was the germ of the city which was to beat back and civilise the Celtic North, to overthrow the rival power of Carthage, and to extend its supremacy over the whole Mediterranean and the lands that bordered it from the Euxine and the Euphrates to the Atlantic sea.

This was the scheme of what we may call the original Aeneid as we may conceive it to have formed itself in Virgil's mind. The first great enlargement which it took was to incorporate with the epic of Italian war and settlement an epic of travel and adventure; to engraft a Latin Odyssey, as we might say, upon a Latin Iliad. The coming of Aeneas to Italy followed upon the fall of Troy: and in the work of his Latin predecessors, Naevius and others, Virgil found this second motive already suggested and partially dealt with. He enlarged the scope of his poem to cover a seven years' wandering between the departure from Troy and the arrival in Italy. His treatment of this part of the poem was suggested, and greatly determined, by two Greek sources. One of these, as I have just said, was the Odyssey; the other was a poem to which Virgil owed much, and a careful study of which is one among the things necessary towards any full comprehension of Virgil's aim and achievement, the *Argonautica* of Apollonius. From the Odyssey he took the idea of a poem in which the first half should end by bringing the hero, after many episodes and adventures, to the place where the main action was to take place. According to a well-authenticated tradition, the adventures of the seven years were originally planned as the poet's direct narrative. They brought Aeneas, towards the end of the period, to Carthage; and there, following again the suggestion of the Odyssey, Virgil found an opportunity to place in the mouth of Aeneas, as told by him at night in the Punic Queen's palace, the story of the Fall of Troy itself.

But meanwhile the Carthaginian episode had been taking further shape and assuming greater importance. Two motives united in it. One was to link up the early history of the two great Mediterranean powers, the long contest between which had been by far the most memorable and dramatic in the whole of Roman history, and had left an indelible impression, as the whole of Latin literature bears witness, on the Roman imagination. The other was to bring into the poem the love-interest which was demanded by the feeling of Virgil's time, and for the expression of which in poetry he must have been fully conscious of his own unsurpassed genius. In Latin poetry as in the Alexandrian Greek poetry which supplied Latin poetry with nearly all its models and with a great part of its inspiration, this interest was dominant over at least half the field; and Virgil was attracted towards it not merely by fashion and tradition, but by the influence of his own special poetical circle in his youth, by his romantic sensibility, and by his profound and delicate psychological instinct. Under the joint influence of these motives the Carthaginian episode grew into an importance which had not been foreseen. It dominates the whole of the earlier books of the Aeneid: and by its combination of intense human interest with extreme beauty of workmanship, makes what had been at first meant for a prologue into what we might almost call a substantive epic by itself, and one which the majority of readers, from St. Augustine to Tennyson, have probably always found the most attractive part of the whole Aeneid. Partly of course this is due to the fact that it comes first and so is naturally read first; but this is not the only reason. The other reason is one which has a direct bearing on the progress and evolution of poetry itself.

Poetry, being vital and organic, never rests anywhere: at the same moment at which, and by the same impulse by which, it has brought any of the forms in which it embodies itself to maturity, it passes out of and beyond that form on a further voyage to search for a new embodiment. The epic, when enriched by new motives into a complex structure, begins at once to develop these motives on their own account; it puts forth new blossoms on new branches, and sends into them the current of its life. Like the branches of the Indian fig-tree in Milton's famous description, they strike root on their own account in the soil, growing round and enshrouding the parent tree, and finally replacing it—

> "Branching so broad and long that in the ground
> The bended twigs take root and daughters grow
> About the mother tree, a pillar'd shade
> High overarch'd, and echoing walks between."

Or we may liken the process to the engrafting which changes the whole character of the old tree and does not so much enrich it as cause it to enrich, and feed, from its own native strength, those new boughs, for the sake of which it now exists: so that, in Virgil's own exquisite lines,

> "Nec longum tempus et ingens
> Exiit ad caelum ramis felicibus arbos,
> Miraturque novas frondes et non sua poma."

The engrafted epic of Aeneas and Dido, with its thrilling story of ill-fated love and its prophetic or mystical import as foreshadowing the fame and fate of Rome and the great historic drama of the Punic Wars, became under the genius of Virgil something even more wonderful and more enthralling than its parent stem, the Italian epic of conquest and settlement. It became, as Tennyson says of FitzGerald's Omar, "a planet equal to the sun which cast it"— equal, and even greater, because even more Virgilian.

As it grew, it absorbed into itself much of what had belonged to the prologue and accessories of the main story. Not only the tale of the Fall of Troy, but nearly the whole tale of the wanderings, was sucked into it, and became a narrative discoursed by Aeneas to Dido, and delaying the development of the love-story only to make it break out with reinforced splendour in the fourth book. So complete and so sufficing is this part of the Aeneid when Virgil had given it its full expansion, that it took all his art and skill to make the transition and keep the whole Aeneid as a single poetic unity. It may even be doubted—as it has been by many, both professed critics and ordinary readers—whether the task had not become one for which no art or skill was perfectly adequate. Something almost but not quite as difficult had been done with triumphant success by the poet of the Odyssey. In that masterly poem—the best constructed, as has been truly said, of all narratives—the prologue of the *Telemacheia*, which occupies the first four books, while fascinatingly interesting in itself, never diverts the attention from the main story. Odysseus, though he never appears until the fifth book, is from the first the central figure. The action remains single, and the poet has the whole of its threads completely under his control. To study the construction and mechanism of the two poems in comparison with each other is a work on which it would be impossible to enter now, but which is an essential part of any vital study of the Aeneid. Just one feature of comparison and contrast I may indicate, as a sort of starting-point for the study. The action of the Odyssey opens in Ithaca; from the first we are at the centre; we stand on the very hall-floor where the consummation is to come. But the Aeneid opens at sea off the coast of Africa—*Italiam contra Tiberinaque longe ostia*. In this line, as in a hundred others, Virgil does all he can to keep Italy the centre, to link up all the action with Italy; yet it is the word *longe*, "far away," on which we find ourselves laying the stress. The action of the Aeneid never does succeed in attaining complete unity. No one can go on from the end of the fourth to the beginning of the fifth book without feeling a lowering of temperature; no one could go straight from the fourth book to the seventh—from the death of Dido at Carthage to the landing of Aeneas in Latium—without feeling a change of subject, a passage from one poem into another.

To bridge over this chasm wholly was a task which, if Virgil did not succeed in it, we may well believe to have been beyond human power. But the means he took to bridge it over are what we have to consider; for nothing throws greater light on the Virgilian art, which in combination with the Virgilian pity makes the quality of Virgil as a poet so incomparable. Of the most obvious means I have just spoken. This is the constant and deliberate reference forward, in the earlier story, to the quest of Italy and the foundation of a kingdom there as the appointed purpose of God, the event towards which the fall of Troy and the adventures of Aeneas were fore-ordained. This note is clearly struck in the seven lines of introduction or argument with which the Aeneid opens; it is emphasised at every turn thereafter; the Trojan exiles are driven irresistibly onward, are continually as one might say being rounded up and headed off towards Italy; they are not allowed to rest anywhere short of it; at first a goal only dimly seen or vaguely surmised, it opens out more and more clearly before them through successive acts of Providence, and direct or indirect divine monitions; the tragedy of Dido itself is brought on by the conflict of merely human love with that unalterable ordinance.

But this was not enough. All these links might have been sufficient to knit up into the main story events which formed a mere prologue; but as we have seen, they became in Virgil's hands and almost, we might fancy, against his will, or at least beyond his intention, something larger than any prologue. Art had been greater than the artist. How was he to recover his hold over a work that had expanded so far beyond formal limits, that had become the first of Latin romances as well as the greatest of Latin epics? What was he to do further that might enable him to pass, within the scope of a single epic structure, from the fascination of Troy and Carthage to the goal of Italy? to disengage himself, like Aeneas, from the romance of strange lands and tragical passions that he may attain the destined object of his poem? The poet, like his own hero, had almost succumbed to that fascination. *Ardet abire fuga dulcesque relinquere terras. Heu quid agat? Quae prima exordia sumat?* And in fact we can see him feeling his way through different devices, postponing his resolution, making tentative advances, until the final inspiration came to him.

His first project was simply to resume the story of the wanderings from the point at which it had been broken off by the expansion of the Carthaginian episode. The earlier portion of that story had already been remodelled from the form of direct narrative and incorporated with the secondary narrative put into the mouth of Aeneas, told by him to Dido in continuation of the tale of the fall of Troy. In the fifth book Virgil resumes the direct narrative, and brings the Trojans from Africa to Italy, to the threshold of the main scene. But he seems to have felt that this was inadequate. The lowered temperature which, as I said, we feel at the opening of Book V. had somehow to be raised, and a high tension regained. Until this could be done, the Aeneid was practically at a standstill. The long episode of the funeral games of Anchises which fills more than half of that book, and gives the effect of filling almost all of it, is generally and rightly considered the weakest part of the poem. The original upon which it was modelled, the episode of the funeral games of Patroclus at the end of the Iliad, is largely at least a post-Homeric addition, out of tone with the rest of the Iliad: and we have a similar feeling about the games of the fifth Aeneid. Partly no doubt the pause in the action is deliberate; but partly it is unwilling. Virgil is waiting, circling round, feeling his way.

Then the transcendent stroke of genius came. The sixth book slips the keystone into the interrupted arch, and locks the whole structure. It is even more than that. The two epics, as by this time we may call them, the epic of Troy and Carthage and the epic of Italy, are brought into unity; but they are brought into unity, if I may borrow a phrase from the mathematicians, through a fourth dimension. The vision of the sixth book does not merely unify, but transcends and absorbs, the whole action of the poem. Aeneas, it has been said, and the saying is at least suggestive, passes in this book through a process analogous to what is known in the language of religion as conversion. But this is true not only of Aeneas but of the Aeneid. The poem passes here out of space and time. It becomes an impassioned vision of the whole of existence. History is merged in what for want of a better word we call philosophy. The vision includes and incorporates past and future. The heroes of the Trojan war are seen in it alongside of the kings and consuls of Rome. Men long dead and men who have still long to wait before they reach the borders of light live here side by side in the still light of eternity. Dido herself moves silently in the same world as Phaedra and Eriphyle, and with them are the daughter of Julius and the mother of Marcellus. The armies that fought at Troy, *Danaum proceres Agamemnoniaeque phalanges*, take their place by those Roman legions which met in the shock of battle at Ilerda and Pharsalia during Virgil's own lifetime. The creative imagination of the poet opens up for us the ultimate secret of existence, the creative processes of the universe. Human life itself is shown as the manifestation, under forms of space and time, of the thought of God, the essential life of the world.

Thus when Aeneas passes back through the gate of ivory into what is called real life, he resumes his place in what is, in the real reality, a world of false dreams—*sed falsa ad caelum mittunt insomnia manes*. But to live in that world and bear his part in it has become, more than ever, his destiny and duty: and over the whole of his life thereafter, as over the whole of Virgil's poetry, rests the light which is also a shadow, the shadow which is also a light, of an invisible world.

This transmutation and spiritualisation of poetry was Virgil's final achievement; and it is this which, in the end, gives him his unique place among the poets. It transcends art, properly so called; for the function of art is to create and embody some image of perfection; and the image which Virgil finally sets before us is of imperfection; the wistfulness, the haunting trouble of his poetry, is of its inmost quality. It is, in the apt phrases used of him by the two greatest masters of modern English prose and verse, his "pathetic half lines" and his "lonely words" through which and by virtue of which he makes his deepest appeal to mankind. But that transcendence, that continual search further and further after what cannot be found, that stretching out of the hands (to use his own words rather than those of any later appreciation) in love of a further shore, is not consistent with the requirements of a complete and finished work of art.

Into the Aeneid Virgil tried to put the riches of a whole world. He loaded the framework of the epic with more, perhaps, than it could bear. He attempted to unite in it the large simple Homeric structure with the later and more specialised refinements of poetry as they had been brought out by the final efforts of the art of Greece. Partly he did this by interweaving into the epic scheme the new romantic motives; in this he followed his own romantic temperament, possibly the instinct of his own Celtic blood, and it made him, for later ages, the fountainhead of romanticism. Partly he followed the Alexandrian fashion, and bettered his examples, by the introduction of those highly finished and richly ornamented episodes to which allusion has already been made, and which are more or less detachable as matters of composition, though skilfully interwoven with the main structure and enhancing the total effect of the poem.

Into the Aeneid, too, Virgil poured his vast and multifarious learning. He made it a treasury of Italian antiquities. For the classical archæologist, as is now fully recognised, the Aeneid is one of the first and most indispensable handbooks, whether his particular study be of the geography and ethnography of ancient Italy, or of its religious practices, its social life, and the growth of its civic institutions. On this side, we are only now beginning to understand Virgil.

To the kingdom of poetry Virgil thus strove to annex the provinces of human knowledge, history, archæology, philosophy. Such an attempt was never made again until Dante; it is never likely to be made again with anything like equal success until a poet of immense learning and genius comes to birth just at the precise time which is, as Virgil's time was, the critical point of passage from an old to a new world. Or it may be that the genius makes his own time rather than is made by it. In any case, the *anima mundi* works both in the poet and in his environment. Virgil received divine honours not long after his death; the Aeneid was gravely consulted by Emperors for omens of their own fate and that of the Empire; and the Christian world for many ages believed that just as the Roman Empire had been established by the direct act of Providence to prepare the way for the coming of the Son of God upon earth, so the Roman poet, *Vergilius Romanus*, was elect and inspired by God as the Prophet of the Gentiles. These beliefs have passed away, but not their effects, and still less their causes; for their causes may be summed up in this, that in Virgil and the Aeneid was heard not only the imperial and prophetic voice of Rome, but the very voice of mankind itself speaking, with majestic tenderness, of patience and obedience, of honour in life, of hope beyond death.

ARABIAN LYRIC POETRY

THE GOLDEN ODES

The lectures which I have hitherto given from this Chair have dealt, at one or another point, and in one or another aspect, with a single subject. That subject is the progress of poetry within what may be called broadly the European or Western civilisation; within the world from which we directly inherit, and to which we primarily belong. But that world is not the whole world. Wherever the human mind is, it strikes inward and outward; it brings with itself the processes of reflection and creation: it seeks instinctively after some interpretation and pattern of life in the forms of patterned and interpretative speech; and the product of that instinct is poetry.

Within the closed field of European poetry there is indeed room enough to expatiate: and for English students and artists the main current of progress to be traced in history is the current which passed, in Gray's brief and pregnant phrase, from Greece to Italy, and from Italy to England. But that current is neither single nor continuous. It is true that the more we study it, the more we are impressed with the element of continuity in it. Of no age in poetry, as of no single poem, can we say that it is isolated and unaccountable that it is a thing which happens. That doctrine has been laid down, not merely of poetry but of all art, by artists whose opinions are not negligible. But it is merely the reaction from another doctrine which is equally partial and equally misleading, the doctrine that poetry, or art in general, can be defined and explained in mechanical terms. Both views put one side of the case so partially and with so much over-emphasis that they are in effect untrue. But among the elements of truth which the former view seizes on and distorts by exaggeration is this: that the springs of poetry are numerous, intricate, and often obscure; that its main current is reinforced by many affluents, and that the very soil over which—or it may be under which—it moves imparts to it a perpetually varying colour and quality.

Between the disappearance of the classical or Graeco-Roman tradition and the new birth which it took in the earlier Middle Ages, European poetry ran underground. But during that period in its progress it was subjected to many influences which profoundly modified it. It sank one thing, and rose again another. Among these influences the most important perhaps, as it is certainly the most subtle in its effect and the most obscure in its working, was that of Arabian art, of the imaginative interpretation of life given by an Asiatic race. The obscurity of that influence is at once the cause and the effect of the fact that insufficient attention has hitherto been paid to it by historians of literature and interpretative critics of poetry. But though obscure, it is vital. Just as the course of European history in the earlier Middle Ages involves and is affected by the Crusades, and all that movement, partly of antagonism, partly of interpenetration, of which the Crusades are the symbol, so the development of European poetry was deeply and organically affected by the Arab poetry which seems so entirely detached from it, and which after it had leavened the art of Southern Europe disappeared again into the East and was forgotten or ignored in the West, except among a few Oriental scholars, until quite modern times.

To trace the historical connexion and the organic effect of this Arabian influence is a task which still remains largely unaccomplished. It is one which requires very wide knowledge and very sensitive artistic perceptions. Even in the more concrete and measurable province of architecture it is still, I believe, a matter of debate how far a distinct Asiatic influence is to be found, alike in matters of construction and of ornament, in the Byzantine work which culminates in the masterpiece of Anthemius; and how far again the Mohammedan architecture of later centuries itself drew from European sources and was engrafted on or varied from Byzantine or Byzantino-Romanesque originals. In the world of poetry we are dealing with causes and effects which are still more subtle and imponderable.

At no time have the European and the Asiatic mind been wholly shut off from one another, but there are whole periods in which the two have been brought into a contact more than usually direct through the movements of national or political history. The earliest instance which bears on extant living poetry is that of the Homeric poems themselves. The Iliad and Odyssey are the product of a region and age whose historical relations and significance we are only now beginning to comprehend. Mr. Hogarth, in his volume on Ionia and the East, has shown with great skill and knowledge how that period in history was marked to an unusual degree by Oriental pressure upon the civilisation to which by that time we may begin to give the name of Greek. Such pressure is never wholly mechanical; it always involves some considerable amount of intellectual, imaginative, and artistic interpenetration, something of what we may call by analogy chemical action and the formation of new substances, or by a closer analogy still, cross-fertilisation and the creation of new species in the organic world. At a later period the effect of the Persian wars on the development of Athens cannot be wholly measured in terms of political and military history; it had also a direct bearing on the development of Athenian poetry.

The Alexandrian school, so immense in its influence as well as in its actual product, was from first to last not wholly Greek, not wholly European; the ambiguous position which Egypt has always occupied in history is reflected in the composite flowerage of the poetry which takes its name from the Egyptian capital. From its beginnings in the reign of Ptolemy II. until its final disappearance about the beginning of the sixth century A.D., a time almost within sight of the Arab conquest, that school was more or less continuous. It on the whole represented the main current of poetic tradition, so far as poetry remained Greek and had not moved westwards into the Latin world. Just at the period when the central life of poetry was transferring itself from Greek to Latin, the Syrian poet Meleager infused into Greek poetry a new tone and colour which are specifically those of Arabia and the Syro-Arabian plateau. Gadara, his birthplace, itself is within that geographical and ethnographical area. Tyre, the place of his education, is just on its edge. In his poetry, as in that of the whole school in which he is the central and the most striking figure, we do not get the new element clean: it is a ferment introduced into Greek poetry and reacted upon by the fresh environment; and in the resulting product—as happened similarly a thousand years later in Provence—there is something of a nerveless and deliquescent quality, something exotic and even unwholesome. But its effect was none the less potent and long-continuing. Further west, once more, in the Roman province of Africa, where the native race and genius were more akin to an Asiatic than a European type, and where the earlier Phoenician colonisation had emphasised the native Orientalism, we meet an analogous phenomenon. The African poets of the fourth century A.D. are, both in form and in substance, the precursors of Romance literature, the beginners, one may properly say, of the Middle Ages.

These earlier influences—and more might no doubt be discovered or noted—are indications of a more or less continuous deflecting force exercised by the East over Western poetry: one which in different ways and to various degrees fertilised, enriched, possibly sometimes warped, the central course of its development. But they are all inconsiderable in comparison with the effect produced by the full impact of the brilliant Arab civilisation which spread behind the great Arab conquests. As Europe owes its religion to Judaea, so it owes its romance to Arabia: and not only that, but the awakening of imaginative and creative force that issued in the romantic poetry of the twelfth and thirteenth centuries. Classical Italian poetry, in which the central current of the life of poetry was once more embodied, was derived historically—this is a matter of common knowledge—from the earlier poetry of Provence and Sicily. But Provence was saturated with Arabic influence; and Sicily was half Saracen, a debateable land on the frontier of the Arabian empire. Ciullo d'Alcamo, reputed the first of the predecessors of Dante, took his name from the Arab fortress near Palermo which was his birthplace. Another of them, in the next century, actually bears the name of Saladin, the hero of the Third Crusade and the destroyer of the Latin kingdom of Jerusalem. The Emperor Frederick II. was an accomplished Arabic scholar as well as a poet. During the Dark Ages in Europe the arts, including the art of poetry, had flourished at the courts and under the favour of the Arab Khalifats, and when they revived again in Europe, their revival, like that of learning generally, took place under strong Asiatic influence. The Spanish school of poetry, which comes to its flower in the *Poem of the Cid* in the twelfth century, derived much, both in form and in substance, from the poetical art as it was practised under the Umayyad Emirat of Cordova—roughly for a period of three centuries from 750 to 1050 A.D. It no doubt traces its parentage on the other side to the French *Chansons de Geste*. But the French epic was itself not produced on a soil unaffected by Arab invasion. The Arabian conquests of the eighth century pushed up into Central France. The *Chanson de Roland*, in its metrical and formal mechanism as well as in its subject, is a sort of symbol of an influence that had been left in the soil then, and had germinated in it.

It is therefore immediately relevant to any large consideration of the progress of poetry to know something about Arabian poetry itself; and the work of modern scholars has recently made it possible to do so even for those who, like myself, derive their acquaintance with it only from translations. Of the many sources available I will only name three, which are all indispensable in different ways, and which taken together and intelligently used give perhaps as much insight into the history, scope, and specific quality of Arab poetry as can well be got by those who cannot go direct to the originals: at least if there be added to their study not only some broad knowledge of history but some amount of that imaginative appreciation—one might almost speak of it as divination—without which the study of poetry as a vital process, an interpretation and function of life, remains necessarily barren.

The first of these is Sir Charles Lyall's volume, *Translations of Ancient Arabian Poetry, chiefly prae-Islamic, with an Introduction and Notes,* published in 1885. It is one of those books of admirable taste and sound scholarship which do not appeal to a large public; but to those who were able to appreciate it, it came, a generation ago, as a sudden revelation of unsuspected riches. So far as its scope extends it remains the classical work on its subject. But its scope is strictly limited; and for a larger view, in which that early Arabian poetry takes its place in the general course of Arab history and letters, it can now be supplemented by another work of great value published quite recently, Mr. Nicholson's *Literary History of the Arabs.* The third of the three indispensable volumes is of a different and even a rarer kind; for it presents us with a version of and commentary on the acknowledged masterpieces of early Arab poetry by one whose acquaintance with Arabia and the Arab mind is unusually great and whose sympathy with them is almost unique; and even more than this, one who is himself a poet. This is Mr. Wilfrid Blunt's rendering of the Golden Odes, also known as the *Muallakât*, into English verse, with an introductory essay which is no less illuminating than fascinating. It was published in 1903.

It may be worth while however to point out another source, subsidiary and secondary indeed, yet also in its way invaluable, which is familiarly known and lies ready to every one's hand. This is a book with which all English readers are or ought to be well acquainted, Lane's *Arabian Nights*. Let me then digress for a moment to call your attention to the fact that the scraps of verse in the *Arabian Nights*, while they differ much in poetical quality, and from the circumstances in which they are introduced tend to confine themselves mainly to brief gnomic or didactic fragments, contain among them pieces of authentic and characteristic Arab poetry. The fascination of the *Arabian Nights* simply as stories is so great that they are but little studied as literature, and insufficient stress is laid either on the time and circumstances of their origin, or on their extraordinary variations of literary quality. In this matter Western readers only follow the bad example of neglect set by Arab scholars themselves. "The native critics of Arabic literature," so Mr. Lane-Poole writes, "paid small attention to a collection of romances which appeared to them (as one of them wrote) only as 'a corrupt book of silly tales.'" The collection was formed by accretion through centuries, and was subject to all kinds of interpolation and corruption, alike in the oral transmission of the stories through a succession of professional story-tellers, and in the manuscript copies which were from time to time made for use or sale. The greater part of it belongs, at all events in its extant form, to a time considerably later than that of Haroun al Rashid, the contemporary of Charlemagne, who has already become in many of the stories an idealised and half legendary figure like his Western colleague in the Carlovingian epics and romances. Some of it may be as late as the sixteenth century. But the original nucleus goes back to the period of the earlier Abbasid Khalifat, and is not later than the tenth, while it may be as early as the eighth century. And the range in the literary quality of the collection is correspondingly great. Together with much work that as art is crude, invertebrate and vulgar, it includes literary masterpieces which have suffered but little through long transmission—stories like those of the City of Brass, or of Nur-ed-din and Enis-el-Jelis, or of Aziz and Azizeh. Among the scraps of poetry quoted in these stories are some which, together with the romantic sensibility of the East, have the pellucid quality of the finest, or all but the finest, Greek work. So far as the romantic poetry of the earlier Middle Ages in Europe remains alive now, it is in virtue of the extent to which it approximates to this combination. And where it has done so, it was under the subtle ferment of Arabian influence.

The lyrical fragments in the earlier and nobler stories of the *Arabian Nights* remind one, again and again, of the Greek epigram as it took its latest new development in the hands of Meleager and his contemporaries, blown over and quickened to a strange beauty by a breath from the East. But these Arabian lyrics have not the exotic and feverish quality of those others: they preserve the simplicity, the genuine flavour, of a native growth. Let me quote one or two instances, in which those familiar with the Greek Anthology will at once recognise the strong likeness and the impalpable yet organic difference. Compare this for instance with the famous Δάκρυα σοὶ καὶ νέρθε, Meleager's lamentation over Heliodora:[1]

"I have lost my existence among mankind since your absence,
    for my heart loveth none but you.
  Take my body then in mercy to the place where you are laid,
    and there bury me by your side.
  And if at my grave you utter my name, the moaning of my
    bones shall answer to your call."

[1] *Anth. Pal.*, vii. 476.

It is the pulse of the Greek elegiac, at its lyric tension, beating in a different blood.

Or again, compare with the mixed languor and passion of Meleager's love-pieces this quatrain from the story of Nur-ed-din:

" Her skin is like silk and her speech is soft, neither redundant nor deficient.
Her eyes, God said to them, Be, and they were, affecting men's hearts with the potency of wine."

Or this other sestet:

"You made a covenant with me that you would remain faithful; but when you had gained possession of my heart you deceived me.
I conjure you by Allah, if I die, that you write upon my tombstone, *This was a slave of love:*
That perchance some mourner who hath felt the same flame may pass by the lover's grave and pity her."

Nearly every single phrase here may be matched from Meleager's epigrams. "We swore, he to love me, and I never to leave him; but now he says that such vows are in running water": "When I am dead, I pray thee lay me under earth and write above, *Love's gift to Death*": "I will leave letters uttering this voice, *Look, stranger, on Love's murdered man*": "Even myself I carry the wounds of Love and shed tears over thy tears."[1]

Or we may set beside the finest examples of the later Greek elegy—whether we are disposed to regard these as sentimentalised and hyperbolical, or as suffused with a new wistfulness and delicacy, a new touch of romantic beauty—the poem engraved on the tomb of the loving and heroic Azizeh:

[1] *Anth. Pal.*, v. 8, 215; xii. 72, 74.

ARABIAN LYRIC POETRY

" I passed by an undistinguished tomb in the midst of a garden,
with seven anemones upon it;
And I said, Whose tomb is this? The soil answered, Be
respectful, for this is the resting-place of a lover.
So I said, God keep thee, O victim of Love, and lodge thee in
the highest stage of Paradise!
Were I able, O tomb, I would make of thee a garden and
water it with my streaming tears."

These lines are earlier than the thirteenth century, but how much earlier we cannot conjecture. There is something in them which hardly reappears in poetry until about a hundred years ago : they have a natural magic which in one way suggests Wordsworth, in another, the more modern neo-Celtic revival. In them, as in other fragments quoted in the *Nights*, the poetry has not only this finer magic; it has also a greater strength and gravity than anything belonging to the later Greek or Hellenistic world. Poetry was to those Arabian poets something solemn and awful: something (as it was also to Wordsworth) not to be touched without a sense of deep responsibility : it was the creation by man of what was more than human. In one of the fragments we read :

" There is no writer that shall not perish ; but what his hand
hath written endureth for ever.
Write therefore nothing but what will please thee when thou
shalt see it on the day of resurrection."

That grave religious feeling about poetry, as about all art, came with the new religion : it was part of the Puritanism which was the strength of Islam and won it its amazing victories. But the Mohammedan Arabs, whether in their own ancient home or in their new capitals, at Cairo or Damascus, at Baghdad or Cordova, regarded their classic poetry as belonging to an earlier age. It had culminated during the Ignorance, and in

Arabia itself. And Arabia was then still, as it always had been, and as it became again soon afterwards, a strangely isolated country, living its own contracted life intensely, but hardly touched by external civilisation or by the movements of the vast empires which almost immediately adjoined it.

"In Europe," as Mr. Blunt strikingly says, "the nearest analogy to it is to be found in the pre-Christian verse of Celtic Ireland, which by a strange accident was its close contemporary, and lost its wild natural impulse through the very same circumstance of the conversion of its pagan bards to an overmastering new theology." The influence of that Celtic and pagan Ireland upon the imagination and art of Western Europe was also undoubtedly great. In both cases it was the new religion that broke the barriers of what had previously been a wholly isolated civilisation. It was isolated, and one might almost use the term in its literal sense of insular, cut off by an impassable sea; for the deserts which divide Central and Southern Arabia from the rest of the Continent are comparable to the ocean, as the ocean was in the infancy of navigation, the *dissociabilis Oceanus*. Both Ireland and Arabia were *extra anni solisque vias*, beyond the known world.

It is also singularly striking that the two bodies of poetry, the Irish and the Arabic, were both considered to culminate at the same time, in or about the latter half of the sixth century of our era. It was a time in which for the rest of the world poetry was almost dead. The Dark Ages had settled down over Europe. In the East, the illusive brilliance of the age of Justinian— the first attempt at a classical Renaissance—had passed away as quickly as it rose; it flowered, and fell away fruitless, within a single generation. In the West but little tradition of letters survived. The monastic chroniclers who were almost the only representatives of literature had to record mere wretchedness; in Italy, the extinction of the Gothic kingdom and with it of the hopes of a new Europe; beyond the Alps, the sanguinary annals of the earlier Franks. Only in two countries, and these both beyond the extreme verge of the Roman Empire at its fullest extent, was there imaginative life. Neither into Ireland nor into Arabia had Rome ever effectively penetrated. From these two remote soils, unbroken and virgin, there rose a flowerage of exquisite poetry. In neither case had it the chance to develop further in its native country. In Ireland it was a desperate protest against the new religion which was already dominant: we hear in it the cry of subjugated heathendom.

"If I were as I once was, the strong hoofs crushing the sand and the shells,
Coming out of the sea as the dawn comes, a chant of love on my lips,
Not coughing, my head on my knees, and praying, and wroth with the bells,
I would leave no saint's head on his body from Rachlin to Bera of ships."

The poetry of Pagan Ireland was crushed out or driven underground by Christianity. To Ireland no doubt, as well as to the kindred Welsh and Breton stocks, some at least of the elements in the Arthurian romance are to be traced. But on a large view we may say that Ireland flooded the world not with poets, but with missionaries. The triumph of Islam in Arabia might have done something similar, but that its normal effect in this way was merged in a much vaster movement. Arabia emptied itself out bodily over half the known world. Until then it had been a blank in history. In one generation it issued in the storm of conquest which broke the Persian empire in a single battle, and hurled the disciplined armies of Heraclius into irretrievable rout; within two generations it had spread its dominion from the Oxus to the Guadalquivir, and Byzantium itself was only saved by its fleet to be for seven hundred years longer the capital of a European empire. An immense exhaustion followed that incredible effort: Arabia has ever since been like a scoria-heap left naked and barren after a volcanic outburst.

The Arab poetry, so far as it survived when it passed out of Arabia, became something different, something weaker. Good poetry was written, according to the Arab critics, down to the end of the second century of the Hejira. But from the establishment of the Abbasid Khalifat soon after the end of the first century—in the year 750 of our era—it took, like the Khalifat itself, a distinctly Persian flavour; it ceased to be purely Arabic and became cosmopolitan. The Golden Age of Islam in the reign of Harun al Rashid was one of splendid culture which was on the verge of decay: a culture which had become fully matured, but in doing so had lost its vitalising force. This was long before Hulagu, with his Mongol hordes and his trained corps of Chinese engineers, stormed Baghdad and made an end of the Khalifat. By that time the mediæval poetry of Western Europe had been made: the period of romance had culminated: there were only seven years more until the birth of Dante.

Even in the first century of the Hejira something was already lost. The fatalism which is fundamental and essential in Islam perhaps laid a numbing touch on the springs of poetry. In any case the world was altered for the Arabs. "All that was best of them," says Mr. Blunt in apt and accurate words, "had passed outside the desert borders and had become city-dwellers in Syria, Irak, Persia, and Egypt. Their old ways of thought had been exchanged for new ones; they were no longer Bedouins; they had intermarried with strangers; their insularity was gone. As far as the rules of the art go, good verse was written; but the special desert flavour of the old is certainly lacking in the new, that splendid realism in regard to natural things, that plainness of speech and that naïveté of passion which distinguish the pre-Islamic from all other poetry, and which we Europeans find of such priceless value." If we make an exception for the early Greek lyric, this statement as to the unique quality of the pre-Islamic Arab poetry is substantially true. There is indeed one other exception, though it is beyond the stricter bounds of Europe. In the marvellous heroic literature of Iceland there are these same qualities, raised by a certain stern greatness to a level as high if not higher. But that literature remained insular; it produced no effect on Europe until it was rediscovered (one might almost say) within living memory: nor at its full height did it embody itself in the forms of poetry, but in those of the classical Icelandic prose.

It is then to what remains of the pre-Islamic poetry, the poetry of the Ignorance, that we must turn in order to appreciate the quality of Arabian poetry at its fullest and finest. Only a little of it survives; but we have at least the satisfaction of knowing that among what survives are the pieces deliberately chosen as its best. The seven Golden Odes, like the seven extant plays of Sophocles, were chosen out and transcribed as masterpieces. They derive that name, according to an unauthentic tradition, from the circumstance that "being judged in the pagan days to be the most excellent compositions of the Arabs, they were written in letters of gold upon pieces of fine Egyptian linen and hung up in the court of the Ka'bah at Mecca." But this story is now regarded as a mere piece of mythology, invented to account for the two titles under which they became known, the *Mudahabât* or Golden Poems, and the *Muallakât* or Suspended Poems.

The date of the earliest and also the noblest of the seven, the *Muallaka* of Imr-el-Kais, is reckoned to be about the middle of the sixth century A.D. It became the model for a school of verse previously unknown to Arabian poetry; and the other six, composed at various times during the fifty or sixty years after it, follow more or less closely its structural arrangement, and also, with various modifications, the general form of its rhythms and metres. Both structurally and metrically the odes are elaborated with great finish and with strict adherence to canon. It is clear that they represent a matured art, and one which, but for the genius of the poet, would be becoming academic. Structurally their nearest European parallel is to be found in the Odes of Pindar: of which they may remind one also by their sudden transitions, and their elaborate figuring upon the motives which succeed one another in a determined, one might almost say a conventional order. But they differ from the Pindaric ode essentially in their vividly personal or autobiographic quality; and they differ from it fundamentally in metrical structure. They are written in a series of uniform stanzas, each consisting of a rhyming or assonant couplet, the same assonance being continued (as the Arabic language permits and even suggests) right through the poem. The first line of each couplet has likewise an internal rhyme, so that we may also think of the couplets as quatrains, each line being a couplet. They have thus a pretty close metrical analogy with more than one familiar European form; with the Greek elegiac; or with the Latin and English trochaic tetrameter, the metre of the *Pervigilium Veneris* and of *Locksley Hall*; or with the metre—which accurately reproduces one of the favourite Arabian lyric metres—of Browning's *Abt Vogler*.

The rigid and elaborate formal rules of the Arabian Ode must have been the outcome of a long tradition and of generations of practice. Both the art of expression and the capacities of the language must have been deeply studied for long before the date of the earliest compositions which are now extant. These show nothing archaic or immature; and in fact, so far as dates are assignable, the earliest are at the same time the most perfect. During the sixth century A.D. poetry was not only fully established as a professional art, but was becoming an appanage of the courts of chiefs and kings. The Arab kingdoms of al-Hirah on the lower Euphrates and Ghassan in the desert south of the Hauran were on the very edge of the Persian and Graeco-Roman civilisation, and were, to some undefined extent, tributary to the Sassanian and Byzantine empires: both were the resort of court-poets, who were highly honoured and lavishly rewarded. As under the outlying Ionian dynasties which were in touch with and subject to the influence of an adjoining great foreign monarchy—the Androclids at Ephesus, or the Neleids at Miletus—the development of the native poetry seems in these surroundings to have been quickened and reinforced, while it did not lose its distinctively native quality. It remained purely Arabian: it retained the fine and austere desert flavour. There is in it a quality which it is difficult to describe by any single word. The word of hardness would be exaggerated, that of crispness would be too feeble: it is a quality of sharp edge, unwavering and yet delicately elastic, such as is found in its highest degree in the sculpture and poetry of Athens at their culminating period. It seems hard, both in outline and modelling, to minds which are accustomed to the infusion of sentiment in imagination. Arab poetry only became sentimental, the best authorities agree, after the Arab conquest of Persia. Then the infusion, or infection, spread rapidly. Acting in conjunction with other causes, particularly with the enormous dilution of blood and character which accompanied the spread of the Arabian conquests, it transformed the substance of the older and more purely native art. "With the fall of the house of Umayyah," Sir Charles Lyall says, "Arabian poetry, rightly so called, came to an end."

The pure, clean, tense quality of that poetry can only be fully appreciated—so we are told, and we may well believe it—by those who know it in the original and who have become to some degree acclimatised to the physical and moral atmosphere in which it was produced. But some idea may be got of it from Mr. Blunt's fine translations, especially if these are compared with other and more prosaic renderings. Mr. Blunt's versions, while they do not seem to fail at all in fidelity, have the immense advantage of reproducing, so far as can well be done in English, the original metres, and preserve in a wonderful degree the sharp accentuation of a language meant (as has been said of it) to be shouted through clear air from hill to hill, full of a strange ring and of strong sudden cadences. Here is one specimen, an elaborated descriptive passage from the *Muallaka* of Antara;

"So is a garden new-planted, fresh in its greenery,
    Watered by soft-falling raindrops, treadless, untenanted.
Lo, on it rain-clouds have lighted, soft showers, no hail in
    them,
    Leaving each furrow a lakelet bright as a silverling.
Pattering, plashing they fell there, rains at the sunsetting,
    Wide-spreading runlets of water, streams of fertility,
Mixed with the humming of bees' wings, droning the daylight
    long,
    Never a pause in their chanting, gay drinking-choruses:
Blithe iteration of bees' wings, wings struck in harmony
    Sharply as steel on the flint-stone, light-handed smithy-
    strokes."

Here again is a specimen in a different manner, showing the gnomic or reflective side of the Odes. It is from the "wisdom," to use the phrase of the Northern Sagas, which concludes the *Muallaka* of Zoheyr. Eighty years, the poet says, have taught him

"That he that doeth for his name's sake fair deeds shall
    further it,
    But he that of men's praise is careless dwindleth in
    dignity:
That he who keepeth faith shall find faith; who in
    simplicity
    Shall pursue the ways accustomed, no tongue shall wag at
    him:
That he who flieth his fate shall meet it, not, though a sky-
    ladder
    He should climb, shall his fear fend him; dark death shall
    noose him down:
That he who shall refuse the lance-butts borne by the peace-
    bearers,
    Him the lance-heads shall find fenceless, naked the flesh of
    him:
That he who guardeth not his tent-floor with the whole
    might of him,
    Cold shall be his hearthstone broken, ay, though he smote
    at none;

> That he who fleeth his kin shall fare far, foes for his guest-fellows :
> That he who his own face befouleth none else shall honour him :
> That whatso a man hath by nature, wit-wealth or vanity,
> Hidden deep, the day shall prove it; all shall be manifest."

Or once more let me quote part of what is perhaps the most splendid single passage from the most splendid single Arabian Ode, the conclusion of the *Muallaka* of Imr-al-Kais. Like all really great poetry it suffers by being detached from its context: and indeed the Ode produces its superlative effect as a whole rather than in its parts. The exquisite descriptions of the lovers meeting at night, of the forsaken desert camp, of the chase and capture of the deer, follow one another in massed harmonic evolution, like the movements in a symphony. The *Coda*, the final movement, is a vividly imagined picture of a storm in the night sweeping over the desert. It comes abruptly, like the storm itself, with a sudden change of key and atmosphere. This on the one hand makes it detachable for quotation : on the other hand it must be borne in mind that on this very change of key depends much of its poetical effect. I do not quote this time from Mr. Blunt's rendering, but (to be on the safe side) from the more literal and perhaps more scholarly though less poetical version of Sir Charles Lyall. It lacks the strong rhythm and ringing cadence of the other; it lacks, too, something of the characteristic Arabian swiftness which Mr. Blunt reproduces so admirably, with its paratactic constructions and its extreme compression of language. The outlines in this English version are a little blurred, the edge a little softened : the whole effect is slightly occidentalised,

"O friend, see the lightning there! it flickered and now is gone,
　As though flashed a pair of hands in the pillar of crownèd
　　cloud.
Nay, was it its blaze, or the lamp of a hermit that dwells alone,
　And pours o'er the twisted wicks the oil from his slender
　　cruse?
We sat there, my fellows and I, twixt Dârij and al-Udhaib
　And gazed as the distance gloomed, and waited its oncoming.
The right of its mighty rain advanced over Katan's ridge,
　The left of its trailing skirt swept Yadhbul and as-Sitâr.
Then over Kutaifah's steep the flood of its onset drave
　And headlong before the storm the tall trees were borne to
　　ground.
And the drift of its waters passed o'er the crags of al-Kanân
　And drave forth the white-legged deer from the refuge they
　　sought therein.
And Taima—it left not there the stem of a palm aloft,
　Nor ever a tower save one firm-built on the living rock.
And when first its misty shroud bore down upon Mount Thabîr,
　He stood like an ancient man in a grey-streaked mantle
　　wrapt.
The clouds cast their burden down on the broad plain of al
　　Ghabît
　As a trader from al-Yaman unfolds from the bales his store;
And the topmost crest on the morrow of al-Mujaimir's cairn
　Was heaped with the flood-borne wrack like wool on a distaff
　　wound.
At earliest dawn on the morrow the birds were chirping blithe
　As though they had drunken draughts of riot in fiery wine:
And at even the drowned beasts lay where the torrent had borne
　　them, dead,
　High up on the valley sides, like earth-stained roots of
　　squills."

There is a touch in this passage of the early connexion, slender enough and almost imponderable, between pre-Mohammedan Arabia and the Western world. The first flicker of the distant lightning is compared with the upleap of flame in a lamp when its keeper pours oil into it: and that is the lamp of a Christian hermit, such as were to be found here and there, in Arabia itself as well as in Syria and Upper Egypt, before they were swept away by the flood of the new religion. They represented almost the whole amount of the penetration of the West into that isolated land.

Not many years before this Ode was composed, a forlorn company of seven philosophers had, after the formal closure of the schools of Athens, sought refuge at the court of Khosru Nushirvan from an unfriendly world. They returned utterly disillusioned. Had their contemporaries, that Pleiad of Byzantine poets who made the last additions to the long jewel-chain of the Greek Anthology, made a like venture into the Arabian desert, they might have returned equally empty-handed. For the flower was of the soil, and would not bear transplantation. It was only after an interval of several centuries, in a vastly diluted form, and through tortuous and circuitous channels, that this strange and potent poetry, so primitive and yet so elaborate in its art, could become communicable, could strike upon and refertilise the West.

In one of his miraculous phrases, phrases created by a power of instinctive divination which seems little less than magical, Keats speaks of

"Asian poppy or elixir fine
Of the soon-fading, jealous Caliphat."

This early Arab poetry is a fine elixir distilled from Arab life, with its vastness, its mystery, its strange combination of vivid colour with immense monotony. Something like it, something wholly lost and only to be guessed at through reconstructive imagination, lies behind the Homeric poems: it belonged to the dawn of that day of which the Iliad and Odyssey represent the magnificent sunset. Let me quote again a fine passage of Mr. Blunt's. "These living wild creatures they described; these and the storms which occasionally wrecked their valleys, blotting out in a night the memorial stones of their encampments; the sun's heat in their long day-marches; the stars hung overhead at night like lamps from the firmament; the ships seen from their sea-coasts; and yet again their camels and their horses, for it was always to these that their thoughts returned, and which they did not weary of depicting." We might be reading here of the earlier poetry that has left its traces indelibly in Homer; the lion-hunt and the boar-hunt, the nine days' rain that blotted out the great Achaean wall, sweat and dust under the strength of the sun, the march of the constellations that guided the mariner and gave sign of the seasons, Sirius and Arcturus and the Pleiades. Only, in that primitive pre-Homeric poetry, it would not be ships seen from their sea-coasts that the poets described so much as sea-coasts seen from their ships, and it was to the horses of the sea—ἁλὸς ἵπποι—that their thoughts always returned, and which they never wearied of depicting.

The formal and finished Ode is not the only product of early Arabian poetry of which specimens survive. Many more are preserved in the *Kitáb-al-Aghâni*, a great collection made early in the tenth century by a distinguished Arab scholar, a descendant of the dethroned House of Umayyah. They consist chiefly of lyrical or elegiac pieces of briefer form and slighter texture than the Odes, but belonging to the same period. Some of these are fragments of longer poems; others are complete in themselves. Their scope and range may be roughly compared to that of the Greek epigram in its widest signification: only to make the comparison just, we should have to include with the epigram the shorter Greek lyrics and elegies. Some may properly be described as pure lyrics: others are descriptive or reflective pieces; but they can only be divided into distinct classes in a somewhat arbitrary way. The Sicilian sonnet, which was afterwards naturalised and perfected in Italy and has remained a distinct poetical form in Europe ever since, seems to derive, partly at least, from Arabian models. In the Spanish *Romance*, which may be dated back at least as early as the eleventh century, the Arabian influence is even stronger and more unmistakeable. In it, as in the *Chansons de Geste*, we find the strongly accentuated rhythms, and the rhyming system of the *laisse* or *tirade* —a series of lines carried on upon the same rhyme or assonance throughout—which are both distinguishing features of Arabian poetry.

The question how far the whole element of rhyme in the poetry of the Romance languages is a native growth derived from Latin, and how far it is also of Arabian origin, is a difficult and complex one, into which I do not now propose to enter. That accentual rhymed verse was in certain specific forms native to the Latin tongue is beyond doubt: there are traces of it under the surface throughout the whole of the classical period, and we can follow its re-emergence in the third and fourth centuries when the quantitative metres imposed on Italy by the genius of Greece were beginning to give way with the general transformation of the world and the loosening of the classical civilisation and culture. Accentual rhymed or assonant verse has already attained a decisive predominance when the Romance languages begin to develop substantive bodies of poetry of their own. But it is no less certain that in this predominance Arab influence had a substantial if not even a decisive share. It is likewise to be noted that while the native Latin rhythms were falling or trochaic, those of the new Romance poetry are rising or iambic: the one therefore is not the direct descendant or derivative of the other. The origin of the ten-syllabled or eleven-syllabled line on rising rhythm which became the norm for the great bulk of European poetry has been accounted for in different ways, but no fully satisfactory account has yet been given. The eleven-syllabled Italian line (the *superbissimum carmen* of Dante) is almost the precise metrical equivalent of the accentualised Latin Sapphic, a form very widely used in ecclesiastical Latin poetry. It is also an approximate equivalent of the Phalaecian hendecasyllabic verse, the favourite metre of Catullus, if that verse became similarly accentual in its structure. But the Italian eleven-syllabled line is historically derived from the ten-syllabled line of earlier literatures, Provençal, and French, and Sicilian: and that decasyllabic line, while it bears little relation to any known Latin metre whether quantitative or accentual, is in fact a metrical form largely used in Arabian and Arabo-Persian poetry.

The problem is technical and historical. It has no direct bearing on the progress of poetry as an interpretation of life. But in poetry, as in all art, form and substance are inseparable, and even technicalities have a distinct value towards poetical interpretation as well as towards the historic sense through which poetry itself becomes more alive and more intelligible. This subject belongs to the province of the Modern Language School which is one of the most important additions made in this generation to the field of University studies: and it is one of those upon which specialists in that School might profitably concentrate their attention.

It is however to the lyrico-elegiac poetry of early Arabia in its inner and more strictly poetical quality that we must for the present return: and perhaps its quality may be even more readily and more vividly brought out by instances than by a formal disquisition. The normal metres of these minor pieces, I may add, are, unlike those used in the formal Ode, in rising or iambic rhythm, corresponding closely to the eight-syllabled and ten-syllabled lines which were established for England by Chaucer, and have remained ever since characteristic and normal for English poetry. Many of these short poems are alike remarkable for depth of feeling, clearness of expression, and intensity of realisation. These qualities set them alongside of the finest European work, whether Italian or Greek.

Here is a lyric of intense and restrained passion, strong without any loss of tenderness, sweet without any tinge of sentimentality:

" O God, if I die, and thou give not my ghost to drink
   Of Lailà, no grave lies thirstier than my grave.
If I forget my pain though Lailà be not for me,
   My comforter is despair: patience no comfort brings.
And if I suffice myself without her, seeming strong and stern,
   Ah! many are the strengths of soul that lie near to lacking sore."

Or take this lyric, which like the other is from the *Hamâsah*, a collection made in Northern Syria about the middle of the ninth century of our era:

" By him who brings weeping and laughter, who deals Death and Life as he wills,
   She left me to envy the wild deer that graze twain and twain without fear.
O Love of her, heighten my heart's pain and strengthen the pang every night!
O Comfort that days bring, forgetting, the last of all days be thy tryst!"

Here again, in a short piece probably belonging to the sixth century A.D., is a vision of the splendour and transitoriness of life. I give Sir Charles Lyall's translation. It is in the metre of the original, but without the rhymes, except in the last verse, where, as they happen to be on proper names, they remain.

> "Roast flesh, the glow of fiery wine;
>   To speed on camel fleet and sure,
> As thy soul lists to urge her on
>   Through all the hollow's breadth and length;
>
> White women statue-like that trail
>   Rich robes of price with golden hem;
> Wealth, easy lot, no dread of ill,
>   To hear the lute's complaining string;
>
> These are life's joys. For man is set
>   The prey of Time, and Time is change.
> Life strait or large, great store or nought,
>   All's one to Time, all men to Death.
>
> Death brought to nought Tasm long ago,
>   Ghadî of Bahm, and Dhû Judûn,
> The race of Jâsh and Mârib and
>   The house of Lukmân and at-Tukûn."

The splendid effect of the names with which this piece ends is to be felt rather than dwelt upon.

Or take this verse from a poem on a dead warrior, where spirit and language are both nearly akin to those of the Sagas, with their heroic iron temper that meets life and death alike with the same clear steady eyes:

> "Slaughter chose from all men born the race of Simmah for her own:
> They chose her, and would none other; so fate goes to the fated end.
> Flesh to feed the sword are we, and unrepining we meet our doom;
> Well we feed him, slain or slaying: joyfully he takes our food."

Or this other from the *Muallaka* of Zoheyr, which is like the death-song of Gunnar in the house of King Atli:

> "I know what to-day unfolds, what before it was yesterday,
>   But blind do I stand before the knowledge to-morrow brings.
> I have seen the Dooms trample men as a blind beast at random treads;
>   Whom they smote, he died; whom they missed, he lived on to strengthless eld."

Or again this passage, drawing, in a few clear firm strokes, the Arab ideal of manhood:

> "Sunshine in winter, and when the Dog-Star burned, coolness and shadow;
> Lean-flanked and thin, but not from lacking; liberal-handed, keen-hearted, haughty:
> He journeyed with Wariness, and where he halted, Wariness halted as his comrade;
> A rushing rain-flood when he gave of his fulness; when he sprang to the onset, a mighty lion.
> Two savours had he, of sweet and bitter, and one or the other all men have tasted.
> He rode Fear alone, without a fellow but only his deep-notched blade of al-Yaman."

Finally let me quote a noble passage of reflective poetry: it occurs in a poem written when the author's tribe were forced under pressure of war to migrate from their ancestral home, leaving nothing in their loved meadows but ruinous tents and penfolds.

> "The righteous shall keep the way of the righteous,
>   And to God turn the steps of all that abideth.
> And to God ye return, ye too: with Him only
>   Rest the issues of things and all that they gather;
> All that is in His book of knowledge is reckoned,
>   And before Him revealed lies all that is hidden.
> Is there aught good in life? Yea, I, I have seen it,
>   Even I, if the seeing bring aught of profit.
> Long has life been to me, and this is its burden:
>   Lone against Time abide Tiâr and Yaramram
> And Kulâf and Badî the Mighty, and Dalfa,
>   And Timâr that towers aloft over Khubbah;

And the Stars, marching on all night in procession,
   Drooping westward as each moves forth to his setting.
Sure and steadfast their course: the Underworld draws them
   Gently downwards, as maidens circling the Pillar;
And we may not know, when their lustre is vanished,
   Whether long be the ropes that bind them or little."

These lines, alike profound and majestic, come in an ode which in main substance is a wild tale of foray and plunder and revenge.

Romance reaches its height in the brilliant opening of one of the seven Golden Odes themselves, the *Muallaka* of Tarafa: where the art is not only (as we are apt to say about anything that pleases us) strangely modern, but unusually complex and subtle. In those lines a motive not uncommon in Arab poetry, the moving of the camp in spring, is transfigured by the romantic spirit into a magic magnificence. The howdahs pass silently at dawn, like a dream moving through a dream: fair women in them, white-armed and supple-waisted, half hid behind the scarlet-lined curtains, "the precious stuffs with fluttering ensanguined borders." "They seemed a white fleet of tall-rigged ships, wandering wide through the night to meet at sunrise: thus clomb they the long wave-lines with prows set aloft, ploughing the drifted ridges of sand." Then, without any phrase of transition, the splendid vision of dawn and dreams melts into an even lovelier daylight.

" Ah, the dark-lipped one, the maid of the topazes,
   Hardly yet grown a woman, sweet fruit-picking loiterer,
   A girl, a fawn still fawnless, aloof in the long valleys:
   The face of her how joyous! the day's robe enfolding her,
   Clean as a thing fresh-fashioned, untouched. . . ."

Love in the Valley has never had a more exquisite embodiment, or been set against a more wonderful background.

We seem, in this early Arabian work, in that epic age so kindled and irradiated by the spirit of romance, to be on the verge of a great poetry, a romantic epic such as has been only achieved a few times in the progress of poetry. It did not come. But what advances were made towards it, how far the lyrical, elegiac, and idyllic poetry of Arabia went in the direction of the larger scope of epic and romantic poetry will be the subject of another lecture, in which also I shall attempt to indicate, or at least to suggest, the bearing which that Arabian poetry and the pattern of life that it drew has on our own Middle Ages and the development of romance in the Western world.

ARABIAN EPIC AND ROMANTIC POETRY

THE STEALING OF THE MARE

THE saying that history repeats itself is one of those provisional theories or approximate generalisations which are useful as stepping-stones towards progress. The object of history indeed, if history be regarded as more than the endless amassing of isolated grains of fact, is to find the pattern in human affairs; for that pattern, if we could find it, is the meaning of the world, or if we prefer to put it so, the manifestation of the thought of God. And the essence of pattern, as we have seen already when we were considering the question of the definition of poetry, is repeat. But that this repeating pattern may become art in the full sense, something else is required. The repeat must be so planned and varied as to become more than a mere repeat; it must become the organic element of a whole which is not an aggregate but an organic unity. In art, as in all vital processes, nothing repeats itself absolutely; even if when abstracted and taken by itself it appears to do so, the mere fact that it has occurred before makes its recurrence something new and different, because bearing a different relation to the whole integrated past out of which it rises, and the whole potential future of which it is both the germ and the soil. But it is seldom that the recurrence bears even superficially the aspect of a mere repetition; the difference, even at first sight, is generally as obvious as the likeness:

and if because of the weakness and imperfect flexibility of language we use the same word for two different things, we are conscious that such language suggests an analogy rather than affirms an identity.

In speaking of the epic age of Arabian poetry we avail ourselves of this loose and approximate application of language. It was the age which was epic, rather than the poetry. Nothing corresponding strictly to the European epic, even if that term be taken at the full stretch of its meaning, was produced by the genius of Arabia. That genius worked for a time on lines presenting a rough parallel—suggestive and illuminating even in its roughness—to the lines on which the poetical genius of Europe grew towards what we call the epic. Then it swerved off, and took a course of its own. But meanwhile its effect, direct and indirect, upon the mediæval epic as well as upon the mediæval romance of Europe was great.

To enquire why it was that Arab poetry never produced an epic may be too curious. Where we have an actual work of art, we can put it into relation with its environment, and can see to some extent at least how, if not why, it came into being. But our knowledge is too imperfect, our analysis not fine enough, to let us see why or how, in art as in other matters, anything did not happen. We can no more do this than we can say how the course of history would have been deflected if facts at any moment had been different from what they were. But we can say this much, that the conditions in which epic poetry has in fact arisen elsewhere, did not hold here. Arabia before Islam was a loose aggregate of small tribes. They had little in common beyond a general resemblance in manner of life and habits. It was only towards the end of the period that they had even a common language. They were without anything that could be called a national self-consciousness, and they could not therefore have a fully developed national poetry. After the tremendous conquests and expansions of the seventh century, anything like nationality was out of the question. The bond of the empire of the Khalifs was one of religion: and that religion was a fierce Puritanism which was jealous of art. The concentration of Arabian poetry in what may be called the epic age never had a chance to expand and dilate itself by any normal course of growth. It is like the wine in the Odyssey that had to be mixed with twenty parts of water in order to be used for drinking and to disengage its flavour. The jar that held that strong heady wine of poetry was violently broken, and the wine spilt before it had been mixed for the larger draught. But where the scattered drops fell they were not all drunk by the sand; still potent in strange surroundings, still capable of immense dilution without losing their virtue, they gave to the poetry of other races not merely a new colour and tone but a new element of life.

The new element was one to which no single word precisely corresponds. It held in it, embodied in a single texture, the two things which we call romance and chivalry: the chivalrous romance which is akin to the epic and distinct from the sentimental romance of a later development: and the romantic chivalry which is different from anything in either classical or Northern literature, but when engrafted on and interfused with these became the imaginative soul of the Middle Ages. Western romance and chivalry derive from Arabian origins much as Western religion derives from Jewish origins. To the kindred stocks of the Arabo-Syrian plateau—for of that single race and region Palestine is also a part—we owe largely or even mainly the vital forces which make the Middle Ages spiritually and imaginatively different from the world ruled over by Rome.

Their influence did not come all at once or through one channel. As we have seen, the Asiatic influence counts for something even as far back as the epic age of Greece. It was present and active in the Alexandrian school, when Egypt, itself according to the division of the ancient geographers an Asiatic country, was the central nursery of Greek literature, as it afterwards became the centre, or one of the chief centres, of Arabian literature also. It acted on Europe at a later period in and through Byzantium and the Greek empire of the East. But its determining impact as regards poetry was more direct. Historians have gone too far in tracing to Byzantine origins what reached and affected the West through a more immediate contact with the East. The formula "à travers Byzance," in which that doctrine was summarised by Gaston Paris, must be supplemented and modified if it is not to be misleading. It is applied by him not only, for example, to *Parthenopeu de Blois* and to the *Châtelaine de Vergi*, but to *Aucassin and Nicolete*. In this last instance certainly, as perhaps in the others, any Byzantine influence or suggestion is remote and conjectural; the immediate Oriental influence is patent and dominant. In the Middle Ages from first to last Byzantium was as much a foreign city as Cairo or Damascus, as Samarcand or Cordova: Greek was as much a strange language as Arabic. The rediscovery of Greek at the Renaissance was a discovery of something of which all touch had for many centuries been lost. To Dante and Petrarch, as to the whole age of their contemporaries and predecessors, Homer was a sealed book. But the knowledge of Arabic literature was for several centuries before them widely diffused in the countries bordering the Western Mediterranean.

> " Era scritto in Arabica, che 'l Conte
> Intendea così ben come Latino "—

so Ariosto says of Orlando reading the inscription left in the cave by Medoro and Angelica, and romance here follows, in a broad way, the facts of history.[1] In a notable passage of *Sordello*, Browning, with a true historical instinct, couples Greek and Arabic as among the accomplishments of Salinguerra, each acquired for its own reason—

> "Speaking the Greek's own language, just because
> Your Greek eludes you, leave the least of flaws
> In contracts with him; while, since Arab lore
> Holds the stars' secret—take one trouble more
> And master it !"

The Western knowledge of Greek was in the main confined to traders and diplomatists; it had nothing to do with literature: while the knowledge of Arabic was not only of much wider use, being necessary in the whole circle of the arts and sciences, but much more intimate and vital. It held the stars' secret in more senses than one.

It is a common and accepted, but a fallacious, belief that Arab romance was confined to prose. Mr. Bourdillon, in his excellent introduction to *Aucassin and Nicolete*, falls into this error. "Fauriel first observed," he writes, "that this poem "—I don't know why he calls it a poem—"has the form of Arabian romances: and the probability of this origin has not been denied. Only, as Dr. W. Herz remarks, there is this difference, that in this work the story continues uninterruptedly, told alternately in prose and verse; while in the Arabian and Persian romances the verses

---

[1] *Orlando Furioso*, B. xxiii. st. 110.

are of a purely lyrical or didactic character, merely illustrating and not continuing the story told in the prose; they could in fact be left out without injuring the course of the tale. In thus departing from his models, the French poet hit upon a most happy and telling method, employed with marked skill." This is true of the *Arabian Nights:* but the Nights are not the whole body of Arabian romances; and we shall see presently that this form was not an invention of the French poet, but had been used, and developed with even greater skill and constructive power, by his Arabian models or predecessors. Even Mr. Nicholson, if I may venture to say so, generalises somewhat too widely, or omits, as for his purposes he was justified in omitting, a qualification which for our purpose is important, when he says in his *Literary History of the Arabs* that Arabian literature " produced no great epic, but only prose narratives which, though sometimes epic in tone, are better described as historical romances." That it produced no great epic is accurately true, but it did not confine itself to prose narratives. In its feeling after the epic, before the romantic period had fully set in and before Arabian poetry, much about the same time, came to an end, it struck upon, and pursued for some way, a form of poetry which is an inchoate epic. That form was not pursued to completion: it remained only half-developed. But the key had been found, and was handed over to the West.

It is to one of the few surviving specimens of this highly significant form of poetry—a new departure which was to have immense issues—that I wish to draw attention. This is the romance entitled *The Stealing of the Mare*. It has been made accessible to English readers by Mr. Wilfrid Blunt's admirable translation. Even among Arabic scholars I find it is but little known. But with the instinct of a poet, he realised its value; and with the skill of a born man of letters he has presented it so as to lose none of its unique fascination, and has thus increased the debt already owed to him by students of literature and lovers of poetry.

The Romance of the Stealing of the Mare was composed in the tenth century. It is one of a cycle composing the Romance of Abu Zeyd. Its author was one Abu Obeyd, of whom nothing but the name is known. The Beni-Helal, the tribe of which Abu Zeyd was the national hero, belonged originally to Nejd. About the end of the ninth century A.D. they migrated under stress of famine (like the Beni-Israel between two and three thousand years before them) to the eastern borders of Egypt, where they remained for upwards of a generation and then, according to tradition, moved on again westwards. Tribes claiming descent from them still exist in Tunisia, and for all we know they may have penetrated into Spain and come into actual contact with the developing poetry of Southern France. An elaborate simile drawn from the flooded Nile, and some other allusions to Egyptian monuments and customs, make it reasonably probable that the romance was composed, in its actual form, during the Egyptian sojourn: and it is in Egypt that it has been orally preserved till modern times. But it contains reminiscences of earlier history: the Chosroes are mentioned in it as though they were still kings in Iran, and the framework and ideas of the poem, with one striking and important exception which I shall mention, are mainly pre-Islamic and take us back to the period of the Ignorance.

The incidents on which it is founded were quasi-historical, as they were with the almost contemporary Charlemagne-epic in France: but as historical documents they are equally valueless. Fact, if there, is overlaid with and transmuted by imagination. The work was transmitted orally through centuries, as in fragments it still is; when it was first written down there are no means of determining, but in the long course of transmission, chiefly through illiterate storytellers, both language and versification became much corrupted. Nevertheless its essential excellence of construction was so great that it has resisted decay; it has become neither greatly debased nor badly mutilated. Arab scholars, we are told, hold it in contempt on account of vulgarisms of dialect and defects of metre. But it is true metal: and we may judge, without straining probability, that its form was originally not unworthy of its substance. Even now it is the best single picture which we possess of romantic chivalry as the Arabs of the ninth and tenth century understood it; and this was also as they created it, and as they handed it over to Western Europe.

The form of the romance is however no less remarkable than its substance; and in form as well as in substance it throws a flood of light on the development of mediæval poetry in the West. It is planned and executed in alternate prose and verse. This form of literature—the *cante-fable*—occurs in a number of independent literatures. It is most familiar through a single European example, the French romance of *Aucassin and Nicolete*. It has been little followed at any time of fully developed art. *Aucassin and Nicolete* is unique of its period. Later Western romances made the choice between verse and prose and stuck to it throughout. In our own time Morris, that great experimenter and rediscoverer, brought the form into use again. The

House of the Wolfings, the earliest, and in the judgment of many the finest, of the romances of his later life, bears a remarkable analogy to the *Stealing of the Mare* in its use of the alternation of verse with prose; and that analogy is the more striking because in both cases the romance may properly be described as a romantic epic: it has the epic concentration and nobility, the tone and colour of an epic age. When *Aucassin and Nicolete* was composed, about the end of the twelfth century (the extant Northern French version belongs to the beginning of the thirteenth) the epic age of France was practically over; the period of the cyclic epic, of literary *rifaccimenti*, had begun. This tenth-century Arabian romance, springing from deeper roots, has what Gaston Paris calls, in an admirable phrase, the "large uninterrupted movement" of the true epic, which does not either move in spasmodic jerks like the *Chanson de Roland* or crawl along like the *Nibelungenlied*. It has the essential epic construction; but it stops short of reaching the full epic form.

Mastery of construction is a quality that can be hardly shown by a sketch; it has to be pursued throughout the complete work. A work of art only shows its constructive quality when the whole is considered as the integration of all its parts, and when the parts are considered as the elements, essential and mutually interrelated, in which the whole receives its substance and creates its effect. But it is worth while giving a sketch—necessarily on this occasion brief—of the *Stealing of the Mare;* both because of the extreme art and beauty of particular episodes, and also because we may thus incidentally emphasise some of the qualities of the work as poetry, the kind of pattern of life which it embodies. In doing so I shall quote freely, as I am permitted to do, from Mr. Blunt's translation.

It will be convenient to say here that as regards its technical mechanism this romance is a poem set in a framework of connecting passages of prose, differing thus from *Aucassin and Nicolete,* which is a prose romance set in a framework of connecting passages of verse. The prose here is only about one quarter of the whole; with one exception the prose passages are brief, not exceeding a page or two in each case. The art of narrative prose had been developed in Arabic to perfection; and read together, the prose passages make a continuous and complete story, short indeed, but as brilliant as the best of those in the *Arabian Nights.* The verse taken by itself does not set forth the story quite completely and continuously, but it covers most of the ground. The prose is all in direct narrative, the verse partly in narrative, partly put in the mouth of the hero by an impersonation which is half lyrical and half dramatic. At the beginning, and for some way on, each section begins with a formulary line, *Saith the hero Abu Zeyd, the Helali Salame.* This line gives the name, the patronymic, and the race of the hero in full: an exactly equivalent line in Homeric language would be, εἶπ' Ὀδυσεὺς Λαερτιάδης μέγα κῦδος Ἀχαιῶν. The sections are likewise introduced by formulary words; "said the narrator" before each section of prose; "and the narrator began to sing," or some variation of these words, before each section of verse: just as in the French romance the respective sections are headed "or se cante" and "or dient et content et fabloient."

The opening of the romance, in its succinctness and swift precision, shows an art already studied and mature. There is no fumbling, no preluding, no getting under weigh. There are indeed a few prefatory lines in prose; but these are something between an epistle to the reader and a title-page: they bear in fact a close resemblance to one of those lengthened title-pages with which we are familiar in old printed books. I may quote this preface because it is at once brief and characteristic: it is a pleasant bush for good wine.

"In the name of God, the Merciful, the Compassionate! He who telleth this tale is Abu Obeyd; and he saith: When I took note and perceived that the souls of men took pleasure in hearing good tales, and that their ears were comforted and they made good cheer in the listening, then I called to mind the tale of the Agheyli Jaber and his mare, and of what befell him and his people. For this is a story of wonderful adventure and marvellous incidents, and a tale which when one hears he desires to have it ever in remembrance as a delight tasted by him and not forgotten. And the telling of it is this."

Then the romance at once begins. In what follows I shall quote from the verse, but borrow from the briefer and more unadorned prose where it can conveniently be used for giving the outline of the story. The first lay or canto opens with the formulary line I have mentioned, and adds to it curiously what does not occur elsewhere, a flourish or cadenza. This seems also to be formulary and to descend directly from the lyric with a refrain, familiar in all popular or ballad poetry.

"Saith the hero Abu Zeyd, the Helali Salame:
(Woe is me, my heart is a fire, a fire that burneth!)

On a Friday morning once I sat with three companions,
I in my tent, the fourth of four, with the sons of Amer.
Sudden I raised my eyes and gazed at the breadth of the desert,

> Searching the void afar, the empty hills and the valleys.
> Lo in the midmost waste a form, where the rainways sundered,
> Wandering uncertain round in doubt, with steps of a stranger."

This form, drifting like a leaf in the wide vast landscape, is Ghanimeh, the widow of a great man among the Arabs. At her husband's death, his brother (like Julian Avenel in the *Monastery*) had possessed himself by the strong hand of his inheritance, driven out the widow, and degraded her boy, the rightful heir, to be a herder of camels. He pacified the indignation of the tribe by engaging that when the boy grew up he should marry his own only daughter, and succeed to his position. But when Ghanimeh returned to claim this promise, and was backed up by the great ones of the tribe, he attached a condition that he meant to be impossible. He required that the boy should bring, as the price for his bride, the mare of the Agheyli chief, Fadel Jaber. When the men of the tribe heard it, they said to one another, "No man alive can do this, unless it were Abu Zeyd." And Ghanimeh disappeared into the desert, and came to the Beni-Helal to ask Abu Zeyd for succour.

The plea was made simply to his chivalry and his spirit of knight-errantry. To undertake an adventure so perilous was in itself a motive to the romantic Arab spirit; and to that spirit not only were the rights of a guest unbounded, but the duty of succouring the weak was imperative, and the request of a woman, at least if she were a woman in distress, was equivalent to a law. "Frank, honest, and approximately equal relations of the sexes," says Sir Charles Lyall in carefully chosen words, "were guaranteed by mutual courtesy and respect": and this courtesy, even to the extreme of what we should regard as knight-errantry, was fostered by the feeling that it was at once the inborn character and the outward proof of noble blood. It had little to do with sentiment, and nothing with physical attraction. Love came otherwise, as we shall see.

This mare was the most celebrated in Arabia,

" The grey mare, the renowned: in the world there is none like her,
Not with the Persian kings, the Chosroes, the Irani."

She was the treasure of the tribe, guarded more carefully than a princess. To attempt the enterprise and fail in it meant almost certain death. But Abu Zeyd did not hesitate for a moment. To the remonstrances of his chief and his tribesmen he only answered, " To leave this adventure were shame; though I were given to drink of the cup of confusion, yet must I go forward." A suggestion that he should be kept back by force was met with a flash of anger that silenced it. His sister Rih, a beautiful figure firmly and delicately drawn in a few lines, tried vainly to dissuade him :

" And Rih cried, ' Woe is me, the burning of my trouble:
How shall I quench this flame? Yet shall he take our blessing.'
And I: ' The word farewell is but a wound to the goer:
Cease therefore from thy tears.' And weeping thus she left me.
But I mounted on my camel and went my way in silence,
Going by unknown paths in the wide trackless desert,
Nor turned my head again when they had turned back silent."

One other touch at this point is notable : for it is very characteristic of that lavish and often ostentatious generosity which was part of the curiously compounded Arab ideal. Before going, Abu Zeyd ordered his slave,

Abul Komsan, to take charge over Ghanimeh during his own absence:

"Go with this lady and build her a pavilion
With breadths of perfumed silk, and bid prepare all dainties,
That she may eat of the best, and serve her in due honour:
For well it is in life to be of all things generous,
Ere we are called away to death's unjoyful dwellings."

So Abu Zeyd went on, fifteen days' journey, till he came to the pastures of the Agheylat. There he left his camel among shepherds, whom he won completely over by his stories, and songs he sang to the Arab lute —the *rebab*, which is one of the few Arabic words used by Chaucer. Music as well as gymnastic was an essential part of the Arab idea of knighthood: and the poetical device which makes Abu Zeyd the singer of his own achievements, while it is dramatic, is dramatically probable.

His first plan had been to make his way disguised as a minstrel or a pedlar right into the encampment. But in an accidental meeting with a girl of the Agheylat outside the camp (we have to note throughout the romance the almost absolute freedom and fearlessness of women, alike married and unmarried) he let drop something about the mare which roused her suspicion. She spoke sharply yet kindly to him in warning:

"Fly for the life thou hast nor linger here for its losing.
Fly ere I spread the word and bring the Arabs upon thee:
And I shall tell them truth, and give thee up to the spear-
    points."

Abu Zeyd tried, with partial success, to throw her off the scent:

"Ha! the mare, what is she that I should wish for or win her?
Never in all my days have I bent my leg to a saddle,
Being of the unskilled, and little apt in learning."

But when she was gone, he was left very uneasy. As night fell, he found himself by a spreading tree with low-set branches beyond the furthest camp-fires; and there he sat down to wait for dawn.

Through the darkness some one approached. Abu Zeyd swung himself up into the tree and lay along one of the low branches, watching. The new comer stopped under the tree; and this was Sahel ibn Aaf. He waited there, looking ever to the right and to the left, till a third of the night was over: then there came softly out of the camp another, an exceedingly fair woman; and this was Zohwa. Sahel was a felon and an outlaw, whose outlawry had come on him however not through any of his crimes, but through an unintentional insult—the story of Artemis and Actaeon over again, and exquisitely described in the poem—that he had offered to the princess Alia, the daughter of Jaber. Under the savage Arab code of honour which was also a code of revenge, this was as much as his life was worth. Jaber had hunted him, and not finding him had killed his father and set a blood-price upon his head. Barbarous as this was, it was within the accepted rules. But Sahel now broke completely through these, and designed to take his revenge, not on the men of the Agheylat, but on Alia herself. By doing this, he broke the code of Arab honour, and put himself not only out of law, but out of sympathy.

In Zohwa, who was secretly his mistress, he found an apt confederate. The prose narrative goes on:

"And they fell to talking, and presently they spoke of Alia. And Sahel became troubled, and he said to Zohwa, 'O that I could behold her! O that thou couldst bring her hither!' And she asked of him, 'Why so? is she then more beautiful than I? are her eyes more fairly painted?' And he said, 'Not so; but listen.'"

He tells his story and ends, "'And now, O Zohwa, I have but this one desire, to soothe my soul with slaying her, and after that I care not what may come, not though they hew me to pieces with their swords. And surely the news of her death at my hand would travel abroad and grieve the heart of Fadel, and wound him so that he too should die.'

"And when Zohwa heard this story, she bade him to be of good comfort, for she would bring him to his heart's desire. And she said, 'I will fetch thee Alia hither, and in a short space. Wait only until I return.'

"And she left him, and returned to the tents, and she sought the pavilion of the Princess Alia. And Alia rose and went forward to meet her, and enquired the cause of her coming. And Zohwa said, 'O my lady, I am in a great perplexity, and therefore am I come to thee.' And she sat down beside her, and told her a long tale and kept her thus talking through the night, and soothed her with soft words, deceiving her and flattering her with fair speeches of praise until she touched her heart with her cunning, nor did she cease from discoursing until a second third of the night was spent, and there remained but these two awake of all the camp. Then Zohwa arose as if to go, and asked leave to depart; but Alia asked her to stay and sleep there in the tent beside her. And Zohwa said, 'Of a truth that would be before all things pleasant, and an honour to me; but I have been at pains to escape unperceived from my people, and to them I must return.' And Alia was moved to pity, and said, 'Go then.' And Zohwa went out of the tent, and on a little way, but presently returned trembling. And

Alia asked her, 'What aileth thee?' And she answered, 'O lady, I am overcome with lack of courage; wilt thou not come with me a little way?' And Alia said, 'If I should go with thee, who should return with me? The guards are sleeping, and all my damsels: nor am I too without danger of enemies who might do me a hurt, and more than the rest, of that dog Sahel ibn Aaf.'

"And Zohwa answered quickly, 'Say not so, O lady. How should Sahel hurt thee, or how should any other, seeing that thou art the daughter of the prince of our tribe? and yet thou speakest thus, thou daughter of the generous? It is no far journey. Listen; between thy tents and ours are but ten furlongs, and if thou wilt come but one half the road, thou canst then turn back and I will go forward, and the way will have been divided between us.'

"And Alia agreed, for her wit failed her; and she arose and went with Zohwa out of the camp: and Zohwa's tongue wagged as they walked, so that the way seemed short, and Alia lost reckoning in the darkness."

So they came to the place where Sahel was waiting in the dim starlight, and Abu Zeyd was still crouched above in the branches of the tree.

"And Alia's eyes misgave her
Seeing a form in the dark: and she called out, 'What thing art thou?
Art thou a passer-by, or one with intent a prowler?'
And he, the approacher, said: 'Now truly art thou taken,
Captured as in a net, and the Maker of earth and heaven
Yieldeth thee to my hand and blindeth thee to thy peril.'
And Sahel began to curse her, and to the tree he drew her;
And she knew her hour was come, and the heart within her was shaken."

Sahel dragged her to the tree by her neck-ornaments, tied her wrists together, and began to prepare to kill her, leisurely, that he might have the full taste of his revenge. She appealed to his mercy and that of Zohwa in vain. The traitress who had lured her out by an appeal to her kindness stood by, taunting her coldly. For Zohwa, a sort of Arabian Regan, cruel, mean and dissolute, no sympathy can be felt from the first. But for Sahel there was more pretext; and the Islamic re-fashioner of what is in its essentials a Pagan and pre-Islamic story has inserted here a touch which is meant to destroy any excuse for him and make him a moral as well as a legal outlaw. Sahel added to his outrage what was to the Mohammedan Arab mind the last and most horrible refinement of cruelty. He refused to say the *Fatha* for her, the dying confession of faith which a Moslem was bound to recite for any other too weak, or too ignorant, or, as here, too terrified to speak the words. This touch was needed to make the refusal of mercy to Sahel's own plea for mercy later unchallengeable even according to the extravagant code of Arab chivalry. To what lengths that code went is well illustrated by an incident in the Romance of Nur-ed-din. When the murderous traitor El Mo'in is put in Nur-ed-din's power, " the Khalifeh addressed him, saying, 'Take this sword and strike off with it the head of thine enemy.' And he took it, and approached El Mo'in : but he looked at him, and said to him, 'I did according to my nature, and do thou according to thine.' And Nur-ed-din threw down the sword from his hand.'"

To return to our own romance.

" And Alia raised up weeping
Her beautiful eyes to heaven, and prayed to him who hath pity.
'O thou searcher of hearts,' she said, 'who knowest the secrets
Even of every heart, to thee I look for compassion.
Thou the Merciful, the Eternal, the Most Mighty,

Thou who art of thyself, the Giver of Consolation,
Thou the Pitiful one, to thee I come in my sorrow
Calling on thee by the name of thy deeds, the might of thy
    wonders
Done for those thou hast chosen against the unbelievers.'"

"But he laughed at her words" (says the prose,) "and said, 'If thou be of the blameless, pray on.' And he went to Zohwa and kissed her, and Alia beheld it."

"And to Ibn Aaf she said, 'I appeal to thee of thine honour,
  So may the Lord spare thee and heal thy soul of blindness.'
But Sahel answered, 'Nay by the Prophet I will not spare thee,
Not though Abu Zeyd were here himself, the Helali:
Let him deliver thee! let him help thee, thou dog's daughter!'
But she, 'Yet if God so willed he were here even now upon
    thee.'
And Sahel, 'Hold thy peace, for to-night thy life hath ending.'
  And Abu Zeyd from the tree heard all the words between
    them:
And my mind rose to her help as a full pot boiling over,
And I heard my name in their mouths, and my heart grew hot
    within me,
Like a pitcher from the well which brims and spills with fulness.
Sahel has drawn his sword and leapt on her with cursings,
The while she crieth aloud. But I too cried, 'Take courage:
Lo, I am here to thy hand, one able for thy burden.'
And of a sudden I dropped and ran to the three that struggled,
And Sahel I seized by the throat and dragged towards destruc-
    tion.
And he cried, 'Who art thou and whence? and what the way of
    thy sending?'
And I, 'From Death the King am I come to take possession:
Life is weary of thee, and Death's edge presseth nearly.'
And he, 'O Sheykh of Afrits, wilt thou not spare the sword-
    stroke?
Lo, I turn from my sin in thought of the day of judgment.'
But I, 'Thou art but a heathen. Thou didst refuse the verses.
Thou hast done a treacherous deed: thou hast angered thy
    Creator,
Purposing death to souls, and therefore will I slay thee.'
  And I put my hand to the sword and drew it from the scab-
    bard,

And it flashed as lightning flasheth, making a flame in the darkness,
And I smote him with its edge, and his head flew from his shoulders.
And turning then on Zohwa I smote her too, while Alia
Watched with the eyes of thanks the issue of the swordstroke.
And I severed the cord from her wrists and she rose and took her bracelets:
And I bade her go in peace nor speak a word of the doings;
For ever the mouth is blest that holdeth its own counsel."

This grim and great scene is followed immediately by another between Abu Zeyd and Alia of such radiant beauty that I shrink from spoiling it by a summary. It is like the breaking of a lovely dawn over the darkness and horror of the night. For restraint, and interplay of humour and emotion, and a sort of delicate purity, it is unsurpassable. When the two clasp hands as a token of the covenant that the doings of the night shall be kept secret, the poet lifts a veil for a moment.

"And I stretched my hand to her hand and touched it with my fingers,
And its softness made me wonder, and its most slender fashion,
And the palm of her hand in mine was cool as a cloud in summer."

From that moment they are plighted lovers. And what love meant to the Arab poet may best be told in his own words. The two, in a moment so charged with emotion, can have no secrets from one another. He tells her who he is, Abu Zeyd, her enemy, the slayer of her kindred.

"And Alia heard me speak and stood up tall before me,
Like to one making a cry; but I shut her mouth with my hand's palm,
And hot tears came to my eyes, and 'Cry not,' I said, 'O Alia,

Cry not for pity aloud, lest I fall in a sea of trouble.'
And she said, 'My cry was unwilled, for thy love my whole
    heart filleth,
And now fear is forgot. And O Abu Zeyd Salame,
Know that we twain must love, for I am of noble lineage
Even as thou thyself, the hero, the lion of Amer.'
And I said, ' Now listen, Alia, to that which I would tell thee.
Love is a building fair, broadbased on sure foundations,
And the builders built it high as was no other dwelling.'
And she said, 'Thou speakest truth. And love is of three
    conditions,
And to men of understanding each hath a sign to know it.
The first compelleth thee to kiss the hand thou lovest:
This is a moment's love. The next is more enduring,
Which kisseth thee on the cheek. But there is yet the
    latest,
Love which shall kiss thy forehead. This is a love for ever.
Mine is of all the three.'"

Alia took Abu Zeyd back with her to the women's tents, where she hid him for twenty days. To the other women, "the daughters of the Arabs," she explained the situation with perfect simplicity. With the same perfect simplicity they accepted it, and there was not a whisper of scandal. "Were we in thy place, so would we do also." On the twenty-first night she brought him the mare (she had access to the keys), and sent him away. At the moment of parting she almost broke down. "She clung to his stirrup, and said, 'Take me also with thee, and leave me not to suffer blame.' But he swore an oath to her that he would return. And she let go the stirrup. And in that guise he left her; and they were both weeping."

Abu Zeyd rode off on the mare to the outer pastures, till he came to a well of water, where he drank and watered the mare, and sat down to think out his plans. Meanwhile the loss of the mare had fallen like a thunderbolt on the Agheylat. Her grooms, when they entered the stable in the morning, found a lantern burning in it, but no mare. The skilled trackers who were summoned found footsteps all ending at the tent of Alia. The truth came out: and then the romance turns to that element of savagery which (as also in the Homeric and the Arthurian stories) is mingled with high chivalry and magnificent courtesy. Alia, like Guenevere in the *Morte d'Arthur*, was "appeached of treason" and condemned to be burnt alive.

Abu Zeyd, after thinking the matter out, had come to the conclusion that her danger was the greatest, and her claim on his honour the first. Ghanimeh must wait, like Lucius in the fifth Act of *Cymbeline;*

> "Alack!
> There's other work in hand: I see a thing
> Bitter to me as death."

He hid the mare in a cave, blocking the mouth with stones, disguised himself like a dervish, and returned to the camp of the Agheylat. "Said the narrator: And when they had lit the fire, while Alia watched the kindling, her fear was great and her eyes looked to the right and to the left; and while she was in this wise, suddenly she saw Abu Zeyd standing in the midst of the Arabs who were around her. But he signed to her to be silent, as it were he would say, 'Fear not, for I am here.' And when she was sure that it was indeed he, she smiled on him very sweetly. And now the flames began to break forth."

The execution was already a thing in which the authorities had little heart; and when a holy man, a stranger, appeared to stop it, there was a revulsion of feeling which no one sought to check.

> "I took her by the hand, while the crowd looked on in wonder,
> And I thrust them back with my hands and stood beside the burning

And cried out, 'Burn me not, O fire, nor seek thou to
  shame me,
For if thou work me ill, I bear to the Lord my witness.'
And I passed out through the fire; and by the Lord's per-
  mission
The flames died and fell down, and I walked forth from them
  scathless;
And I came to the side of Alia, of her with the plaited
  tresses,
And I undid her bonds while all the world beheld us.
And they said, 'He is a Sheykh, a holy man of wonder.'"

The next stage in the story is an episode which is one way like that of Theoclymenus in the Odyssey, in another like something out of the fantastic *diablerie* of the *Arabian Nights*. There came to them, says the narrator, a swift horseman, and his name was Bedr-ibn-Saleh, the sand-diviner, and he came from the land of Baghdad, a knower of things hidden. And when he had lighted down, he said to Jaber: "Prince of the people, the news has reached me of the loss of thy mare, nor have I come save for her sake." Then he made divination, first by the sand and then by an image of gold in the form of a son of Adam: after fumigations and invocations a smoke rose, and there came to him of the Jinns crowding round him, and the image began to speak.

What follows is very dramatic and exciting, but too intricate to be made clear in a short summary. In the end the image speaks again, and this time plainly: "'O Fadel, the prince Abu Zeyd saved thy daughter; and he slew Sahel and Zohwa for her sake, and she helped him to obtain thy mare and gain that which he desired of thee.' And in making an end of speaking it said: 'If thou wouldst hearken to my bidding, thou wouldst make fellowship and friendship with him; for to thee he were the truest of companions and helpers.' And when the Emir Fadel heard these words of the image, then he cried with a loud voice, and his cry filled the assembly and all the tribes heard it, and he swore a great oath and said, 'Yea verily will I, though he be the first of my foemen.' And when he swore that oath, the prince Abu Zeyd started to his feet and cried with a loud cry, 'I am here, even I, Salame.' And he told his tale from the beginning; and Fadel rose and pressed him to his heart, and all his trouble passed from him."

Abu Zeyd told where he had hidden the mare; she was brought back, " and Fadel gave her to Abu Zeyd, and other noble gifts, and said, ' What wilt thou at my hand?' And he said, 'That which I would have of thee is Alia thy daughter.' And Fadel answered, ' By the faith of the Arabs, that also is my desire.' "

Then the pledge for which the quest of the mare was undertaken is fulfilled. Abu Zeyd rode back with the mare to his own people and handed her over to Ghanimeh, and sent Abul Komsan with her to En Naaman, the usurping uncle. Naaman flatly refused to carry out his promise. He bullied and stormed, threatening to kill on the spot any one who interfered. Abul Komsan, like Dickie of Dryhope when he met fause Sakeld, had little skill in arguing, and as little inclination:

> " The ne'er a word had Dickie to say,
>   Sae he thrust his lance through his fause bodie."

"But Abul Komsan," says the narrator, "struck him with his spear upon his breast and pierced him through, so that the spear shone beyond him. And he called out to the tribe, and defied them: but they said, ' Nay, but thou hast done us a service, for this one refused to do according to our counsel.' So Abul Komsan bade them bury him."

The boy Amer, Ghanimeh's son, was reinstated in his sovereignty, and married to his cousin amid general rejoicings.

" And they said, ' O Abul Komsan, thou art a man of honour,
   For thou hast slain the wicked, and we are thine, thy protected,
   And thou hast befriended Amer. Do with us as thou desirest.'
But he answered them, 'O people, peace be with you, O people:
Salame is my lord, to-day and now and for ever.'
And Amer brought him the mare, and with it gifts and treasures,
And said, 'Thou didst bring this gift. A gift of me shalt thou take her.'
So he took the mare at his hand, and the gifts, and he departed.
And when he came to his tribe he told Abu Zeyd the story:
And Abu Zeyd gave thanks. And this is the end of the telling."

So the poem ends. It is the epic manner of ending; the reconciliation is effected, the tension relaxed; the story of the Stealing of the Mare is at an end with her return to Abu Zeyd, just as the story of the Wrath is at an end in the Iliad with the burial of Hector under the truce guaranteed by Achilles. At this point the epic poet instinctively and unhesitatingly ends also. The romance-writer finds it more difficult to stop here. For a romance, or at least a romance which is no longer capable of being described alternatively as a romantic epic, has no inevitable structural unity; it prolongs itself from delight in itself, as its less organic character and its fainter and more diffused vitality enable it to do. In this case the prose continues to linger on over the story: it was meant for a popular audience, and such an audience does not care for unity of action; it wants to know what happened next, and next, and yet again next; and so the narrator proceeds to tell how Abu Zeyd went back to the Agheylat with two thousand horsemen, how he married the Princess Alia, and how they went back to the Helalat after a while, and lived there in happiness until the end of their time.

The Homeric analogies in the Arabian poem are manifold and striking; some of them have come out incidentally in this sketch of its contents, and I need not labour them. But what is more important than particular analogies, of incident or treatment or language, is the common quality of epic elevation and largeness. We are almost forced to ask the question, whether this is the nearest to a fully-developed epic poetry that the Arab genius reached, and if so, how it is that it stopped here.

One of the first questions that occur is whether this romance, in the actual form in which we possess it, is on the line of ascent to, or on the line of descent from, a realised epic form. Whether it was committed to writing as originally composed we cannot tell; it has certainly reached us mainly through a long oral tradition, and has suffered some amount of wastage and deterioration in the process. It is then at least theoretically possible that it originally existed in the shape of a continuous poem; the interstitial prose being the later work of rhapsodes, of professional story-tellers who recited portions or lays of the original poem, but brought these in incidentally, here and there as they felt inclined, in the course of telling the story as a story. The actual verse certainly is the work of a poet who had the power of producing an *œuvre de longue haleine*, who was capable of putting a long and complex narrative into structural form, and keeping up his work at high tension; the mechanism of an epic poem in the full sense does not seem beyond him. Nor is the process thus suggested without parallels elsewhere. Some such disintegration of the Iliad for popular use had taken place before the Iliad as a whole was brought together again, and in a sense effectively recreated, at Athens in the sixth century B.C.

But a more exact appreciation of the poetical quality of the *Stealing of the Mare* does not bear out this hypothesis; it leads one to see that we are dealing not with an epic in disintegration, but with the epic in the making. We have here the epic well on the way towards being made, but lacking yet the critical lifting movement, the decisive effort of genius that was needed to bring it fully into being. It is still attached organically to the earlier organism, out of which it had to be born in order to launch itself and attain substantive life of its own. It still partakes of the nature of the lyrico-elegiac poetry of a previous age. Throughout the greater part of the poem, as I have said, the hero narrates in his own person, and indeed there are whole passages in the earlier part of the romance which, standing alone, might be classified with those lyrical or quasi-lyrical fragments which are among the precious relics of the Poetry of the Ignorance. It is always on the point of slipping over into the direct narrative form, and attaining the objective quality of epic. Every now and then it does actually so pass over. But it has not freed itself from the subjective quality of lyric. Homer worked on analogous material; and Books IX. to XII. of the Odyssey show in the most striking way, among many other instances on a smaller scale, how subjective and quasi-lyrical narrative could be fused and merged in the large epic structure by a poet of immense genius.

This tendency towards crystallisation into the authentic epic form becomes more marked as the romance goes on. The half-lyrical and half-dramatic impersonation is wholly dropped after the point at which the sand-diviner comes on the scene. The canto in which he appears is introduced by a line in which the poet for the first time speaks clearly in his own person:

"Now doth my song return to the Emir Agheyli Fadel."

From that point on to the end the poem is all pure narrative, comparable to Homeric narrative in its ease, swiftness, and lucidity. The secret of the epic has been found: even some of its specific devices are used, and used with complete skill: for instance, the artifice of repetition or recapitulation. This is admirably used in a passage where the whole of the first part of the story, from the arriving of Ghanimeh to the rescue of Alia, is told in summary by the golden image. Another device is of more fundamental importance, for it is of the essence of the epic. This is the artifice of completing the structure without closing the pattern. It is of the essence of the saga that it goes on to the end of the story: it is of the essence of the epic that it does not. The story of the Iliad, as a story, does not end where they went about the burial of Hector the knight: the story of the Aeneid, as a story, does not end where the life of Turnus flies indignant into the dark. But the Iliad and the Aeneid end there, rightly and inevitably. One of the chief reasons for believing that the end of the Odyssey either is a later addition, or at the least represents material which had not been fully wrought into epic shape by the poet, is just this, that it trails off into telling the end of the story. So likewise the prose *Völsungasaga* does not stop until the whole story has been told to the end: the saga-writer does not stay his hand until he has brought the whole kin of the Volsungs to their destruction, root and stem. When he reshaped it as an epic, Morris, the greatest master of structure among modern poets, made his poem end at the epic ending. And similarly, the poet of the *Stealing of the Mare* had the intuition of an epic poet when he ends the poem where he does; while the prose story-teller, as we have seen, continues it with the intuition, no less just for its own purposes, of the story-teller. We can see in the *Stealing of the Mare* what I do not know that we can see elsewhere in literature, the actual process of the invention and creation of epic poetry going on, like the precipitation in a chemical solution, like the determination of an embryonic structure, before our eyes. To see poetry in the making is a rare and a fascinating privilege; but here we see a sight rarer still, a whole generic form of poetry in the making, and that one of the noblest of its forms, perhaps even the noblest of all, according to the view ably presented and somewhat inconclusively refuted by Aristotle in the *Poetics*.

It was this Arabian poetry, charged and saturated with the potentialities of a supreme poetical art, which kindled the new life of poetry in Europe. That was its last achievement. Its own day of frost and sun was over. "The wild desert flavour ebbed out of it." Its romance did not long survive its conquests. Its chivalry, its splendid courtesy and magnanimity, hardened and dwindled: and its constructive and creative power, divorced more and more from actual life, became dissipated in the fluid material of what the world has agreed to call Arabian Tales. By the twelfth century of our era, the chance for an Arabian epic was over. What survived of the instinct for narrative poetry was wasted on monstrous and formless romantic chronicles, still from time to time flashing up into fine episodes, but in the mass invertebrate and insufferably tedious. Some of these survive; one, the Romance of Antar, has even been printed. Few people have ever read it through; and this is not surprising when we learn that it fills thirty-two printed volumes. The historical Antar was a pre-Islamic warrior and poet, the author of one of the finest of the Golden Odes. In the romance, which shows a strong Persian influence, he has been transmuted into a full-blown hero of chivalry. The process of transmutation was gradual; the date of the romance, which used to be put as far back as the end of the eighth century, is now ascribed to a much later period, perhaps not before the end of the eleventh. In any case it would appear to be the earliest example now known of the *roman chevaleresque* in its full development. The scene of the death of Antar, alike by its romantic incidents and its epic magnificence, is not inferior to anything in Homer or the Icelandic Sagas. The poisoned arrow, shot across the river at midnight by a blind archer; the retreat through the desert, led by the dying hero's heroic wife mounted on his horse and dressed in his armour; the last stand in the pass; the dead man sitting all night on his motionless steed propped on his terrible spear, the thirty pursuing horsemen not venturing to approach him: all this, for splendour and concentration, is unsurpassed by any death-scene in literature. The inchoate Arabian epic, already stricken with decay, flamed up into this momentary brilliance before it fell to pieces.

Greek poetry, from the sixth century B.C. onwards,

was based on Homer; but the whole body of Arabian poetry was organically and structurally what we may call pre-Homeric. And if we ask why it stopped there, while many reasons may be plausibly named as contributory, the central truth is this, that history does not repeat itself, and that Homer was not born twice.

THE DIVINE COMEDY

ALL those who have studied Dante's great poem as poetry—a class which includes at least a respectable minority among his readers—must I fancy have at one time or another asked themselves two questions: first, Why did he call it a Comedy? and secondly, In what sense is that name rationally or poetically applicable to it? And all who have asked themselves the questions must have found some little difficulty in answering the first, and a great deal in answering the second.

Byron in 1821 writes, with his usual incisive swiftness and lucid common sense, that there are in poetry "compositions which belong to no class at all. Where is Dante? His poem is not an epic: then what is it? He himself calls it a divine Comedy; and why? This is more than all his thousand commentators have been able to explain." How far Byron had looked into the "thousand commentators" is a question which need not be pressed. He could not have gone far into them without knowing that the substantive, without the adjective, was Dante's own title; nor, probably, had he ever read Dante's own explanation of it. But these are details; Byron's question "What is it?" is what matters: and the answer to it, so far as an answer can be given, involves an enquiry of no little interest, which affects the definition of poetry itself as well as that of the formal "classes" or subdivisions of poetry.

To the first of the two questions, why Dante called the poem a Comedy, we have Dante's own answer, in

THE DIVINE COMEDY

his letter to Can Grande; or at least if this is not exactly an answer, it is his explanation, and in effect the only explanation he has vouchsafed to give. The second question, that of the scope and applicability of the name, was raised and discussed by Boccaccio a generation afterwards; the discussion comes towards the end of his Life of Dante. Boccaccio felt the difficulty fully, and stated it fully. Since then, the question has remained pretty much where it was. Later commentators appear to have done little more than repeat, in various forms of words, what Dante and Boccaccio had said already, and Byron's sweeping statement, even if carelessly made, is in fact justified. It is worth while to restate the case now in simple terms and to see whether in the first place any fresh light can be thrown on the facts, and whether in the second place any fresh inference or suggestion can be drawn from them. Probably there is little to be done in either direction; but there is something. And consideration may open up some suggestions, not without interest, as to the bearing which the problem has on another and a more general question: that is, on the position and function—if I may so express myself—of the Divine Comedy in the field of poetry.

What Dante himself says, in section 10 of the Epistle to Can Grande, is in effect this:

"The title of the book is, the Comedy of Dante. Comedy is a kind of poetical narrative, differing from all others. It differs materially from tragedy, in that tragedy begins in peace and ends in horror, whereas comedy opens with a distressing circumstance, but brings it to a prosperous conclusion. This may be seen in the tragedies of Seneca and the comedies of Terence. They likewise differ in their language; that of tragedy being elevated and sublime, while that of comedy is lax and humble; though as Horace lays down in his Poetic, each may occasionally adopt the language proper to the other. It is accordingly clear why the present work is called a Comedy; for if we regard its substance, it begins with horror, in Hell, and ends beautifully and happily, in Paradise: while if we regard its language, it is in the vulgar tongue, such as is employed even by women. There are other kinds of poetical narrative, such as the pastoral, the elegy, the satire, the dedication; but on these I need not dwell here."

There are several points which call for special remark in the passage which I have thus paraphrased. As will be noticed, I have omitted some portions of the passage which are parenthetical and have no particular bearing on the main point: and exception might perhaps be taken to my translation in some particulars: the meaning for instance of the phrase *votiva sententia*, which is taken from Horace, has been from very early times a battle-ground of commentators on Horace himself, and we cannot tell what meaning Dante attached to it, if indeed he attached any definite meaning to it at all. But my abbreviated paraphrase gives I think with sufficient accuracy all in Dante's own statement which is strictly relevant.

Now the first thing which any one would say on reading this passage would probably be to remark on the strangeness of calling either comedy or tragedy a "poetical narrative." The distinction between narrative and dramatic poetry is to us fundamental, just as it was to Aristotle. It would seem that to Dante, at all events, it was so far from being fundamental that it was not even noticeable. "Nothing"—said a capable critic a century ago—"can more strongly prove how little dramatic ideas or associations were afloat in the time of Dante, than that he should have ventured to call his shadowy and awful panorama of Hell, Heaven and Purgatory a comedy." In the main, this observation still holds good.

Again, if Dante was mentioning other kinds of poetry, why should he omit altogether the principal among them all, the epic? Of the five great poets in Limbo, three are epic poets: so is Statius. He cannot have meant here to ignore Homer, Lucan, Statius, Virgil himself. Once more, what does he mean by speaking of the language or diction of his own poem as "relaxed" or "low"—*modus loquendi remissus et humilis*? These are just the opposite, one would suppose, of the terms by which the style of the *Divina Commedia* would be described. Human language has never been used with a greater elevation, at a higher tension. In the poem itself Dante is continually laying stress, in the most marked way, on just this quality. *Lo bello stile, che m'ha fatto onore*, he says at the beginning of the *Inferno*. *Qui la morta poesì risurga*, he says again at the beginning of the *Purgatorio*. The *alta fantasia* of the *Paradiso* is such as lets him crown himself with the authentic laurels of Apollo, the wreath of supreme sovereignty "per trionfare o Cesare o Poeta": as poet, he is the equal of an emperor. But it is needless to multiply citations. Even in this same epistle he has already used the term *sublimis* of his poem; specifically, no doubt, of the *Paradiso*, but that is because it is the *Paradiso* of which he has set himself to give a particular account.

We may now turn from this to Boccaccio's comment, in which the commentator does not seek to conceal his perplexity. "Vogliono alcuni," he says, "mal convenirsi a questo libro questo titolo"; and then proceeds to set forth, very lucidly and very fairly, the substance of their objections, with which he was clearly in a good deal of sympathy.

He begins by repeating, substantially in the same terms, the twofold distinction between tragedy and comedy, as regards matter and as regards manner, already drawn by Dante in the passage cited. Both he and Dante took it pretty much as they found it in Uguccione's dictionary, which appears to have remained a standard work since it was produced somewhere about the year 1200: and it is worth while giving it again in Uguccione's terse and precise Latin, the more so because he adds a distinction which both Dante and Boccaccio pass over, but which, as we shall see, is both relevant and important.

"Comedia," says Uguccione—again I do not quote in full, but only what is immediately to the point— "id est villanus cantus, qui . . . affinis est cotidianae locutioni . . . Differunt tragedia et comedia, quia comedia privatorum hominum continet acta, tragedia regum et magnatum. Item comedia humili stilo scribitur, tragedia alto. Item comedia a tristibus incipit sed in laetis definit, tragedia e contrario."

Starting from and commenting on this accepted general definition of comedy (so far as it is strictly to be called a definition) Boccaccio proceeds to set forth under six heads the reasons which may be, and are, urged for the inappropriateness of calling Dante's poem a comedy. These are as follows: first, the matter is not low: secondly, the style is not low; thirdly, the poet speaks throughout in his own person; fourthly, similes and episodes are freely introduced; fifthly, the story or plot does not deal with fictitious characters and events; sixthly and lastly, the poem is not in scenes but in cantos.

First, as to the matter: "Canti villeschi"—the

villanus cantus of Uguccione—"come noi sappiamo, sono di basse materie . . . a' quali in alcuno atto non sono conformi le cose narrate in alcuna parte della presente opera": village or rustic poetry (the derivation of the word comedy then accepted being from κώμη and ᾠδή), as we are all aware, deals with low subjects, to which the things narrated in the work before us have no conformity anywhere or in any part of the action.

Second, as to the style or diction: "Lo stilo comico è umile e rimesso, acciochè alla materia sia conforme; quello che della presente opera dire non si può . . . quantunque in volgare scritta sia . . . è nondimeno ornato e leggiadro e sublime": the style of comedy is low and relaxed, to be proportionable to its matter: this cannot be said of the work before us, written in the vulgar tongue though it be; the language is nevertheless ornate, brilliant, and sublime. The word *leggiadro* is not easy to render; "light" in English fails to convey its meaning. It conveys the sense of something which moves in a lighter element, or which is a lighter element itself, the "air and fire" of Shakespeare's Cleopatra. The three epithets taken together are an accurate description of the style of the *Commedia*, with its rich though grave ornament, its elastic radiance, and its general though not uniform nobility.

Third, as to the absence of the specific dramatic form which is common to both tragedy and comedy: "Mai nella Commedia non usa introducere sè medesimo in alcun atto a parlare, ma sempre a varie persone": it is the uniform practice of comedy that the author does not speak in his own person, but through the characters, who speak in their persons. In the *Commedia* Dante speaks in the first person throughout; this to be sure varies from the usage of epic, in which the poet only speaks in the first person rarely and occasionally, but varies still more fundamentally from what is not only the usage, but the essence of drama.

Fourth, as to the enrichments: "Nelle commedie non s'usano comparazioni nè recitazioni d'altre storie": both formal similes and episodic narratives are alien to the dramatic method. This is true and well observed. Any large use of similes is undramatic, because except in the rarest instances they do not help, but obstruct and retard what is the end of dramatic art, the representation of action. Any large use of them therefore means bad dramatic quality. In all the seven extant plays of Sophocles, for example, there are only about half a dozen. Used sparingly and with judgment, they may be dramatically justifiable and even dramatically valuable in either of two ways: by momentarily suspending the representation of action and so creating a dramatic pause; or by accumulating ornament on a point of the action where it is so swift and intense that it can carry this added weight without any loss of life and speed, and only with a resulting increase of momentum.

So too with Boccaccio's remark on episodic narratives; these are undramatic, in the first place because they are narratives (though it is doubtful whether Boccaccio meant to make this point), and in the second place because they are episodic. The art of the dramatist is nowhere more expressly shown than in the skill with which he contrives to avoid narration, to make the action act itself instead of telling us about it. The conquest of this feature of the art is really, one may add in passing, the main distinction between Greek and modern tragedy; and that there is no similar distinction (or at least none nearly so strongly marked) between Greek and modern comedy indicates that Greek comedy belongs to a later evolutionary stage than Greek tragedy—partly no doubt because the latter was from first to last subject to a much more rigorous hieratic convention. And again, it is of the essence of a well-constructed dramatic work that it shall have no episodes, that it shall confine itself strictly to the action with which it deals, to the setting and solving of a single problem. The romantic drama may from its looser texture indulge in episodes; they have no place in the perfect tragedy or in the perfect comedy. On the main issue it is needless to say that Dante's poem is crowded with similes, often most elaborately expanded, and nearly always of extreme beauty. And the whole texture of the poem may in a way be called a continuous series of episodic narration, though the episodes, like the rows of figures in the finest primitive painting, fall into place in the rhythm of a single vast pattern. The unity of the *Commèdia* is a unity of progressive design: it is not the dramatic unity, which is a unity of completed action.

It would not be too much to say that most lovers of poetry begin by reading Dante for the sake of the similes and episodes; and even when to a more trained appreciation these have taken their place as detail subordinate to the larger design, they do not lose by that in their separate and specific charm. A real and full knowledge of Dante, of the *Commedia* as a single and complete whole, was until a generation ago confined to comparatively few persons. It has since then been spreading enormously; yet even now the dozens and scores of text-books and commentaries nearly all take for granted that this knowledge does not come naturally, that people need to be coaxed or driven into it. The world-wide reputation of Dante has rested in the main on certain particular episodes, and not very many even of these—such episodic narratives, *recitazioni d'altre storie*, as those of Francesca, of Ugolino, of the last voyage of Ulysses, of Pia de' Tolommei. This is a fact of which account must be taken in any attempt, if I may so put it, to place Dante; to indicate his position in, and his effect upon, the whole progress and evolution of poetry.

Fifth, as to the invention: "Sono le cose che nelle commedie si raccontano cose che peravventura mai non furono, quantunque non sieno sì strane dai costumi degli uomini che essere state non possono": the drama (for this statement of course applies to tragedy and comedy alike) deals not with things that have actually happened, but with things such as might happen. Whether with or without some indirect knowledge of Aristotle's *Poetics*, Boccaccio here almost reproduces Aristotle's words: οὐ τὰ γενόμενα λέγειν τοῦτο ποιητοῦ ἔργον ἐστίν, ἀλλ' οἷα ἂν γένοιτο καὶ τὰ δυνατὰ κατὰ τὸ εἰκὸς ἢ τὸ ἀναγκαῖον. In effect he might go on to say, following the next sentence in the *Poetics*, εἴη γὰρ ἂν τὰ Δάντου εἰς μέτρα τεθῆναι καὶ οὐδὲν ἧττον ἂν εἴη ἱστορία τις μετὰ μέτρου ἢ ἄνευ μέτρων. This is not the sort of difficulty that troubles us much now, any more than it troubles us with regard to *Paradise Lost*: partly because we do not any longer believe in the narration as a narration of fact, partly because we have come to see that even if it were a narration of fact, fact as passed through the processes of poetic imagination becomes transmuted or rather transubstantiated. To Dante no doubt, as to Milton, the substantial facts of his poem were literally true; what matters to us in both cases, what makes them and the poem alive, is that they are imaginatively possible. So likewise we regard tragedies, as tragedies, with little regard to the degree in which they reproduce recorded facts of history. We read *Coriolanus* or *Antony and Cleopatra* in precisely the same spirit as we read *Othello* or *Hamlet;* we attach to them precisely the same sort of poetical value.

Sixth, as to the technical form: Comedies, Boccaccio goes on, are in scenes, where the actors (the *mimi*) transform themselves into the people who are to act or speak; but our author calls the parts of his comedy not scenes, but *canti*, cantos, and there is no impersonation: even where there is dialogue, it is narrated dialogue, not acted dialogue. This is really the third difficulty over again, only put in a more technical and limited way. The bondage of words, always great, was in the Middle Ages and to persons brought up in the severe traditions of scholastic philosophy, prodigious; and one might almost fancy that Boccaccio would have waived this last objection if he had found the divisions of the poem headed *scene* and not *canti* in the manuscript that lay before him.

The cumulative effect of all these points, thus concisely and lucidly set forth, was so great on Boccaccio's mind that he felt tempted to think that there was some mistake, and that those who thought *mal convenirsi a questo libro questo titolo* were right. But he was faced with the fact that the poet, who surely must have known best, expressly calls it a Comedy twice over in the poem itself, and that in the most pointed way: *per le note di questa commedia, lettor, ti giuro*; and again, *parlando che mia commedia cantar non cura*.[1] He probably had not Dante's letter to Can Grande before him for confirmation, but it was not needed. He finds himself accordingly driven to the conclusion, as the only possible solution of the difficulty, that in giving his poem this name Dante looked only to the broad fact (*al tutto*) that comedy, according to

[1] *Inferno*, xvi. 128; xxi. 2.

the orthodox definition of the dictionary, " begins in discord and ends in tranquillity." " E questo," he concludes rather lamely and without any accent of strong conviction, " dee poter bastare a fare che così fatto nome si possa di ragione convenire a questo libro" —notice the hesitating way in which he slowly piles word on word—" this ought to be able to be sufficient to justify the possibility of the title being reasonably appropriate to the work." It is hardly the Q.E.D. of a mathematician, or the precise conclusion of a syllogism.

What, then, may we suppose Dante to have had in his mind beyond what appears on the surface of the words in his own explanation as given in the letter to Can Grande? The question is not an easy one to answer; for in order to be able to answer it at all fully we should have to succeed in putting ourselves more or less at Dante's own point of view: and that would be not only as regards the scope and function of poetry in its different kinds, but also as regards the amount and nature of his actual acquaintance with the ancient writers—with the poets and dramatists in the first place, and in the second place with the critics who had divided poetry into its specific kinds and settled a terminology for them. It is difficult—at least I always find it so—to remember where the line runs, in Dante or in any mediæval writer, between vast and most carefully organised knowledge on the one side, and on the other what we should now call gross ignorance. Even among the works accessible in his own time Dante's reading shows curious gaps. When we are enquiring what the term comedy really meant to him, apart from dictionary definitions, clearly the first or almost the first question which we have to ask is, What first-hand knowledge had he of classical comedy, or of what had been written about comedy by classical critics?

In the first place, the whole of the Greek drama, tragedy and comedy alike, was a sealed book to him. He could not read the originals, and there were no translations. He never even mentions the name of Aeschylus or Sophocles, of Aristophanes or Menander. Nor is there any evidence that he was acquainted with Aristotle's *Poetics*, even through the channel of such obscure and partly unintelligible translations into Latin from the Arabic abridgement as unquestionably existed at the time: in fact the negative evidence seems conclusive in the other direction. Of the Latin dramatists, Plautus was extant, at least as regards eight of the plays, but in the Middle Ages he was to all intents and purposes unknown. The casual mention of his name in the *Commedia* means no more than the mention of the name of Euripides a little further on.[1] A generation later we find him in fact unknown to a trained scholar of high reputation. Giovanni Andrea of Bologna, Professor of Canon Law in that University, "did not believe there was no such person," and actually accused Petrarch[2] of inventing an ancient author and giving him that name; just as Chaucer, a generation later again, did for his own purpose invent an ancient author and give him the name of Lollius.

The two ancient dramatists who were effectively extant, and whose works formed or were supposed to form part of the reading of all scholars, were Terence in comedy and Seneca in tragedy. It is here that we come on one of the curious gaps in Dante's scholarship. There is no distinct trace in any of his writings of his ever having read either Terence or Seneca. When I say Seneca, I mean of course the tragedies, not the moral or philosophical works. If this is so—and

[1] *Purgatorio*, xxii. 98, 106.
[2] Petrarch, *Familiar Epistles*, iv. 15.

apparently it is so, however strange it may seem—the only ancient source left is Horace's *Ars Poetica;* and it is an obvious remark that Horace in the *Ars Poetica* takes the distinction between tragedy and comedy for granted and does not either define or elaborate it. The phrases in the letter to Can Grande, *ut patet per Senecam in suis tragediis,* and *ut patet per Terentium in suis comediis,* have all the air of being mere transcripts from Dante's dictionary authority, Uguccione or some one else. Clearly if Dante had never read either any ancient plays or any systematic ancient exposition and criticism of the dramatic art, it is not surprising that he should use the terms of that art in a very loose and vague way. Drama of a rude sort was being produced in his own time in the vernacular; the *giuochi di scena* are mentioned by chroniclers (*e.g.* in the *Cronica Bolognese* of the thirteenth century). But this he would not take into account, because, according to the whole tenor of the argument in the *de Vulgari Eloquentia,* it was not literature.

In that treatise, Book II. chapter 4, *de varietate stili eorum qui poetice scribunt,* he had already opposed "tragedy" to "comedy" and spoken of their essence, both in distinction from one another and in distinction from other kinds of poetry, as consisting not in form but in substance. I may quote part of this passage also as relevant and rather illuminating.

When we propose to write poetry, he says, we must discriminate whether the *canenda,* the subject-matter of the poetry, should assume the tragic, the comic, or the elegiac manner, *utrum tragice sive comice sive elegiace sint canenda.* For the first, the *vulgare illustre* is the proper language; for the second, either the *vulgare mediocre* or the *vulgare humile* according to circumstances; for the third, the *vulgare humile.* As regards the *comice canenda,*

THE DIVINE COMEDY 167

he promises a further discussion in the fourth book of the treatise: unhappily the treatise as we possess it breaks off in the middle of the second book. In the meantime he proceeds with further remarks on the tragic style. This exists where three things are combined with *gravitas sententiae*, with weighty subject matter; namely, *superbia carminum*, "magnificence of versification," *elatio constructionis*, "height of design," and *excellentia vocabulorum*, "distinction of language." This tragic style is the *summus stilorum*; it is the only one appropriate to the three greatest subjects of poetry (*summe canenda*), Salvation, Love and Virtue: *quando tria haec*, he goes on, *pure cantare intendit, vel quae ea directe ac pure secuntur, prius Helicone potatus, tensis fidibus, adsumptum secure plectrum tum movere incipiat.* No description could be more appropriate to the *Divina Commedia*: and the phrases of this last sentence give an echo to those of the poem—the "a buon cantor buon citarista" of the *Paradiso* (xx. 142), the "or convien ch' Elicona per me versi" of the *Purgatorio* (xxix. 40), or the double invocation to Apollo at the beginning of the first and second cantos of the *Paradiso*. But there is some clue to his use of the term comedy in the remarks on language. We know from other sources that Dante in the *Commedia* did deliberately what the most cursory reading shows he did in fact, namely to enlarge the poetic vocabulary far beyond what had hitherto been considered its limits. For his purpose, nothing in language was to be common or unclean. The *vulgare mediocre*, and even to some extent the *vulgare humile*, was swept in and fused. He did not confine himself to what might be called classical Tuscan; he did something infinitely more, made the whole of Tuscan classical. In this he broke away from and superseded the Virgilian or "tragic" tradition.

It is noticeable that he makes Virgil himself speak of the Aeneid as *alta mia tragedia;* and it is the more significant, because it is on the very next page, twenty lines further on in the poem, that he expressly refers to his own work as *mia commedia*.[1] The juxtaposition, though we need not suppose it to be deliberate, is not accidental in the sense that we can suppose it to have escaped Dante's notice. Partly no doubt this is according to the common mediæval usage in which the name of tragedy was applied to any great story of the deeds or fates of great men and princes. The familiar instance is in the Monk's Prologue in Chaucer:

> "Or elles first tragedies will I tell
> Of which I have an hundred in my cell.
> Tragedy is to say a certain story
> As olde bookes maken us memory,
> Of him that stood in great prosperity
> And is yfallen out of high degree
> Into misery, and endeth wretchedly.
> And they been versifyed commonly
> Of six feet, which men clepe exametron.
> In prose eke been indited many one,
> And eke in metre in many a sundry wise."

Here there is no distinction between dramatic and epic form, but the *exametron,* that is to say the epic, is casually mentioned as the normal type. The Monk's Tale itself begins,

> "I will bewail in manner of tragedy
> The harm of them that stood in high degree:"

and ends,

> "Tragedy is none other manner thing,
> Ne can in singing crye ne bewail
> But for that fortune alway will assail
> With unwar stroke the regnes that been proud:"

[1] *Inferno,* xx. 113; xxi. 2.

in both of these passages the implication being of what Dante calls the *cantionum modus*, the form of the *canzone* or regular lyric, which "excellentissimum esse pensamus." This *cantionum modus*, the "singing cry" of Chaucer, roughly corresponds to what we call lyrical poetry. But lyric and dramatic poetry tend to coalesce; at all events their dividing line cannot be sharply defined. There are dramatic lyrics and lyrical dramas. Tennyson invented for his *Maud*, which is a series of lyrics, all in the first person, and conveying in their sum the substance of a dramatic narration, the name of monodrama. That name, if legitimate at all, as to which I express no opinion, might also be applied to Dante's poem. It is interesting to note too, that of the seventeen "tragedies" which Chaucer's Monk recites, one is the story of Ugolino, "Erl Hugelyn of Pise," out of the *Inferno*. And another remark may be made by the way: among the reasons that Dante gives[1] why the *cantio* is the most excellent of poetical forms is that *cantiones per se totum quod debent efficiunt*, and *in solis cantionibus ars tota comprenditur*—just the doctrine which Aristotle lays down about tragedy, or rather, although he is speaking of tragedy specifically, about the drama.

Modern writers most generally, when they have occasion to give the *Commedia* a name, call it an epic. Byron, in the letter I have already quoted, with his slashing accuracy, his way of hitting the nail hard on the head, had tersely denied this: "it is not an epic." But here, though he was perfectly right, he stood almost alone. Shelley for instance in his *Defence of Poetry*, where he is using terms with great care, calls Dante an epic poet. And very possibly Dante might have done the same himself had the name epic been ready to his hand: but he was

[1] *Vulg. Eloq.*, ii. 3.

probably ignorant of it. It does not occur in the *Ars Poetica:* and if we read the *Ars Poetica* attempting to remove from our minds all that we instinctively read into it from other sources, we shall be struck very much by the way in which Horace fluctuates back and forward between dramatic and epic poetry in his rules and criticisms. One could not infer with certainty from the *Ars Poetica* itself that Homer was not a tragedian. Horace's "observations follow one another," to quote Addison's demure and exquisite words, "without that methodical regularity which would have been requisite in a prose writer"; and to the mediæval mind, accustomed as it was to excessive parade of logical arrangement and subdivision, they must have been more than usually perplexing.

The only word which Dante himself uses so as in any way to suggest epic as opposed to drama is *Storia.* Statius' *Thebaid* is called the "Tebana storia" in the *Convito* (iv. 25). The absence of any definite conception of narrative poetry as such, and of a fixed term to express it, is still more notable in the list given by Boccaccio in his life of Dante: "Le poetiche narrazioni," he says, "sono di più e varie maniere, siccome è tragedia satira e commedia, buccolica, elegia, lirica ed altre." Dante again, also in the *Convito* (i. 5), when speaking of the supremacy of the Latin language, says "onde vedemo nelle scritture antiche delle commedie e tragedie Latine che non si possono trasmutare." Here the "Latin comedies and tragedies" simply mean Latin poetry, and both are named simply in order to cover the whole of that poetry, whether more familiar or more august.

Similarly when towards the end of the *Paradiso* Dante, after he has entered the Empyrean, speaks of his subject having at this point become ineffable,

THE DIVINE COMEDY 171

he employs two phrases which express the same meaning.

> " Da questo passo vinto mi concedo
> Più che giammai da punto di suo tema
> Soprato fosse comico o tragedo ":

"Conquered more than ever comedian or tragedian was overcome by a point of his theme." "Comedian or tragedian" simply means here "any poet": and so Dante goes on, a few lines later, to say:

> " Ma or convien, che il mio seguir desista
> Più dietro a sua bellezza poetando,
> Come all' ultimo suo ciascun artista ":

"Now must my pursuit needs fall back from before her beauty and cease making poetry, as every artist must from before his ideal." The "tragedian or comedian" of the first of these two passages is the same as the "every artist" of the second: and *poetare*, "to make poetry," is the common work of both.

There is however another point to notice, and it is one which without attention might easily be forgotten. To us, Dante is a classic; in his own day he was not a classic, but the initiator of a daring and doubtful innovation. Of reaching the greatest heights of the classical poetry, he thought any language but Latin essentially incapable. This feeling runs through the *Vita Nuova*: it comes out strikingly in another passage of the *Convito* (ii. 13)—"della donna di cui io m' innamorava non era degna rima di volgare alcuno palesemente poetare." The feeling is like that of the famous passage in *Hyperion*:

> "Words she spake
> In solemn tenour and deep organ-tone:
> Some mourning words, which in our feeble tongue
> Would come in these like accents: O how frail
> To that large utterance of the early Gods!"

Of the whole of modern poetry, not merely of his own, one can seem to hear Dante saying:

> " Vidi questo globo
> Tal, ch' io sorrisi del suo vil sembiante,
> E quel consiglio per migliore approbo
> Che l' ha per meno " :

and he might say this even when he let his eyes rest on

> " L'aspetto di suo nato, Iperione."

Speaking in Oxford, and to scholars, I need not spend many words in saying that this doctrine is less than a paradox, that to the civilised world Latin is still a mother tongue, " perpetuo e non corruttibile," " sovrano e per nobiltà e per virtù e per bellezza," and that modern poets may well hesitate, as Dante did, before they apply to their own work a title appropriated to the highest work of those whom we still call the classical poets. Few indeed would be inclined now to justify the title of the *Commedia* in the way in which it was justified by my predecessor Thomas Warton, as appropriate to " a compound of tragical and comical incidents, of familiar and heroic manners, and of satirical and sublime poetry." Yet the description is not without an element of truth. And as we turn from Dante to Virgil, from poetry often unsurpassed in ardour and brilliance, yet unequal, often harsh and mannered, sometimes—dare I say?—laborious and even tedious, to the golden cadence and majestic rhythm of his master, we shall feel that his own definition of the title, " qualunque componimento poetico in stile mezzano," has more to be said for it than we might at first have been inclined to think.

Yet even on the ground that is common to Dante and Virgil, the name of comedy has a relevant application; for it was applied by ancient critics—I do not think the point has ever been noticed in this connexion—to certain parts of the Aeneid. This is a fact of peculiar interest; and the more so, because it is probable that Dante himself knew it, though his commentators have been ignorant of it. Dr. Moore has proved, beyond all reasonable possibility of doubt, that the *Divina Commedia* shows, in several passages, knowledge of the Servian commentary on Virgil. In that commentary, the introductory remarks prefixed to the fourth book contain a striking passage, which in this connexion is of much significance.

"Est paene totus in affectione, licet in fine pathos habeat. Sane totus in consiliis et subtilitatibus est: nam paene comicus stilus est: nec mirum, ubi de amore tractatur."

The wording here requires and repays careful appreciation. "The whole book, broadly, deals with mental states, although at the conclusion it contains tragic incident. It is completely occupied with mental processes and delicate psychological touches. The style approximates to that of comedy, as is natural, since love is the theme."

The terms *affectio*, *subtilitas*, and *comicus stilus*, are all highly technical. The word *affectio* is by itself of ambiguous meaning: as Servius uses it here, and placing it as he does in antithesis to the word *pathos*, it conveys a sense almost equivalent to our term of sensibility. The phrase *in subtilitatibus est* conveys the idea which we should express in the words "it is concerned with the refinements of psychology." These two qualities, the sensibility appropriate to poetry dealing with love, whether that love be human, as in the Aeneid, or divine, as in Dante, and the concern with a study, at once profound and minute, of the human soul, do not belong, in the view here indicated, to the epic or tragic sphere; they belong to the sphere of something larger, something that has the largeness and freedom of comedy, and that we may call a sort of comedy, *paene comicus*, " comedy with a difference," for fault of a better word. And these two qualities, it is needless to say, are of the essence of Dante's poem from beginning to end. It is *totus in affectione*, and *totus in subtilitatibus*; and the style follows the matter. Only, both the *affectio* and the *subtilitas* are more than merely human; they are attached to and incorporated with a theology, as though the fourth Aeneid were incorporated with the sixth. In the sixth Aeneid the subject of the fourth has become dim and distant; the silent phantom of Dido in the myrtle-wood is just seen, like the thin crescent of the moon faintly revealed or surmised through clouds. But the Beatrice of Dante expands and brightens as the poem moves up from circle to circle of Paradise, and his last sight of her is

"Che si facea corona
Riflettendo da sè gli eterni rai."

Comedy and tragedy alike are transcended and merged in vision.

Thus it was only natural that the epithet "divine" became attached to the title "comedy" within less than a generation after Dante's death. Suggested no doubt by actual expressions used in the *Commedia* itself—*sacrato poema* and *poema sacro*[1]—the attached epithet was also found necessary to redress the balance and remove the implication which the title *Commedia*, standing alone, inevitably suggested. It placed Dante formally in the same class (to say on the same level would be going too far) with Virgil; for there can be no doubt that it bore express reference to the established application of the epithet to Virgil himself. Origi-

[1] *Paradiso*, xxiii. 62; xxv. 1.

nating with the *divinam Aeneida* of Statius, the term of "divine poet" had become an understood equivalent for Virgil's name: Dante's own phrase *divinus poeta noster* in the *De Monarchia* merely follows common usage.

The epithet, once attached, became permanently incorporated in the title; indeed to the ordinary and instinctive appreciation the stress laid on the epithet diverts attention from any close questioning as to the force and application of the noun. It was a lucky stroke on the part of whoever it was that invented it before Boccaccio. For the reinforced title indicates very appositely the character of the poem as at once complex and unique. It has been pointed out that the damned cannot be in more places of Hell than one, and that therefore they have to be placed where their most conspicuous sin is punished. Somewhat analogously, Dante's poem could not well be called by more names than one; and so the name selected for it is one which lays stress on what is, in some ways at all events, its most conspicuous quality, namely, its width of range and all-inclusiveness. For here we touch a point not perhaps always sufficiently emphasised by the interpreters, that whether the name of comedy be apposite or not, the name of any form of poetry covering a narrower scope than that of comedy would be less apposite still. If we turn again to the Epistle to Can Grande, we shall find in it another sentence of the utmost relevance and significance. *Est subjectum operis,* Dante says, *literaliter, status animarum post mortem; allegorice, homo.* The *status animarum,* in the literal sense of these words, is what the analytic poets—Browning very notably and very insistently—have taught us to regard as the real subject of poetry. And when Dante wrote *Subjectum operis est homo,* one can hardly doubt that he had in his mind, consciously or subconsciously, the famous line of the Terentian comedy, the *Homo sum, nihil humani a me alienum puto* of Chremes which is the complete and permanent motto of comedy itself. Thus too Quintilian—though Quintilian was unknown in the age of Dante—uses not of the tragedians nor of the epicists, but of the master of the New Attic Comedy, the striking phrase, offering another suggestive parallel to Dante's words, *omnem vitae imaginem expressit*. It is the phrase which we should use of Shakespeare; and of Shakespeare also we might, if we reverted to the scholastic forms of language, use Dante's words with but one word changed: *est subjectum operis literaliter, status animarum ante mortem; allegorice, homo*. Change the *post* into *ante* and you have the *Humana Comedia*, the volume of 1623.

John of Salisbury, whom Dante had probably read, uses a striking phrase, or pair of phrases, that is not irrelevant in this connexion. *Comedia*, he says,[1] *est vita hominis super terram;* and he goes on to explain this aphorism by the exegetic or interpretative words, *ubi quisque sui oblitus personam exprimit alienam*. He uses the term *comedia*, that is to say, instinctively and without reflection, to cover the whole field of what has dramatic quality. But a little further on, he returns on the phrase and feels obliged to correct or modify it: *vita hominum*, he says, *tragediae quam comediae videtur esse similior, quod omnium fere tristis est exitus, et extrema gaudii luctus occupat*. The two sentences between them give the doctrine and the practice of Dante in his use of the term Comedy.

The great truth implied in, latent in, these fragmentary yet illuminating sentences is that in the evolution of poetry, comedy tends to displace tragedy, or tragedy to merge in a higher and wider tragi-comedy.

[1] *Policraticon*, iii. 8.

THE DIVINE COMEDY

Only in that larger and wider scope can the expression of life be given, the pattern and interpretation of life be found. For life is, as it was called by Marcus Aurelius, the μείζων σκηνή, a theatre more extensive than that of tragedy. What is true of life is true of poetry also; and it is true of poetry because it is true of life: μὴ τοῖς δράμασι μόνον, says Plato in the *Philebus*, ἀλλὰ καὶ τῇ τοῦ βίου ξυμπάσῃ τραγῳδίᾳ καὶ κωμῳδίᾳ. So Chaucer at the end of his *Troilus*, when his head and heart are both full of the sorrow and splendour of his tragedy, prays to God his Maker that he may yet "make some comedy" before he die. So Shakespeare passed on from the period in which he scaled the heights and plumbed the depths of life under its tragic aspect to those later tragi-comedies or romances which in their wider scope and freer handling present the whole spectacle of life, of things as they happen, not as a conflict but as a pageant or vision. So likewise all the more tense and exclusive forms of poetry gradually translate themselves into a larger pattern and looser texture. The modern Greek word for ballad—to take one instance—is, as Mr. Ker has recently reminded us, τραγοῦδι: and the essence of the ballad is that it has a fastidiously narrow limit of theme, and rigorous restrictions of treatment. Like tragedy, it gains its effects by concentration and rejection. So, up to a certain point, does formal comedy, which indeed is framed in the main on the tragic model. But the larger comedy gains its effects by inclusion; its breadth is its distinguishing quality. Dante meant to include everything in his poem; and the title of Comedy is to that extent relevant and appropriate.

He meant to include everything; but that would be to attain finality, and in poetry as in all vital processes there is no finality. He summed up all that had gone before him, but he did not see forward. The mediæval system, so rounded and seemingly complete, was actually on the verge of changing its life: the new world, unsuspected, was at the doors. The founders of modern poetry, Petrarch and Boccaccio, were both born before Dante died; and the new world came with them. Dante was left, a solitary and superb figure, the monument of a day that was gone.

> " Facesti come quei che va di notte,
> Che porta il lume dietro, e sè non giova,
> Ma dopo sè fa le persone dotte."

The *status animarum ante mortem* became the theme of the new comedy, which was the creation of that liberating, enlarging, and expanding movement known as the Renaissance. Dante's influence waned and almost disappeared in a world to which his art seemed inverted, like the back of a tapestry where the live figures, the real forms and colours, were on the other side. Only for those to whom the real reality still lay behind, to whom the actual world (as it is called) was the shadow and human life a rude and imperfect symbol of things invisible, did he retain the full quality of the artist, the interpreter and designer of life. For these the *Divina Commedia*, so far from its name being a contradiction in terms, is the only real comedy, in the complete sense of the term, that exists. It is for them that Dante carries his light.

SHAKESPEARE'S SONNETS

Habent sua fata libelli: and of no book is this more true than of the little quarto volume entitled *Shakespeare's Sonnets* which came into the world, irregularly and under ambiguous auspices, in 1609. Shakespeare, at the age of forty-five, had then already produced nearly all his greatest plays. He was loosening his hold on London and the world of letters and preparing to resume the life of a burgess of Stratford. The singular carelessness which, except in the case of the two juvenile pieces with which he graduated as a poet, Shakespeare always displayed towards his own work, is not the less surprising because it is so familiar. The Sonnets were printed from an imperfect and faulty MS. They were very probably brought out by what would now be called a pirate publisher, though this is taken for granted rather on general grounds than on any sufficient evidence. However this may be, Shakespeare never took the pains either to stop their publication or to issue an authentic edition. They stole into the world, in both senses of the phrase. There are no allusions to their appearance in contemporary literature, and there was, as it would seem, little demand for them among the public. A collection of Shakespeare's poems brought out in 1640 included a garbled, incomplete, and disarranged version of the majority of them. Except for this it was exactly a century from their first appearance before they were reprinted; and it was a century more before they attracted much attention, or were recognised as having a place among the masterpieces of English poetry. What Shakespeare thought of them himself we know as little, except from what may be inferred from the Sonnets themselves, as we know what he thought of *Much Ado* or of *Hamlet*. Towards his own work he preserved uniformly a close silence, as of some *Deus absconditus*, some power that created merely for the sake of creating, and of whom it might be said as in the line of Menander, ἅπαντα σιγῶν ὁ θεὸς ἐξεργάζεται. In one of two purposely enigmatic sonnets which stand at the end of the main body of the collection (124 and 125) we may infer or surmise a momentary intermission of that sphinx-like silence; the phrasing at all events is singularly applicable to the Sonnets themselves and the history of their fortune. For two hundred years after its appearance, the volume seemed as though

> "It might for fortune's bastard be unfathered,
> As subject to time's love or to time's hate,
> Weeds among weeds, or flowers with flowers gathered"—

the illegitimate issue of the press of a thievish publisher, little regarded, little mentioned for either praise or blame. But for the next hundred years which are now expiring the words in which that sonnet goes on are as strikingly applicable:

> "No, it was builded far from accident;
> It suffers not in smiling pomp, nor falls
> Under the blow of thralled discontent
> Whereto the inviting time our fashion calls:
> It fears not policy, that heretic,
> Which works on leases of short numbered hours,
> But all alone stands hugely politic,
> That it nor grows with heat nor drowns with showers."

SHAKESPEARE'S SONNETS

The Sonnets have not in effect suffered either from the pompous and unsubstantial edifices of guesswork that have been erected upon them, or from the narrowing criticism which finds in them a set of purely literary exercises. Towards this latter heresy the fashion of the time has called some of our ablest modern students. Sir Sidney Lee has applied his vast and minute knowledge of the European poetry of the sixteenth century, and in particular of the French sonneteers of that age, to enforce the doctrine that Shakespeare's Sonnets are derivative, artificial, and even academic. The work he has done is of great value; but it hardly touches their quality as a work of art; it does not even affect to any considerable extent the question how far they are a transfusion into poetry of Shakespeare's personal experience.

Scholarly criticism of the Sonnets began, in a tentative way, with Malone's edition of 1780. Poetic appreciation of the Sonnets, towards which the work of scholars is ancillary, may be said to have begun with Wordsworth. The celebrated and familiar passage in Wordsworth's Supplementary Essay to the Preface to the Lyrical Ballads, published in 1815, is worth quoting even now: for it is the starting-point for all subsequent appreciation of the Sonnets as poetry.

"There is extant a small volume of miscellaneous poems"—the Sonnets had been reprinted in full, from the original edition, by Lintott in 1709-10 among "all the miscellanies of Mr. William Shakespeare which were published by himself," and two or three times subsequently, though the mutilated text of 1640 was reissued as late as 1775—" in which Shakespeare expresses his own feelings in his own person. It is not difficult to conceive that the editor, George Steevens, should have been insensible to the beauties of one portion of that volume, the Sonnets; though in no part of the writings of this Poet is found in an equal compass a greater number of exquisite feelings felicitously expressed. But from regard to the critic's own credit, he would not have ventured to talk of an act of parliament not being strong enough to compel the perusal of those little pieces, if he had not known that the people of England were ignorant of the treasures contained in them."

Wordsworth was hardly the person to appreciate the impish humour of George Steevens, who was never so happy as when he was making some preposterous statement with an air of deep gravity, and to whose ghost this passage must have given deep and malicious satisfaction. But it is true that the Sonnets were then little known, and less appreciated. To most of their readers they seemed, pretty much as they seem to some critics now, little more than literary exercises in a manner which had become obsolete. The new eyes with which the romantic revival regarded our older poetry at once fastened upon them as being, in the words which Wordsworth here uses, alike exquisite in feeling and felicitous in expression.

The study which originated in this fresh poetic appreciation was enormously reinforced by the discovery in the Sonnets of what seemed to be an autobiography, and one which had the double enchantment of a strange romance and of a tantalising and partially insoluble enigma, even apart from the added interest which it received in some minds from the suspicion of something in the story which was morbid, if not worse. The Shakespeare-worship initiated by Coleridge and Lamb united with the general movement of literary research to originate a minute study of all documents which could throw any light on Shakespeare's personality, or on the facts of his life. It also united with the new mysticism which was one of the by-products of the romantic movement to give birth to a whole crop of allegorising interpretations, and to find in the Sonnets, as in the plays, secret meanings, and latent philosophical or quasi-philosophical systems. First mythologising Shakespeare's works, this latter movement then sought in them some key to all mythologies. But these movements have spent their force. A treatise on the hidden meaning of the Sonnets would probably now attract but little attention. In the dry light of the comparative method, to which Shakespearian study, like all other studies, owes much, the Platonism of the Sonnets, or whatever other name we may give to their supposed esoteric meaning, is seen to be a fashion of the age, a passing mode of poetic expression. But another change, and one much more important, has come over the methods of criticism. The nature of poetry, as a function and interpretation of life, has come to be better understood. It is understood, not yet fully, but more and more as the science of criticism advances, that poetry does not record, but creates. The germ of actual fact, of tangible personal experience, is but a nucleus round which that creative process goes on. In art, and in poetry as one of the arts, there is no such thing as a narrative of facts. The facts, so far as they were the origin of the creative process, have become transmuted; they have dissolved into the created work of art. This essential truth is very clearly stated in some words of Tennyson's quoted in his Life. "Since it is so much the fashion in these days," he says, "to regard each poem and story as a story of the poet's life or part of it, I may be allowed to remind my readers of the possibility that some event which comes to the poet's knowledge, some hint flashed from another mind, some thought or feeling arising in his own, or some mood coming he knows not whence or how, may strike a chord from which a poem evolves its life, and that this to other eyes may bear small relation to the thought or fact or feeling to which the poem owes its birth."

In reading the Sonnets then it is necessary, if we will not go all astray, to keep sharply distinct from one another the considerations of their poetical quality and of their autobiographic value. That they contain personal experience, nay more, that they are saturated with personal experience, may be fully conceded. The creative processes of art do not make anything out of nothing: *ex nihilo nihil fit* is as true in art as it is in physics. And that this personal experience was no mere experience of books, was not anything merely secondary and derivative, is no less clear to any sound insight. But the experience was transmuted into poetry, and we cannot, where any such vital and not mechanical process is in question, reverse the action, uncreate the creation, and retrace and reconstitute the original experience. In virtue of their extraordinary poetical quality the Sonnets stand alone; as an instance of the transmutation of experience they have many analogies. I need only mention two, belonging to modern times, and both, as in Shakespeare's case, sonnet-sequences. One is Meredith's *Modern Love;* the other is Mr. Wilfrid Blunt's *Esther*. Both are poetry of a high order. Both bear relation to facts, to experiences which their authors had passed through. But it is not necessary to enquire in either case what the precise personal experience was out of which the poems grew, or what precise relation they bear to facts in the lives of their authors as to which we may have knowledge from other sources.

Of Shakespeare's Sonnets at least, in this respect, the best word that has been said, if not the last word that can be said, is in the line and a half of Sophocles prefixed by Francis Palgrave to his edition more than forty years ago:

$$\mathring{\omega}\ \theta\epsilon o\acute{\iota},\ \tau\acute{\iota}\varsigma\ \mathring{a}\rho a\ \kappa\acute{\upsilon}\pi\rho\iota\varsigma\ \mathring{\eta}\ \tau\acute{\iota}\varsigma\ \mathring{\iota}\mu\epsilon\rho o\varsigma$$
$$\tau o\hat{\upsilon}\delta\epsilon\ \xi\upsilon\nu\acute{\eta}\psi a\tau o\ ;$$

The words, like all Sophocles at his finest, are untranslateable: and like Sophocles at his most characteristic, where he goes to the very heart and centre of life, they have two qualities: first that they are extraordinarily simple and direct; and secondly that they settle upon the note of wonder, the endless and fathomless miracle of existence; not explaining, not passing judgment, but seeing the wonder of life with that clear and yet impassioned vision which is the last reward that life has to give.

What we know about the date and circumstances of composition of the Sonnets, as distinct from more or less plausible guesswork and more or less illogical inference, comes within very small compass. They were published, together with *A Lover's Complaint*, in June 1609. The only certain allusion in them to contemporary history is in Sonnet 107, where the reference to the death of Elizabeth and the peaceful accession of James, though it has been questioned, is, I think, unmistakeable. A possible allusion to the Gunpowder Plot of 1605 in Sonnet 124 is merely conjectural, and not probable even as a conjecture: and there is no reason to think that 1603 or 1604 is not the posterior limit of their composition. As regards the anterior limit we find critics plunged into a sea of controversy. Internal evidence of style supports the numerous allusions in substance which indicate that they were written at various times over a space of several years, three or four at least, if not more. Shakespeare is named by Meres in 1598 as the author of sonnets which were in private circulation: but that these were the sonnets which we possess is only an inference, though one which has a *prima facie* probability. In the next year, 1599, we have one solid fact, namely that two of the Sonnets, 138 and 144, were then published in the collection entitled *The Passionate Pilgrim*, but with a text varying from that of the volume of 1609, the variations in 144 being merely verbal, but in 138 amounting to substantial revision. For a date three years earlier we have a piece of evidence which may be interpreted in two ways. In the play of *King Edward III.*, first printed in 1596, there is a line which is verbally the same as one in Sonnet 94, and a phrase "scarlet ornaments" which occurs in Sonnet 142. The author of the play is unknown, and whether Shakespeare himself had some hand in composing or retouching it is a question which is much and inconclusively debated. In any case the mere facts of these coincidences are equally consistent with the theory that the phrases were transferred from the play to the Sonnets, and with the theory that they were transferred from the Sonnets to the play. But it is worth remarking that the "scarlet ornaments" of the Sonnet bear a different meaning from those of the play and imply a different metaphor. The line in the play is:

"when she grew pale
His cheeks put on their scarlet ornaments."

It is the same pretty fancy as in the familiar passage of *Esmond:* "When I came a-courting, you would see miss blush. She said herself, when I joked with her about her d——d smiling red cheeks, ''Tis as they do at St. James's: I put up my red flag when my king comes.'" But the scarlet ornaments of the Sonnet are the lady's wax-red lips which, in one of the many figures of speech drawn in the Sonnets, as in all Shakespeare's work, from the terminology of law, are compared here to the wax seal on a deed:

> "those lips of thine
> That have profaned their scarlet ornaments
> And sealed false bonds of love."

The strong presumption is that the phrase in the play, whether Shakespeare's own or another's, had clung in his mind and was here reproduced by him in a new application.

So far, the natural conclusion to be drawn would be that the Sonnets were in the main composed at intervals over a space of some five years, 1598–1603. This is the period which includes the great central group of the comedies, *Much Ado*, *As You Like It*, and *Twelfth Night*; following almost immediately on them, the full maturing of Shakespeare's dramatic power in *Julius Caesar*; the strange inverted romance of *Troilus and Cressida*; and the slow gestation of *Hamlet*. At its end we are opening on the culminating period of the great tragedies, from *Othello* and the second quarto of *Hamlet* in 1604 to *Coriolanus* in 1609.

But here we are at once faced by a formidable body of criticism which assigns the bulk of the Sonnets to a much earlier date, one contemporary with or immediately following that of the poems in which Shakespeare had first appeared before the public in his own name, the *Venus and Adonis* of 1593 and the *Lucrece* of 1594. Both of these poems were dedicated to the

Earl of Southampton; and on this slender basis has been piled a mountain of misinterpretation.

Further evidence, if it can be called evidence, rests chiefly on three possible identifications. These are, taken in their order, the identification of Mr. W. H.: that of the boy, to whom, or about whom, the bulk of the Sonnets are written; and that of the rival poet to whom allusion is made in a group of Sonnets, 78 to 86, which stand by themselves and seem all to have been written about the same time.

A fourth identification has been attempted, that of the Dark Lady of the later portion of the Sonnets, who is assumed to be the same person as is alluded to, in carefully veiled terms, in Sonnets 40 to 42. It may at once be said that no such identification is possible, and that all the labour that has been spent upon it is pure waste. It is best to dismiss it at once, and to return to the other three, which are all to a considerable extent implicated in one another, and make up a single very complex problem.

On the question of the rival poet I do not propose to spend any time: for the fact is, as to his identity we are wholly in the dark. Attempts have been made by one investigator or another to identify him with at least six of Shakespeare's contemporaries—Barnes, Chapman, Daniel, Drayton, Jonson, and Marston: I give the names in alphabetical order, because any one of them appears to me to be almost as unlikely as any other. The apparent plausibility of the case made out for Chapman will not bear investigation. The case for Barnes and Daniel rests almost wholly on the fact that Barnes was a protégé of Lord Southampton's and Daniel of Lord Pembroke's, and falls to the ground if we reject, as I think we must do, the connexion of either of these noblemen with the Sonnets. For the other three there is really no argument beyond the fact that they all were Shakespeare's rivals in the sense that they all shared a certain jealousy of his success as a dramatist. It seems to me most likely that the reference in the Sonnets is to a poet to whose identity all clue is lost, though it is not impossible that we possess at least one poem written by him. We must remember that the Elizabethan poetry which has come down to us, large as its amount is, is only a small fraction of the poetry which was actually written. Much even of what was printed is lost: an immense amount was never printed at all. Shakespeare's Sonnets themselves have only been preserved by an accident. Had not Thorpe got hold of the MS., years after they were written and when Shakespeare himself would seem to have lost all interest in them, they also (except the two, and these not of the best, independently preserved) would have gone to oblivion.

Until recently it was generally taken for granted that the W. H. to whom the volume of the Sonnets is dedicated, and who is spoken of in the dedication as their only begetter, was the same person as the boy of the Sonnets themselves. Sir Sidney Lee is the originator of a theory, worked out by him with much learning and ingenuity, that this is not the case: that W. H. was simply some acquaintance or accomplice of the pirate publisher; that it was through his hands that the MS. from which the Sonnets were printed came into Thorpe's possession, and that this dedication is merely a compliment paid, in the way of business, by one more or less disreputable tradesman to another. In one William Hall, a printer and publisher in a small way, who meets the requirements of his theory sufficiently well, Sir Sidney Lee is confident that we have the W. H. of Thorpe's dedication.

But the theory itself is wholly unconvincing. Taking words in their plain meaning, we are bound to hold that Mr. W. H. was, or at least was understood to be, the person without whom and apart from whom "the ensuing Sonnets" would not have been written. If it were possible to believe that the Sonnets are from first to last a mere literary exercise upon a prescribed theme, it would also be possible to suppose that W. H. was merely the person who had suggested the theme to Shakespeare, and had no further connexion with the series of dramatic situations and vividly realised moods which the Sonnets convey. But if we believe, as it seems to me we are bound to believe, that the Sonnets convey more than this; that they convey, however largely transmuted by the creative imagination as well as by the influence of an overwhelming literary fashion, the effect of a poignant and remarkable personal experience, it will follow inevitably that W. H. either was, or was understood to be, the boy of the Sonnets himself.

Further than this we cannot go; for the boy of the Sonnets is unidentified, and unidentifiable. Of the many theories which have been started and run to death, three only are worth serious consideration, and none of these three rests on a shred of evidence. These are, the theory which identifies the object of Sonnets 1 to 125 and of the short poem in couplets which follows them as an *envoi* and is printed in the series as Sonnet 126, with Henry Wriothesley, Earl of Southampton; that which identifies him with William Herbert, Earl of Pembroke; and that, the most fancifully ingenious of the three, which identifies him with an otherwise unknown William Hughes.

The Southampton theory is based on little more than the fact that Southampton, who was nine years younger than Shakespeare, was one of his early patrons, and that the *Venus and Adonis* and the *Lucrece* are dedicated to him in terms of eulogy which follow the common convention of the time. In order to make the theory tenable, it is necessary to believe, in the first place, that the bulk of the Sonnets were written as early as 1594 or 1595, and in the second place, that in substance and tone they are such as might be addressed by a young poet to a wealthy and powerful nobleman whom he was at the same time addressing publicly in the ordinary terms used by struggling men of letters towards magnificent patrons. Both of these positions make impossible drafts on credulity. As regards the first it is sufficient to say that in the large majority of the Sonnets, the power of thought, the charged fulness of language, the mastery of compressed and allusive style, are qualities not of the Shakespeare of *Venus and Adonis* or *Lucrece,* not of the Shakespeare of the *Midsummer Night's Dream,* not even of the Shakespeare of *Love's Labour's Lost* after its revision in 1597: they are those of the Shakespeare who has fully mastered his art in the great comedies, who has deepened his hold on life and the human soul to the potency of the great tragedies; they are those more particularly of the Shakespeare who is face to face with the whole vexing sorrow of the world, the Shakespeare who was writing or was preparing himself to write *Hamlet* and *Troilus and Cressida.* These two plays and the Sonnets are the three works of art which their author left enigmatic, irritating and fascinating beyond all the rest.

As regards the alternative Pembroke theory the dates fit well enough. Pembroke came to London in 1598 at the age of eighteen; it is not impossible that Shakespeare may have met him earlier, at Wilton or at Penshurst; and the fact that in the previous year a project of marriage was under discussion between Pembroke and Bridget Vere, daughter of the Earl of Oxford, but came to nothing, agrees as well with the theme of Sonnets 1 to 17 as does the record of Pembroke's subsequent life as a young man about town with the tragic or squalid story, according as one may choose to regard it, which is revealed, clearly enough in its main motive though enigmatically in its details, in Sonnets 40 to 42, and apparently also, though this cannot be taken for granted without reservation, in Sonnets 133 and 134. But all this falls short of evidence; it might supplement and confirm any evidence that existed, but of such evidence there is none.

There is indeed the further coincidence that Pembroke's name was William Herbert, and his initials W. H. It was this fact which led the first investigators of the problem of the Sonnets, early in last century, to propose the identification. It is not preposterous, like the identification of Mr. W. H. with Southampton on the ground that the initials of the latter were H. W., or W. H. read backwards. But apart from the fact that nobody would ever have thought of calling Pembroke Mr. W. H. any more than of calling the late Lord Salisbury Mr. R. C., these particular initials are so common that they would fit dozens and scores of persons. A cursory examination shows about a hundred Mr. W. H.'s in the index to the Oxford University Calendar, and over three hundred in the Dictionary of National Biography. If, with the supporters of the Southampton identification, we allow W. H. to include its reversed form of H. W., the field for choice would be doubled. Sir Sidney Lee, it may be well to remark, though he believes that the "boy" or "friend" of the Sonnets was a literary patron, and that this was Southampton, expressly rejects the identification of Southampton with the W. H. of the dedication. But his own theory, that the dedication is a mere whim of the publisher's, and that W. H. is the printer William Hall, is to me and I think to many others as unconvincing, though not so absurd, as those which make W. H. into William Herbert Earl of Pembroke, or Henry Wriothesley Earl of Southampton.

The third, or William Hughes, theory, first suggested by that able critic Thomas Tyrwhitt, is founded on suggestions in the Sonnets themselves. Briefly the argument is this: that the punning Sonnets 133 to 136 indicate that the friend's name, as well as Shakespeare's own, was Will; and that an obscure line in Sonnet 20,

"A man in hew, all Hews in his controlling,"

can be best explained, or possibly can only be explained, by supposing another pun on the name Hughes. In support of this latter point stress is laid on the fact that the word *Hews* is printed with a capital and in italics, like *Will* in Sonnets 135 and 136, where the play on the name is obvious and admitted.

The Hughes theory, as Dean Beeching drily points out, has this advantage over some others, that if it cannot be proved, neither can it be disproved. It has the disadvantage, that even if it were proved, it would leave us exactly where we were. For nothing is known of any William Hughes to whom the description implied in the Sonnets could apply; and if we frankly admit, as I think we are bound to do, that the boy of the Sonnets is an unknown Eros, it does not matter whether we call him William Hughes or John Stiles. It may however be worth observing, as regards the "Will"

Sonnets, that while they are not merely compatible with the view that the friend's name was Will, but distinctly suggest that view, they do not necessitate it: if analysed closely, they will be found to contain no thought or phrase which is not satisfied by a play of words between the poet's own name and the various senses which the word *will* bears as a common noun. The case for supposing a play on the name Hughes is even slenderer. The text of the crucial line in Sonnet 20 is confessedly corrupt, for, whether the play on the name be assumed or not, the first four words of the line as they stand in the quarto do not make sense. No argument can be safely based on the capital and the italics, for these are found elsewhere, in such common words as *autumn*, *informer*, *heretic*, and *statues*, and are clearly a mere irrelevant eccentricity of the type-setter in a very irregularly and carelessly printed volume, which is full of typographical blunders, and was not corrected in proof either by the author or by any competent reader.

Indeed if we are to give rein to fancy, a much stronger case might be made for another name for the boy of the Sonnets; for the name, not of Hughes, but of Rose. Had the initials in the dedication been W. R. instead of W. H., there is little doubt that this clue would have been eagerly traced and would be an accepted theory with a whole faction of editors. *Hews* only occurs once in the Sonnets: the singular, *hew*, indeed occurs five times, but without the least suggestion either by context or typography of a double meaning. But *Rose* occurs no less than ten times, always spelled with the initial capital, and with a plausible suggestion of a play upon words in more than one instance. Let us just look at these. How does the first Sonnet open?

> "From fairest creatures we desire increase
> That thereby beauty's *Rose* might never die."

There you have it at once, italics, capital and all. Again in Sonnet 67, one of those where the personal note is most passionate and unmistakeable:

> "Why should poor beauty indirectly seek
> Roses of shadow, since his Rose is true?"

And again in Sonnet 95, he cries out, in the full bitterness of a love that is proof even against shame, on the vicious life

> "Which like a canker in the fragrant Rose
> Doth spot the beauty of thy budding name."

Once more, and perhaps most remarkably, towards the end of the series, in Sonnet 109:

> "For nothing this wide universe I call
> Save thou, my Rose: in it thou art my all."

Here are the elements of a theory: I only lay stress on them in order to show what a fabric may be raised out of mere fancy when once we move along the perilous path of conjecture, and try to wring Shakespeare's secret from him, to pluck out the heart of his mystery. Of his relations, actual or imagined, with the enigmatical κύπρις-ἵμερος of the central group of the Sonnets, "the master-mistress of my passion," as he calls him in Sonnet 20 with a singularly close approximation to the Sophoclean phrase, we know exactly as much as Shakespeare himself has chosen to tell us. He might have been making fun of his own interpreters in the passage of *Twelfth Night* where Malvolio puzzles over Maria's letter.

> "I may command where I adore,
> But silence, like a Lucrece knife,
> With bloodless stroke my heart doth gore:
> M-O-A-I doth sway my life.

M-O-A-I doth sway my life: nay, but first let me see, let me see, let me see. What should that alphabetical position portend? if I could make that resemble something in me—softly! M-O-A-I: M—why, that begins my name. M—but then there is no consonancy in the sequel; that suffers under probation: A should follow, but O does: and then I comes behind. M-O-A-I: this simulation is not as the former; and yet to crush this a little, it would bow to me, for every one of those letters are in my name."

Over the Sonnets Shakespeare has in effect written the superscription of Malvolio's letter, "To the unknown beloved."

In one of the concluding pieces of the collection, Sonnet 121, the one beginning

"'Tis better to be vile than vile-esteemed
When not to be receives reproach of being,"

Shakespeare himself emphasises the same note, not humorously, but with an indignant gravity, and a claim for himself as superb as it is justified.

"For why should others' false adulterate eyes
Give salutation to my sportive blood?
Or on my frailties why are frailer spies,
Which in their wills count bad what I think good?
No, I am that I am, and they that level
At my abuses reckon up their own.
I may be straight, though they themselves be bevel,
By their rank thoughts my deeds must not be shown."

"I am that I am": these words are in effect Shakespeare's single and final self-criticism. They are almost appalling in their superb brevity and concentrated insight; beside them even the pride of Milton dwindles and grows pale: for here Shakespeare, for one single revealing moment, speaks not as though he were God's elect, but as though he were God himself.

"With this key Shakespeare unlocked his heart": so Wordsworth wrote of the Sonnets in 1827. The words have become a sort of battle-cry between conflicting schools of criticism, and like most battle-cries have become a good deal distorted from their original meaning. The scornful " Did he ? " of Browning is a counterstroke not to what Wordsworth said, but to what his phrase had become extended and interpreted to mean. As he wrote it and meant it, it expresses the truth with precise and almost punctilious accuracy. A strange and vast mass of experience, passion, imagination, was the central heat under that rich surface out of which the Shakespearian drama bloomed. Of that mass of experience the author of the Sonnets might say to his readers in Ophelia's words:

" 'Tis in my memory locked,
And you yourself shall keep the key of it."

But to hold the key is a different thing from holding the casket which it unlocked and locked again; and no poring over the wards, no fingering and balancing of the key itself will tell us what were the contents of the casket. He says himself no doubt, in Sonnet 76, in words which are a little startling at first sight, that every word of these Sonnets almost tells his name.

"Why is my verse so barren of new pride,
So far from variation or quick change?
Why with the time do I not glance aside
To new-formed methods and to compounds strange
Why write I still all one, ever the same,
And keep invention in a noted weed,
That every word doth almost tell my name,
Showing their birth and where they did proceed?"

Now and then, but rarely, as in Sonnet 111, where he breaks out into a bitter cry against the degradation involved in his own profession as a purveyor of popular amusement, "public means, which public manners breeds," he speaks quite frankly about himself. In the group of Sonnets dealing with the rival poet or rival poets—for Dean Beeching may be right in holding that the reference is not to one poet only—he clearly speaks of matters of fact which must have been common knowledge in his own circle. But these points only touch the fringe of the experience which he locked up in the Sonnets.

As bearing on the question of the date of the Sonnets, the passage from Sonnet 76 which I have just quoted has a special significance. For it indicates clearly, what on other grounds we might suspect, that Shakespeare was deliberately using a poetical form which was passing out of vogue, but in which his genius saw hitherto unreached possibilities. The history of the English Sonnet in the sixteenth century has been fully set out by Sir Sidney Lee in his masterly essay prefixed to the two volumes of Elizabethan Sonnets reprinted from Arber's English Garner in 1904. The sonneteering craze had spread through Europe in the middle of the century. The output of sonnets in Western Europe in that century may be estimated from the fact that the number actually extant now in print is computed at not less than three hundred thousand. The fashion took some time to reach England, where its career was violent and rather brief. It did not break out in its full volume until the publication, in 1591, of the Sonnets of Philip Sidney. The effect of that publication was to give the sonnet, for some five years, an overwhelming vogue. Sonnet-sequences poured from the press: Daniel's *Delia* and Constable's *Diana* in 1592; Lodge's *Phillis*, Barnes' *Parthenophe*, Giles Fletcher's *Licia* in 1593; Drayton's *Idea* and Percy's *Celia* in 1594; Spenser's *Amoretti* and Griffin's *Fidessa* in 1595; Smith's *Chloris* and Linche's *Diella* in 1596; Tofte's *Laura* in 1597. These collections, numerous as they are, probably do not represent a tenth or a twentieth part of the sonnets which were being produced and circulated in print or MS. during these five years. Then the reaction came, as far as one can judge, almost suddenly. It is not until 1604 that we come on the next sonnet-sequence in Sir Sidney Lee's lists, the Earl of Stirling's *Aurora*; and that was the aftermath of Scottish poetry following at some interval, as it had done in the age of the Chaucerians, after English models. The same remark applies to another body of sonnets brought out three years later by Drummond of Hawthornden. Last of all come Shakespeare's, in effect closing the roll of the great sonnet-writers of the Elizabethan age. From that time forward the sonnet did not bulk largely among the forms of English poetry until it was reinstated, two centuries later, by a new school of poets who revived, in this as in other respects, the genius of the Elizabethans. If we read the 76th Sonnet in the light of these facts, it assumes a fresh and clear significance. Shakespeare had been writing sonnets, like everybody else, during the years of the sonneteering fashion; there are sonnets in his earliest plays, from 1591 onwards. But he took up this poetical form for the first time seriously and consecutively just when it was beginning to fall out of fashion, and seemed exhausted by an immense over-production. In the plays, as has been noted, there are a number of more or less sarcastic references to sonneteering, ranging from *Love's Labour's Lost* in 1591 to *Much Ado* in 1599. These references throw ridicule in particular on the fashion of poets promising immortality through verse to the subjects of their sonnets, which had been similarly ridiculed by Sidney in 1581 in his *Apology for Poetry*. This was the face Shakespeare put upon it to the public. But all the while he was quietly practising the scorned art. Up to 1603 at least he persisted, as he puts it, in "dressing old words new, spending again what is already spent." The apology he makes is not only, is not even mainly, for any deficiency in his own powers; it is for persisting in the use of a poetical manner which was regarded as obsolete, a poetical form which had fallen out of fashion. "My gracious numbers are decayed," he writes, "and my sick Muse doth give another place": "thou art enforced to seek anew some fresher stamp of the time-bettering days." But in these phrases there is an accent, if not of sarcasm, at least of pride, of consciousness of his own immense genius. "I was not sick of any fear from thence" he says of the new school of poets, just after he has spoken of his own sick Muse. And the promise of immortality which he gives is too splendid to be insincere; it is no mere flourish of rhetoric, but the authentic and inspired voice of poetry, which sounds in these noble lines:

> "Your name from hence immortal life shall have
> Though I, once gone, to all the world must die:
> The earth can yield me but a common grave
> When you entombed in men's eyes shall lie.
> Your monument shall be my gentle verse
> Which eyes not yet created shall o'er-read,
> And tongues to be your being shall rehearse
> When all the breathers of this world are dead."

So in effect it has been and will be. And if any one should be inclined to say, "Small thanks to Shakespeare, considering how little pains he took to preserve the Sonnets," we must recollect that the same inconsistency meets us in the case of other great artists. Throughout the Sonnets we constantly find the fluctuation of mood—if it be not rather an antinomy of thought—between the feeling that art is immortal and the overwhelming sense of the transitoriness of all art as of all earthly things. In *Lucrece* Shakespeare had already given splendid expression to this latter thought. There, apostrophising Time as the "lackey to Eternity," he speaks of blotting old books and altering their contents as one phase of that universal process whose task it is "to feed Oblivion with decay of things." Years later, in the famous speech of Prospero in the *Tempest,* he gave expression in terms of unequalled gravity and beauty to the same thought, with a hardly veiled allusion to the world of his own creation as included under the sentence. And when he was writing the Sonnets he was particularly possessed by the thought, recurrent in all philosophies, of a cyclical revolution of the universe which repeated itself, at vast intervals, down to the most precise detail. This thought has weighed heavily on some of the greatest artists, and made them regard the products of their own art as something not merely transitory, but phantasmal. Such a feeling is strongly marked in Lucretius; it is at the base of the beautiful chorus at the end of Shelley's *Hellas,* with its wonderful change of key from the exultant opening—

> "The world's great age begins anew
> The golden years return"—

to the bitter cry at the end,

> "O cease! cease! cease!
> The world is weary of the past;
> O might it die or rest at last!"

Under the obsession of this thought it is not so wonderful that Shakespeare should have left the Sonnets, as he left the plays, to take their chance.

For that he left them to take their chance there

is no doubt. Careful analysis of the Quarto text shows convincingly, not only that it was carelessly printed and not intelligently corrected, but that it was printed from a rough MS. containing alterations, erasures, and in some cases alternative readings. There is not time here to go into this point in the full detail through which alone the proof can be given; it is a point not fully taken as yet by the editors, and leaves something to be added even to Dean Beeching's admirable and otherwise almost faultless edition. From the fact as established, more than one conjectural inference may be drawn. We may suppose either that the Sonnets were printed from Shakespeare's own MS. before it had received his final revision, or that they were collected for printing from various MS. sources, autographs or copies. There are indications, not very certain, but highly probable, that the MS. before the printers was not all in the same handwriting.

This question is connected with another, of which indeed it forms part, and which gives it its main interest, whether the Sonnets were arranged by Shakespeare in their present order, and whether, or to what extent, they form a continuous sequence. As to this we must distinguish sharply between the main series, Sonnets 1 to 126, and the appendix of twenty-eight sonnets which follows, and which deals in the main with the sinister and elusive figure known as the Dark Lady. This appendix is arranged in no traceable order. It ends with two Sonnets which have no connexion with the rest. These are purely literary exercises. They are alternative versions of a sixteenth-century Latin epigram itself rendered from a Greek epigram of the Byzantine period in the Anthology, and judging from style I am inclined to think that they are not by Shakespeare at all. The remaining twenty-six vary very much in style and quality. They include some, like 129, 140, 146, which are unmistakeable Shakespeare and in Shakespeare's finest manner; others which are quite Shakespearian in style, but of little poetical merit; and at least two, 128 and 145, which are both trivial in substance and undistinguished in style. From a general consideration of the facts one is inclined to believe that this portion of the volume is a miscellaneous addition, which may have reached Thorpe from the same source as the main body of the Sonnets or may have been put together by him from more than one source. Short poems, we must remember, were at that time multiplied very largely in MS.: they passed from hand to hand, and people selected and transcribed them, for their own use or pleasure, in MS. volumes such as are mentioned in Sonnet 77: that sonnet is an occasional one extraneous to the series, and is sent with a blank book in which the friend to whom it is presented is urged to transcribe what his memory cannot retain. Two extant specimens are described by Sir Sidney Lee of such "blank books" in which collections including one or more of the Sonnets have been transcribed; one of them was written in or about 1610, the other twenty years later.

Of the main body of the Sonnets, 1 to 126, I see no reason to doubt that they were arranged by Shakespeare, or at all events that they left his hands, in their present order, and that this order is substantially the order of their composition. But this belief is subject to two reservations: in the first place, those Sonnets which constitute a consecutive group may have been arranged by him in an order different from that of the dates of their writing; in the second place, he may have been working on more than one of those groups contemporaneously. As the Sonnets extend over a period of several years, and as different groups of them were clearly sent to their recipient at different times, it was obviously possible either for him, or for some third person into whose hands they had come before they went to the printer, to alter the arrangement; but there is no proof, and no probability, that this was in fact done.

As regards their grouping, there are no formal subdivisions in the Quarto, and the numbering is continuous from 1 to 126, as it is also with the Sonnets 127 to 154 which follow. But on the internal evidence, this main body of the Sonnets clearly falls into three parts. The arrangement is as follows:

I. A first group of twenty-five Sonnets (1 to 25); then a considerable gap of time.

II. A second group of fifty Sonnets (27 to 76), ending in Sonnet 76 with a vindication of the charge of monotony and old-fashionedness made against the writer. Sonnet 26 is an introductory or covering Sonnet prefixed to this group; and at the end of the group is attached 77, an occasional Sonnet sent with the gift of an album, and not properly belonging to the series at all. From the persistence in these fifty Sonnets of a misprint due to misreading of the MS.—"their" for "thy" (and once also in Sonnet 31 for "thee")—it is highly probable that they were set up from a MS. in a different hand from that of the rest. The mistake is made fourteen times in this group, and nowhere else in the Sonnets except in 128.

III. A third group of forty-eight Sonnets (78 to 125), opening with the famous rival-poet series (78 to 86), a prolonged and elaborate development of the theme touched upon in the concluding Sonnet of the second group, and ending with the four great Sonnets of self-vindication, 121, 123, 124, and 125. Between the first and second of these four is intercalated, without any obvious relevance, another occasional Sonnet of inferior merit and little interest. At the end of all come the six couplets of *envoi*, which, though not a Sonnet in form, are numbered in the series as 126.

It may be taken as not improbable, though we are here only moving among conjectures, that this main body, Sonnets 1 to 126, is what Thorpe specifically meant by "the ensuing Sonnets" in his dedication; and if we are to yield to the fascination of guess-work, it is tempting to believe that W. H. himself handed them to Thorpe, though there are of course other ways in which they may have come into Thorpe's possession. Together with them, in any case, Thorpe also became possessed of a MS. copy of the Dark Lady Sonnets, and of various others which he printed to fill out the volume. Of these twenty-eight additional Sonnets, I have already indicated my belief that two at least, and possibly four, are not by Shakespeare.

At the end of the volume of Sonnets, and after the *Finis*, is printed the curious poem entitled *A Lover's Complaint, by William Shakespeare*. This piece deserves closer study than it has yet received; for it raises problems, as regards its authorship and its relation to the other contents of the volume, which are of no little interest and intricacy. But these problems are subsidiary, and discussion of them here would be irrelevant.

I have not yet approached, except incidentally, what is most relevant and central in the whole matter, the quality of the Sonnets as poetry, their value as art. But of this it is the less necessary to speak in any detail, because for once we are dealing with something of which the appreciation is as large as it is sound, and on which all critical opinion is at one. Extremists from all quarters meet here. Those who profess to find in the Sonnets a body of metaphysical or mystical doctrine; those who extract from them, with as much violence to psychology as to the rules of evidence or to common propriety, a Procopian Secret History of Shakespeare's own life; those who argue that they are mere literary exercises on a conventional theme; all at least agree that they are an unequalled masterpiece of imaginative power, of psychological skill and pictorial vision, of mastery in rhythm and phrase. They combine, with a perfection of which Shakespeare alone had the secret, the most sumptuous richness with the most direct simplicity. Beside them the whole of that mass of Elizabethan sonnet-literature of which they are the crown grows pale, mannered, and thin. Here all is at a higher power; it is poetic quality distilled and concentrated. That this quality is mixed with the conceits and mannerisms of the age is true, as it is true of all Shakespeare's work even at its finest, as it is true of *Much Ado* or of *Hamlet*. This much must be allowed and even emphasised if we are to keep our feeling for Shakespeare sane, and on this side idolatry. It is true too that in some of the Sonnets Shakespeare is sounding on a dim and perilous way; of this he has given, in words which I have already quoted, his own vindication.

The concentration of poetry in the Sonnets is so great, its sweetness so condensed, that we can only appreciate it fully through a sort of process of separation and dilution. This is not the case with the Sonnets only. It is shown more generally in the extraordinary effect which Shakespeare produces in quotation. The poetry as it stands is so close-packed that it must be disengaged to give out its full effect. "Roses, damask and red," says Bacon in his Essay of Gardens, "are fast flowers of their smells, so that you may walk by a whole row of them and find nothing of their sweetness." They must be approached closely and singly, if their "royal scent" is to produce its full effect. The effect of Shakespeare's poetry is indeed universal and immediate. Yet a line or phrase thus disengaged from it always thrills one with unsuspected depths of beauty. It expands, takes colour, becomes as it were a live thing. And the only way to appreciate the Sonnets fully is, I think, to know them by heart, to become saturated with them, and then to let passage after passage, phrase after phrase, line after line, expand and germinate as memory recalls it, association touches it, imagination kindles it. Then an enhanced richness, a subtler grace, a more essential beauty will flash upon that inward eye which is the bliss of solitude; then Shakespeare will not have written for us in vain. But in saying this I speak not of Shakespeare only, but of all great poetry.

THE NOTE OF SHAKESPEARE'S ROMANCES

"THE best actors in the world," Polonius calls the troop of strolling players who when they arrive on the scene are consciously identified with Shakespeare's own company: "the best actors in the world either for tragedy, comedy, history, pastoral, pastoral-comical, historical-pastoral, tragical-historical, tragical-comical-historical-pastoral, scene individable, or poem unlimited." Polonius was a fool, or so at least he seemed to Hamlet: but he was not, like Patroclus in the play to which I shall presently have occasion to refer, a fool positive. He had a large experience, and the remains of what once had been a good average critical faculty. Sometimes, as in his advice to Laertes and in this passage, he says things that are by no means devoid of good sense and even of insight: the trouble with him is that he has lost all power of applying maxims and definitions, which may be sensible and just in themselves, to the circumstances in hand. Though both Laertes and Ophelia deceased without issue, the family of Polonius is still largely represented among men of letters.

In this curious enumeration Shakespeare no doubt meant to introduce a tinge of burlesque. But it has clearly in view a fact of some importance, namely that the drama, being a mirror and image of life in its whole aspect and working, cannot be sorted out under the two ancient divisions of tragedy and comedy; and that even if to these two names we add two more, history and pastoral, we do not in fact cover the scope of the Shakespearian drama. The thing has become too mixed and complex for this treatment. It has taken to deal with the whole of life, and it has become like life itself, something that cannot be shut off into separate compartments.

Hence the division of Shakespeare's plays roughly made by his first editors into three groups called respectively comedies, histories, and tragedies, though convenient for reference, and based on real distinctions so far as it goes, is inadequate and a little unsatisfactory. It is all right as concerns the central group, the ten plays founded on English history, from *King John* to *King Henry VIII*. But the other two groups each contain certain plays of very various type, which can only be put under a single name by some forcing of terms. There is no need to labour this point. I may just in passing call attention to the difficulties which the division involves by ignoring tragi-comedy as a distinct species, although the name is a very necessary one and was in fact freely used in Shakespeare's own time: one result of this is that in the first folio, and in all subsequent usage, we find a serious and essentially tragic play like *Measure for Measure* wedged in between two farces, the *Merry Wives of Windsor* and the *Comedy of Errors*, as though they belonged to the same division of dramatic art. But the point in the tripartite arrangement of the folio to which I wish to call particular attention, is this: that the sections classed as Comedies and Tragedies begin and end, in each case, with plays which are of an essentially different character from those which constitute the main body of the two

o

sections. One may assume, or conjecture plausibly, that these plays were placed where they stand with a distinct feeling that this difference existed, and that there was a real difficulty felt in assigning them their proper place among the rest. The contents of the volume, you will remember, are as follows: first, the *Tempest*, twelve comedies, and the *Winter's Tale*: then the ten English Histories: then *Troilus and Cressida*, ten tragedies, and *Cymbeline*. The *Tempest* and the *Winter's Tale* are not specifically entitled comedies, but then neither are any of the other plays in the first section. *Troilus and Cressida* and *Cymbeline* are both specifically entitled tragedies, as are all the plays which come between them, with the single exception of *Timon of Athens*, which by what must be a mere freak or accident is called "The Life of Timon of Athens"—not even the "Life and Death." There is the further interesting point to remark, that *Troilus and Cressida* is inserted where it stands by an afterthought: its pages are not numbered, and it is omitted from the table of contents at the beginning of the volume. It had been meant, when the printing of the Folio was first put in hand, to follow *Romeo and Juliet:* and it must have been removed from that place for some considered reason, a reason of what may be broadly called an æsthetic or critical kind. This is one of several indications which show that the arrangement of the plays in the Folio, whether it is a good one or not, was not made at random or left to the printers.

Three of these four plays, namely, the *Tempest*, the *Winter's Tale*, and *Cymbeline*, constitute a section of Shakespearian dramatic work which differs materially, both in tone and in treatment, from the rest. All three may be confidently assigned, alike from external

SHAKESPEARE'S ROMANCES

and internal evidence, to his latest period. I do not know who first hit on the happy thought of giving them the distinctive name of Shakespearian romances: but it is now an accepted and convenient term. *Troilus and Cressida* belongs to an earlier period, about contemporary with *Hamlet*, and (at least according to my view of the matter) a little after the main body of the Sonnets. The unplaced manner in which it appears in the First Folio is a sort of symbol of its unique and enigmatic character as a play. To this I will return later, only saying now that it may be called a sort of inverted romance, and that it has a close affinity in some respects with the other three plays known as the romances.

No study of the Shakespearian romances can be complete which does not take account of two other plays, *Pericles* and the *Two Noble Kinsmen*. But for the purpose of bringing out the special point I have in view, it will be simpler to omit these, or only speak of them incidentally. The *Two Noble Kinsmen*—I speak of the part of it written by Shakespeare—is a fragment only; it is a fragment of great magnificence, including some pieces of Shakespeare's finest writing, and it is further notable as the only instance in which Shakespeare set himself to dramatise the romantic epic, while at the same time preserving its tone and colour. But inferences, and still more generalisations, drawn from a dramatic fragment are insecure, and very likely to be erroneous. *Pericles* is also a play of mixed authorship. As regards its undoubtedly Shakespearian parts it bears a strong affinity to the romances proper of a few years later; one scene, the recognition of Marina by Pericles, may indeed be called the culmination of Shakespeare's romantic manner; it is as miraculous in language and movement as anything in the *Tempest* or

Cymbeline, and as distinct from any manner to be found in the tragedies or comedies.

This last point may perhaps be emphasised. Shakespeare is, from first to last, a romantic poet in one of the senses of that very ambiguous term; and in some of the plays, particularly in the more serious comedies, there are passages conceived and written in a highly romantic manner. An element of romance runs through the *Midsummer Night's Dream*; there is a strong touch of it in Act iv. scene 3 of *As You Like It*, and in the lovely lyrical interlude at the beginning of Act v. of the *Merchant of Venice*. But this is not the romantic manner as we find it in the romances proper, or induce a definition of it from these. And the element is incidental, not essential; we may notice that the instances just cited occur in plays all of which, in their different styles, are strict comedies, and comedies of the first order. In the romances proper we are in a different world, and one the note of which is as distinct from comedy as it is from tragedy.

The difference, the distinguishing note of the romance, is as concerns the artist, one of purpose, as concerns the work of art, one of tension. To put it broadly and simply, we must somewhat overstate it; but the qualifications can be made later, and in some measure are self-evident. Broadly then, and if you like, exaggeratedly, it may be put thus: in the romances you have Shakespeare writing not to satisfy his art, but to please himself; and the life or action in the romances is not the tense, concentrated, idealised life of tragedy or comedy, but life as it actually happens.

This statement may sound not merely exaggerated, but paradoxical. In any case it requires explanation. This I will now try to give. Clearly in the three romances Shakespeare shows himself an accomplished, even a consummate artist. Clearly too, the action in them (what used to be called the "fable") is not such as takes place in the life of ordinary people. The *Tempest* moves among enchantments and impossibilities. The Mediterranean island on which the action passes is not solid land, like the Cyprus of *Othello* or the Britain of *King Lear*. It is ten leagues beyond man's life; it is inhabited by witch-spawn and airy spirits; phantoms of the old mythology appear upon it in visible shape. The scenes of the *Winter's Tale*, with its Bohemian sea-coast and its embassage to the oracle of Apollo in the island of Delphi, are almost as fantastic and shadowy. Even in *Cymbeline*, in spite of the familiar names, Lud's town and Milford Haven, we are in a sort of fairyland. But the life presented in these strange romantic surroundings is actual life. It does not consist in action and passion, stripped of accident and closely knitted into the structure of essential tragedy: or, it may be, into the structure of essential comedy; for comedy is almost as tense as tragedy, and idealises or sublimates real life almost to as great a degree.

It is this tension—involving as it does the rejection of accident and the subordination of incident—which is the fundamental idea of high dramatic art. It is at the basis of the so-called doctrine of the unities, which represents an attempt to express it in some of its more obvious aspects. The unities are an empirical rule for indicating the concentration that is necessary in order to make it possible to secure the requisite tension throughout a play. To do this the action must all be brought within compass; it must deal only with what is essential as cause and effect in transforming the situation with which the drama begins into the situation with which it ends. A tragedy, or a comedy, is not *ondoyant et divers* like actual life; it gathers up out of life, or abstracts from life, what is requisite for its own artistic purpose, and no more.

I said, for its own artistic purpose. I do not mean to hint at any esoteric doctrine of art for art's sake. By artistic purpose, or the purpose of art, I mean the creation of something complete in itself and satisfying the laws of composition—the laws, as Aristotle names them, of " size and arrangement." In actual events—in the life of the individual, or in history, which is the life of the various complex interacting associations of individuals that make up the human race,—there is no limit other than that set by the accidents of birth and death, and no clearly perceptible arrangement. The law of causality exists everywhere; everything has its cause, and produces its effect; but cause and effect are so vast in their own complexity that they do not make a pattern. It is the function of art to make patterns out of life.

In tragedy and comedy these patterns are closely woven, intelligibly shaped, precise. A problem, we may say, is in each case set and solved. In order to set the problem, and in order to solve it when set, everything must be put aside which does not bear upon the problem, or is not a step towards its exposition and solution. Further, the dramatic art, like all arts, works in a certain medium and has to work according to the nature and limits of that medium. In dramatic art that medium is the stage, and representation by actors on the stage; its action is what can be acted.

Romance represents the tendency to transcend or ignore these limits. In the Shakespearian romances we have the artist playing with his art. He neglects the rules of the drama. He does not apply his constructive faculty to the creation of a composition possessed of dramatic unity and dramatic concentration. He follows not so much the chain of causality as the stream of circumstance. He begins the action capriciously, almost accidentally: he ends it in a situation that does not necessarily arise out of the movement impressed upon the play at its beginning. Of all Shakespeare's plays we may say boldly that the romances are the least imitable. For they are the product of a strenuous, highly trained and consummate artistic genius which has let itself loose to move at ease. The *Winter's Tale* is the by-product of *Othello* and *Much Ado*: the *Tempest* is the by-product of *As You Like It* and *Macbeth*. *Cymbeline* is the by-product of the whole of the volume of plays which it ends. To produce work like Shakespeare's romances it would be necessary that the artist should have already produced work like the finest of Shakespeare's comedies and tragedies. *Ne faict pas ce tour qui veult.* Most people have perhaps felt, more or less indistinctly, that some explanation was needed, some reason had to be sought, why these romances have so superb a beauty and so overpowering a charm. They are—I speak in broad general terms—ill-constructed, slackly knitted, full of irrelevances and exorbitances. In the *Tempest* there is properly speaking no dramatic action at all. In the *Winter's Tale* there are several, but they are all fragmentary. In *Cymbeline* the dramatic action is like that of an unusually coherent dream. This is felt in reading: it is still more obvious (if one may judge from modern performances) when the plays are acted. Yet these three plays are, each in its own way, unsurpassable. In parts of the *Winter's Tale* a sort of golden beauty is reached which is almost if not quite unequalled in Shakespeare. The *Tempest* is admittedly—so much so that one is tired of hearing the thing repeated—the fit crown to be set for a finish on Shakespeare's work. For the last of the three, it does not require Swinburne's noble lines to convince us that the death of Tennyson with *Cymbeline* in his hand, his burial with *Cymbeline* in the coffin, was just as lovers of Tennyson and of Shakespeare would have had it. The reason is this; that in these plays we have a superlative artist, a master of dramatic construction, a poet of profound weight and unsurpassed concentration, writing as he likes, carelessly, following the suggestion of circumstance and the play of fancy. Shakespeare had passed through the furnace-fire, like Dante on the Mountain of Purgatory.

> " Come fui dentro, in un bogliente vetro
> Gittato mi sarei per rinfrescarmi ;
> Tant' era ivi lo incendio senza metro."

When he issued from it, the Muse said to him as Virgil had said to Dante :

> " Tratto t'ho qui con ingegno e con arte :
> Lo tuo piacere omai prendi per duce ;
> Fuor se' dell' erte vie, fuor se' dell' arte. . . .
> Seder ti puoi, e puoi andar tra elli ;
> Non aspettar mio dir più, nè mio cenno."

Or, as the lines are finely rendered by Cary :

> " I with skill and art
> Thus far have drawn thee. Now thy pleasure take
> For guide. Thou hast o'ercome the steeper way,
> O'ercome the straighter : thou mayest seat thee down
> Or wander where thou wilt. Expect no more
> Sanction of warning voice or sign from me."

He obeyed her: he took his pleasure for guide, and wandered where he would. One is tempted to go on with the Dante; so apt it is to the occasion.

"A little glimpse of sky was seen above,
  Yet by that little I beheld the stars
  In magnitude and lustre shining forth
  With more than wonted glory. . . . About the hour,
  As I believe, when Venus from the East
  First lightened on the mountain, she whose orb
  Seems alway glowing with the fire of love,
  A lady young and beautiful, I dreamed,
  Was passing o'er a lea; and as she came
  Methought I saw her ever and anon
  Bending to cull the flowers; and thus she sang."

Her name in Shakespeare is Miranda, Perdita, Imogen.

But this radiance of beauty illuminates plays which are weak or loose in structure, fantastic in detail, irregular in proportion; and in portions of which Shakespeare is—if I may say so with due respect—all abroad, and writing anyhow. Let us go into this a little more in specific instances, taking the romances in the order in which they come in the First Folio.

The *Tempest* has been called a masque rather than a drama. Names prove nothing. But it is clear that it has little if any dramatic action, in the sense of interplay of human will or character. The events are brought about by magic. Prospero, directly or through his instruments, Ariel and Caliban, moves the other persons of the drama like a chess-player. In order to get the scene set at all, Shakespeare has to assume a long-continued absence of interest in the whole affair on Prospero's part: in order to make the play last out through the normal five acts, it is necessary that Prospero should in its course be subject to fits of abstraction or lapses of memory. At the opening of the second act the play stands still while Shakespeare throws into the form of dialogue a discussion on the general principles of politics which had interested him in reading Montaigne. The wonderful lines in which Prospero speaks of the masque within the masque as a baseless fabric, melted into thin air before it was ended, are too well known to quote. But another speech of his, a little earlier, which is less often quoted, is no less notable in the tone of easy carelessness about the dramatist's art which it conveys. "I must use you," says Prospero,

> "For such another trick. Go bring the rabble
> O'er whom I give thee power, here to this place:
> Incite them to quick motion: for I must
> Bestow upon the eyes of this young couple
> Some vanity of mine art."

Prospero in these lines is speaking of the play within the play: Shakespeare through Prospero's mouth is speaking of the play itself. The persons of the play are a rabble over whom he has power; he incites them to motion, and uses them to bestow some vanity of his art upon the eyes of a delighted world. "It is my promise," he goes on, "and they expect it from me": the usual excuse made by all of us for doing something we like, when we have a feeling that we might be doing, or should be doing, something more serious.

Turning now to the *Winter's Tale* we find the same characteristics showing themselves, and even more remarkably, because the play is engrafted upon, or expanded out of, a tragic drama of normal type. With a few trifling excisions of passages which anticipate the later action, the first three acts of the *Winter's Tale* are a play by themselves. That play is a tragedy of jealousy. But it is without its beginning. The first scene of Act i. is a short explanatory preface: then in scene 2 we are suddenly in the middle of the complication: the jealousy of Leontes is presented full-blown, unexplained, perfectly irrational. We have the feeling that at least a whole act has been omitted: and so it would be, if the *Winter's Tale* was a formal tragedy, for it is the essence of a tragedy that effects follow from causes, and that the fatal action is neither unaccountable nor motiveless. To a certain extent there is this same, or a similar anomaly at the beginning of *Macbeth*. It is one of the features which make *Macbeth* unique in structure among Shakespeare's regular tragedies. It forms part of a complex puzzle together with certain other facts which have been held, not without strong reason, to prove that the beginning of Shakespeare's play is either lost, and replaced by some fadged and abbreviated stage-version, or at the least gravely mutilated.

But in the *Winter's Tale* there is no question of mutilation. The play is deliberately begun at a point which is well after the dramatic beginning of the action presented in the first three acts. This is because two separate plays, two separate though connected actions, are forged or beaten into one. The beginning of the first play is cut away that there may be room left for the second; that is to say, for Acts iv. and v. A short connecting piece consisting of the last scene of Act iii. forms the transition. You will notice, if you dismiss this latter half of the composite play from your minds, that the former half ends, in the exact tragic manner, upon the formal tragic finishing-note. The final speech is that of Leontes:

> " Prithee bring me
> To the dead bodies of my queen and son.
> One grave shall be for both: upon them shall
> The causes of their death appear, unto
> Our shame perpetual. Once a day I'll visit

> The chapel where they lie, and tears shed there
> Shall be my recreation : so long as nature
> Will bear up with this exercise, so long
> I daily vow to use it. Come and lead me
> Unto these sorrows." *[Exeunt.*

It is the precise motive, at once in its dramatic and its musical quality, of the concluding speech of Aufidius in *Coriolanus,* of the concluding speech of Fortinbras in *Hamlet,* of the concluding speech of Octavianus in *Antony and Cleopatra.*

Of the great adroitness with which Shakespeare interlinked the second part of the *Winter's Tale* with the first it would be superfluous to say anything in praise. Whatever he chose to do, he could do with the ease of immense power and trained skill. The point is, that here he was using this power and skill, I will not say at random, but for his own—and for our—amusement. In the lines spoken by Time as chorus at the opening of Act iv. there is a note of the same feeling which is expressed so wonderfully in the *Tempest*—the feeling that art itself, even the greatest art, is transitory, and that the artist, even the greatest artist, is a child playing with toys, a pattern-designer whose patterns dissolve almost as soon as they are drawn. It is of a piece with this, that when Shakespeare gets among his rustics in that fourth act, he plunges into the sheep-shearing festival with such abandon, such enjoyment, that he can hardly tear himself away from it. That single scene—the fourth of Act iv.—is nearly nine hundred lines long. That is the length of a short play by itself. It is about half the length of *Macbeth.* It is not much shorter than six out of the seven tragedies of Aeschylus. It is actually longer than Terence's *Hecyra.* In writing it, Shakespeare clearly threw the reins on the neck of his genius and went on and on from sheer delight in writing it: it is endless, and endlessly delightful; for the rest, he does not care.

So it is too with the substance as well as the form of the play. As a study of jealousy in its action and effects it gives an interesting contrast to the treatment of a similar motive in the sphere of tragedy, in *Othello*, and in the sphere of comedy, in *Much Ado*. It is all at a lower pressure, more ordinary. The action has not the dramatic concentration of either tragedy or comedy. As a tragedy it would have to be pronounced a failure, and what is more, a deliberate failure. There is no great conflict between will and fate. Leontes acts violently and irrationally, but not with the sort of fatal error which is the essence of a tragic situation. He does not awaken pity or fear. The same is true of the subsidiary characters. Paulina is a figure from daily life, very nearly the common scold. The fundamental difference between tragedy and romance is well brought out by a comparison between her and the Emilia of *Othello*. Emilia, slight and shallow as she is, is swept up into greatness by the intense tragedy in which she is involved, and towards which she has innocently, or at least ignorantly, given the fatal impulse. She has to die for it, by a sudden, a cruel, and yet an inevitable doom. Paulina is subject to no such necessity. She lives on, her tongue clacking from first to last. The second marriage huddled up for her at the end of the play is just what would happen. Camillo replaces the husband whose death was so far from being a tragic issue that we have hardly noticed it, otherwise than with the languid interest with which we might read a newspaper paragraph headed "Strange fatality in Bohemia." Things happen in this play as in life, coming near tragedy and then sliding away from it again. As in life, effects do not visibly or demonstrably follow from causes: things happen: and time heals all, or covers with his dust and oblivion what was unhealed. One generation comes and another goes; time remembered is grief forgotten. The peace which falls is not the awed hush of a tragic ending; it is the peace that life brings in its ceaseless progress, when the tragedy of the past has itself become numbered among old, unhappy, far-off things. This is the upshot and significance of the wonderful lines spoken by Time as chorus at the beginning of Act iv.

> "I, that please some, try all, both joy and terror
> Of good and bad, that make and unfold error,
> Now take upon me, in the name of Time,
> To use my wings. Impute it not a crime
> To me or my swift passage, that I slide
> O'er sixteen years and leave the growth untried
> Of that wide gap; since it is in my power
> To o'erthrow law, and in one self-born hour
> To plant and o'erwhelm custom. Let me pass
> The same I am, ere ancient'st order was,
> Or what is now received: I witness to
> The times that brought them in: so shall I do
> To the freshest things now reigning, and make stale
> The glistering of this present, as my tale
> Now seems to it. Your patience thus allowing,
> I turn my glass and give my scene such growing
> As you had slept between."

Tragedy does not leave gaps untried, or let us fall asleep in the progress of the action. It does not overthrow law or supplant it by custom: it establishes law. It declares the ancient order as that which has been and is and shall be: "not of now or of yesterday," in the words of Antigone, "but that lives for ever, and no man knows whence it was born."

Cymbeline, which for several reasons into which it is not possible to enter here one is inclined to think the latest of the romances, and of Shakespeare's plays, comes in some ways nearer the scope of a single dramatic action; but in its details it is even more strikingly marked than the others by waywardness and a sort of careless following of fancy. The action has in its main course something of the tragic gravity, and even rises at certain points to the tragic intensity. But it is not stripped like a runner: it is overlaid and embroidered with collateral incident, amid which it moves in a leisurely, one might say in a pleasurable way. It is the most striking instance of the faculty Shakespeare has, through his complete mastery of stagecraft and dramatic structure, of combining high-tension and low-tension work into one fabric. If we possessed the full earlier draughts of his tragedies it may be conjectured that we should find a great deal of this in them. Traces of it are left even in the completed form of *Hamlet*. But as a rule, in the great tragedies, the low-tension work has been nearly all distilled away or brought up to high tension.

Exactly the same thing is noticeable as regards the language, the actual writing. The style in *Cymbeline* is distinguishable, on a broad view, from the characteristic finished style of Shakespeare's mature work. Many passages show clearly what is a very fascinating thing in the work of a great artist, and one but rarely seen, his work in the making. The superfetation of thought, as it has been called, which makes Shakespeare's style different from that of any one else, is expressed in *Cymbeline* by a new verbal notation. It stands midway between the redundance of his earlier work and the peculiarly Shakespearian quality of his greatest work, in which the imaginative intensity is so enormous that it fuses all the threads of thought into a single continuous element—for so we must call it rather than a fabric or a structure, since these words convey the idea of something which can be analysed or separated. The most obvious note of this Cymbeline-style is the immense number of parentheses, and of parentheses within parentheses. It is as though Shakespeare's mind were working at its full compass—on three or four lines abreast as one might say—but not at its full tension or concentration in which the concurrent processes of thought become molten into one. He is writing with obvious pleasure, and obviously for his pleasure. The fires are drawn, and the beautifully adjusted engines go on running under a lower steam-pressure, and almost by their own momentum.

It is of a piece with this, that we can trace in all these three romances some amount of reversion towards his earliest work in method and subject. This kind of reversion is noticeable in other great artists towards the end of their life; it is of course a general law of life in all matters, not only in art. There is just this note of reversion, very subtle and not to be pressed —it is to be felt rather than stated or explained— in *Cymbeline* to the *Two Gentlemen*, the earliest of the plays: subject to the caution however, that the *Two Gentlemen* itself, which remained unpublished until it appeared in the First Folio, may have been retouched and retoned by Shakespeare himself at a comparatively late period; there are a few lines in it which suggest this as the easiest explanation of what would otherwise be very remarkable anticipations of the author's mature style. There is a similar note, fainter but still traceable, in the *Winter's Tale* of reversion to the *Midsummer Night's Dream*. In *Cymbeline*, as I have already hinted, the reversion is more of the nature of recapitulation, and extends over the whole field of Shakespearian dramatic work.

The notes of Shakespearian romance on which I have thus touched—to work them out would be a matter for much more minute and prolonged study—may serve even in this sketch for guidance, or at least for suggestion, in the problems presented by other plays. Let me take an instance in the *Two Noble Kinsmen*.

Professor Herford, in his excellent introduction to that play, has the following passage: "Even where style and metre are most persuasively Shakespearian, the design and motive of a scene often suggest rather Fletcher's careless and superficial technique, his eye for sensation and effect, his carelessness of connexion and continuity." This is quite true, and admirably said, of Fletcher: but it is also true, though in a different sense, of romance as distinct from closely wrought high-tension drama, be it tragedy or comedy. In both there is the careless technique, though in the one case it is the carelessness of inferior artistic sense and inferior grasp of life, and in the other case the carelessness of the master who is, in words which one might hesitate to use were it not they have been used by one great artist of our own time in speaking of another equally great,[1] "making art to please himself," for his own enjoyment. In both there is the eye for sensation, though in the one case it is the shallow eye that does not see much below the surface, in the other the eye, at once wide-ranging and profound, that can plunge into the deep bases and hidden springs of life, but chooses now rather to play over the complex coloured surface with which life in fact passes visibly before us.

[1] Burne-Jones of Morris.

Again, Professor Herford says of the Theseus of the *Two Noble Kinsmen*: "There is more of Fletcher's ethics than of Shakespeare's in the conception that a man may possibly, in the face of crying need, if piteously entreated, consent to postpone his marriage for a day or two, but not without some lofty self-gratulation at the close:

'As we are men
Thus should we do: being sensually subdued
We lose our human title.'

Theseus' extraordinary severity again, in the last scene of the act, to the prisoners whose prowess he admires, remains unaccountable. He combines with touches of the godlike wisdom of Prospero and Pericles a peculiarly aimless ferocity."

As to the first of these points, it is sufficient to point out that the Theseus of the *Two Noble Kinsmen* is precisely the Theseus of the *Midsummer Night's Dream* over again; this is indeed one of the most convincing arguments for the Shakespearian authorship of these scenes, and one may commend those who are disposed to attribute them to Fletcher to the conversation which passes at the masked ball in *Much Ado* between Antonio and Ursula. It is Shakespeare's Theseus, and there's an end. As to the second point, it is not easy to understand in what sense godlike wisdom is to be attributed to either Prospero or Pericles, two very human characters. But the aimless ferocity complained of here, whether or not it is properly so described, is found both in Leontes and in Cymbeline. As regards Leontes this is self-evident. Cymbeline shows it not only at the beginning of the play in the interview with his daughter and her husband, but at the end in his cold arrangement to massacre the Roman prisoners, and in his furious order for this immediate execution of Belarius. These gusts of ungovernable temper do not, however, as in *King Lear* work out tragic consequences. They are part of the shifting, apparently inconsequent, surface of life which is dealt with in the large scope of romance.

It is not, to be sure, by arguments like these that the authorship of certain parts of the *Two Noble Kinsmen* has to be finally decided. But a consideration of the essential features of Shakespearian romance goes to show that the points singled out as arguments against that authorship in these instances are really, so far as they go, arguments in its favour.

The upshot of what I have been saying is this; that romance has a constructional or artistic quality of its own differing from that of tragedy and comedy, and that it is this quality, and not the serene temper of the group of the three late romantic plays, nor their happy endings, on which criticism may most profitably lay stress when it distinguishes them as a group standing by themselves. The happy ending, in the technical sense of the phrase, is common to *Cymbeline* and the *Winter's Tale* with *Measure for Measure*, which no one would call a romance, and many would be inclined to call a thwarted tragedy. The serene temper, the mellowness and indulgence, which critics find in these romances is no doubt in sufficiently striking contrast with the storm and agony of the great tragedies. But it is a note of these particular romances, not of romance as such.

We may now turn back to Shakespeare's other romance, which has an unhappy ending—the unhappiest among all his plays—and which, so far from having an atmosphere of placidity and a tone of indulgence towards human life, is from first to last restless, bitter, and angry. This is *Troilus and Cressida.*

Yet like the others, *Troilus and Cressida* is a romance, not a tragedy. It is not merely that the subject is one taken from the romantic mediæval epic. It is that here, as in his other romances, Shakespeare is writing not to satisfy the laws of dramatic art, not towards the intense embodiment and strenuous evolution of a tragic problem, but to please himself. But what pleased him in those later romances was to handle the large beauty of the surface of life: what pleased him here was to handle its large ugliness. In *Troilus and Cressida* there is a sort of inverted indulgence, a desperate serenity which throws helve after hatchet and does not attempt even to save a solid fragment out of the welter of a world lying in wickedness. It develops no great problem, no vital contest between great forces, no great manifestation of human will or even of human passion: it ends in no hush of peace and awe. Indeed it hardly ends at all, except with such an ending as nightfall might bring to a confused battle fought for no reason. Shakespeare flung material of all kinds into it, following the impulse of a sort of acute restlessness, we may imagine, such as often accompanies temporary mental or physical exhaustion. It includes scenes which take their place among his most remarkable work: the debates in the Greek and Trojan councils of war, the love-ecstasy of Troilus in Act iii., the great speech of Ulysses in the following scene. But in spite of these passages with their high intellectual or spiritual elevation, the atmosphere throughout the play, taken as a whole, is thick and oppressive. The pattern of life presented in it—so far as it can be called a pattern at all—is tawdry, squalid, ugly. That Serbonian bog swallows up and effaces even the chivalry of Hector, even the beauty of Helen. The action moves through petty chicane and petty cruelty, petty selfishness and jealousy and unfaithfulness. Over it all we feel the cold sarcastic eyes of Ulysses, the man with no illusions. Among all these littlenesses and meannesses, the one great permanent force that we are made to feel is that which we are expressly asked to feel in the *Winter's Tale,* the force of time. But it is not here, as in the *Winter's Tale,* Time the healer: it is Time the annihilator; the force which feeds oblivion with the decay of things, under whose hand those conflicts which make tragedy, with all their tension and splendour, dwindle away and are as small dust in the balance. Perhaps the most significant passage in the whole play, as it is the most romantic in its accent of strangeness kindling into beauty, is the brief dialogue between Hector and Ulysses when they meet in the Greek camp, and speak to each other for a few minutes seriously, from outside as it were and from overhead of the action.

"*Hector.* I know your favour, Lord Ulysses, well.
Ah, sir, there's many a Greek and Trojan dead
Since first I saw yourself and Diomede
In Ilion, on your Greekish embassy.
 Ulysses. Sir, I foretold you then what would ensue:
My prophecy is but half his journey yet.
For yonder walls that pertly front your town,
Yond towers, whose wanton tops do buss the clouds,
Must kiss their own feet.
 Hector. I must not believe you.
There they stand yet, and modestly I think
The fall of every Phrygian stone will cost
A drop of Grecian blood: the end crowns all,
And that old common arbitrator, Time,
Will one day end it.
 Ulysses. So to him we leave it."

So in effect it is left. But to leave it so gives up the game. It makes the strictly dramatic handling of life impossible. *Troilus and Cressida* is the reaction from

Hamlet: it is the sort of play, one might say, that Hamlet himself might have written. It represents a temporary phase in Shakespeare's art. After it, he addressed himself to the problems of art and life anew. He wrote the great series of tragedies. In them, time is not the arbitrator, and life is not the endless unrolling of a transitory pageant. When he returned to romance in his latest plays, it was as one who had earned the right to deal with life as he chose, because he knew it all, and had traversed it from surface to centre. We may be grateful that he chose as he did.

THE POETRY OF OXFORD

OXFORD has always been the mother or nurse of poets. But this itself would not entitle us to speak of the poetry of Oxford: when we give the name of Oxford poets to poets who were educated at Oxford, we are doing little more than pleasing our fancy and flattering our local patriotism. One does not call Virgil a Milanese poet, nor Goethe a Leipsic or Strasburg poet. Normally the place of a poet's education has little direct bearing on his poetry, nor has his poetry much direct bearing on the place of his education.

But the poetry of Oxford, as a term used in the stricter sense, may bear two meanings. In the first place it may mean poetry written about Oxford; description of Oxford, either in its outward aspect or in its intellectual and social life, raised by some touch of melody or imagination into the sphere of poetry and forming the figured background upon which some image of life is set in relief. This kind of poetry falls under one or other of two divisions, according as the treatment is substantive or episodic: on the one hand the occasional piece, often a mere sketch or fragment, which consists of description coloured by imagination; on the other, the passage in some larger imaginative composition which gives the picture of Oxford incidentally, as ornament included in and subordinated to a larger design.

In the second place, the poetry of Oxford may mean

something quite different; it may mean the poetical quality of Oxford itself, the image of perfection which Oxford embodies; or rather, does not embody but holds within itself like a latent energy, that can be made active and embodied in language by the imaginative power of a poet. This latter sense is the more important, as it is the subtler and more vital.

If we turn over the pages of one of the many modern collections of poems relating to Oxford, such as the *Minstrelsy of Isis*, which is I fancy the fullest and most varied of them all in its contents, we cannot fail to be struck by two things. One of these is the persistence, from generation to generation, of certain motives, the treatment of which varies but little except in so far as it follows general changes, such as are set forth and discussed in any history of literature, in manner and diction and what may be called the rhetorical evolution of style. The other is the emergence from time to time, in that superficial uniformity, of a new imaginative quality: a new power of vision, one might call it, on the part of a poet, or, in another way of regarding the matter, a new power of making itself visible on the part of Oxford. The eye changes; but what makes the eye change is (among other causes) the effective impact on it of new vibrations.

Of the persistent physical charm of Oxford this is the last place where there is any occasion to speak: and hardly less obvious is her persistent sentimental charm, the charm which she exercises over even the stupidest and most prosaic, and which, or some fragment of which, they all take away with them when they leave as her parting gift. Both of these have always been a theme for poetry. Among the colleges there have never failed to be nests of singing-birds. In presence or in absence, each breaks into some variation of the familiar theme:

> "And I'll be sworn upon't that he loves her:
> For here's a paper written in his hand,
> A halting sonnet of his own pure brain."

The theme is throughout nearly the same: it is set out in its barest form by a minor Elizabethan when he writes of

> "Ancient Oxford, noble nurse of skill,
> A city seated rich in everything,
> Girt with wood, water, pasture, corn and hill."

Here a few straightforward words are used to convey the meaning. The art is primitive. Detail is ignored; sentiment, rhetoric, romance, introspection are all absent. On that simple theme successive ages and fashions have woven their descants, their methodical figurings, their *fioriture* and their massed chromatic harmonies. We pass gradually to the rhetorical involutions of the seventeenth century, to the sober and restricted clarity of the eighteenth, to the sentimental, introspective and romantic handling of the nineteenth, and finally to the composite eclecticism of our own day.

In any style and at any period the great mass of Oxford poetry—as indeed is true of the great mass of any poetry—has no light proceeding from itself and of its own, no imaginative and creative value. It is only of interest historically; but that interest is often very great. Let me cite two characteristic examples, one at the beginning, the other towards the end, of the eighteenth century.

> "Wheresoe'er I turn my wandering eyes
> Aspiring towers and verdant groves arise;
> Immortal greens the smiling plains array,
> And mazy rivers murmur all the way.

> Aloft in state the airy towers arise,
> And with new lustre deck the wondering skies.
> Lo, to what height the schools ascending reach,
> Built with that art that they alone can teach!
> The lofty dome expands her spacious gate
> Where all the decent Graces jointly wait.
> Here colleges in sweet confusion rise;
> There temples seem to reach their native skies.
> See how the matchless youth their hours improve
> And in the glorious way to knowledge move!
> Pure to the soul and pleasing to the eyes,
> Like angels youthful and like angels wise."

It is hardly surprising that Isis should, as the author of these lines goes on to say it does, "boast more bards than Helicon," if work of this quality is all to which they aspire.

Eighty years later, the Muse of Tickell is succeeded by the Muse of Hurdis.

> "So on thy banks too, Isis, have I strayed
> A tassel'd student. Witness you who shar'd
> My morning walk, my ramble at high noon,
> My evening voyage, an unskilful sail,
> To Godstow bound or some inferior port,
> For strawberries and cream. What have we found,
> In life's austerer hours, delectable
> As the long day so loitered? Ye profound
> And serious heads, who guard the twin retreats
> Of British learning, give the studious boy
> His due indulgence. Let him range the field,
> Frequent the public walk, and freely pull
> The yielding oar."

I have chosen these passages, from among scores of others, for two particular reasons. In the first place, they are by Professors of Poetry (or to be strict, the latter by a Professor, the former by a Deputy-Professor) and thus bear the hall-mark of what was considered, in their time, the proper manner in which the poetry of Oxford should be handled. In the second place, you can hardly have failed to notice that they sound like deliberate parodies of Pope and Wordsworth. The same might be said of many unsuccessful imitations. But the interesting thing here is that these are not imitations at all. The only curses that Pope and Wordsworth could call down on them would be the curses invoked on those *qui ante nos nostra dixerunt*. When they were written, neither Pope in the one case nor Wordsworth in the other had appeared on the horizon. Oxford was exploring, was showing the way.

The sense of the poetry of places, as distinguished from mere description on the one hand or from a purely ethical or philosophic treatment on the other, is one of the things we owe to that great germinal age, the latter half of the eighteenth century. Panegyrical pieces (to use a term the convenience of which may justify its employment) hardly come into account; for it is seldom that under any but a very loose definition they fall within the sphere of poetry at all. Apart from these it is not until the eighteenth century that the poetry of places becomes important: and it is not until the middle of the century that it takes on itself the inner and finer spirit of poetry. If we accept the common and roughly accurate statement that Denham's *Cooper's Hill*, which appeared in 1642, is the first of purely descriptive English poems, it is exactly a century from that point before we come to the beginnings of a new poetical method, which did not, as purely descriptive poetry does, impose a poetical treatment on places, but sought to bring out from them their own latent poetical quality. Gray's Eton Ode, written in 1742, was the earliest distinct example of the new method. It is still overweighted by the ethical treatment characteristic of its age; but in its fusion of description and sentiment, and still more, in the imaginative sympathy by which it merges both in something different in kind from either, it is the prelude of a new era. The voice we hear in it is not only that of Gray speaking of Eton; it is also, and very vitally, the voice of Eton speaking through Gray. We can speak thenceforth, as we could not have spoken before, of the poetry of Eton. A little later, Gainsborough began to do the same thing in the sister art of painting.

It is not so easy to fix a precise date, or to name a single poem, which enables us to say in this sense that the poetry of Oxford begins there. But the name which marks the turning-point is that of another Professor of Poetry, Thomas Warton. He is better known now as a historian than as a poet. But his poetry, though not great in amount and hardly of the first quality, is by no means negligible, and is historically very significant. Percy's *Reliques* were published during Warton's tenure of the Chair of Poetry; and Warton took up the history of English poetry where Gray's hesitation and fastidiousness had dropped it. The three names stand together in the movement which created a revolution in taste, and prepared the way for a new age of poetry. To some extent all three suffered from being in advance of their time. It was only the next generation that came into their inheritance, and it was only much later that the effect of their work was realised. It is a small matter but rather suggestive, and I have never seen it noticed, that the exquisite motto from Euripides prefixed by Palgrave to the *Golden Treasury* had already served the same purpose on the title-page of Warton's *Miscellaneous Pieces*.

In Warton's poems, several of which deal either expressly or incidentally with the poetry of Oxford, we can see not merely the growth of a new sensibility, but the creation of a new imaginative value. He had begun, as a young man, in the convention of his predecessors. Take, for instance, the characteristic passage from the *Triumph of Isis*, written in 1749, beginning:

> "Ye fretted pinnacles, ye fanes sublime,
> Ye towers that wear the mossy vest of time,
> Ye massy piles of old munificence
> At once the pride of Learning and defence;
> Ye cloisters pale that length'ning to the sight
> To contemplation step by step invite;
> Ye high-arch'd walks where oft the whispers clear
> Of harps unseen have swept the poet's ear;
> Ye temples dim where pious duty pays
> Her holy hymns of ever-echoing praise;
> Lo! your lov'd Isis from the bordering vale
> With all a mother's fondness bids you hail."

Such a passage, with its clattering movement and mechanical enumeration, might have been written by any one at any time during the previous fifty years— or for that matter during the following fifty, and even more; for the persistence of the old tradition among Oxford versifiers is remarkable. But a dozen years later, in the *Complaint of Cherwell*, the breath of a new imaginative movement is distinctly perceptible through a rhythm and diction which still remain largely those of the Augustan school.

> "All pensive from her osier-woven bower
> Cherwell arose. Around her darkening edge
> Pale eve began the steaming mist to pour,
> And breezes fann'd by fits the rustling sedge."

Not only is there direct and loving observation of nature in these lines; there is also the germ of that imaginative sympathy with nature which was to give poetry a new language and a revived life. We can foresee the time coming when a poet could say of a place or scene that it haunted him like a passion. But the imaginative passion had first to throw off from itself, to burn its way through, layer after layer of sentiment or of convention.

The two Oxford poets of the end of the eighteenth century are Russell and Bowles. They were contemporaries and schoolfellows. Russell, the higher of the two in promise and the finer in accomplishment, died at twenty-six, having written but little, although that little included what Warton's biographer calls, in terms of eulogy which are not so extravagant as they might seem, "sonnets than which are none better in the English language." But of these his Oxford sonnets are not the best, and would not by themselves justify any such claim.

Russell died before he had established a reputation: Bowles outlived his. What keeps him from being altogether forgotten is the fact that his little volume of sonnets was what gave a decisive impulse to the developing powers of Coleridge. In its time it had a most unusual success and influence: it passed through nine editions between 1789, when it first appeared, and 1805. In the sonnets on Oxford the new note tentatively struck by Warton is now sounded quite clearly. They are sentimentally imaginative; and the formal classical diction is fading away before a new simplicity and harmony.

"Peace be within thy walls!
I scarce have heart to visit thee"—

the elegiac grace of such a cadence as this points forward to the age of romanticism. In his beautiful elegy on the death of Russell, we hear the note which was to be struck with a fuller tone long afterwards in

Arnold's *Thyrsis*, especially in the contrast between the eternal and serene youth of Oxford and the passing away of youth and serenity from those whose life, for a few brief years, made one music with hers; when, as Bowles writes,

> "We heard the merry bells by Isis' stream
> And thought our way was strewed with fairy flowers."

Forty years later, Bowles writes again, in the bewilderment felt by a survivor from an earlier age, of a new world in which

> "All are poets in this land of song,
> And every field chinks with its grasshopper."

The chinking of those grasshoppers has now long ago faded away, has become forgotten and inaudible. We can hear now, uninterrupted by their din, the few nightingale notes. In May 1820 Wordsworth, passing through Oxford on his way to London and the Continent, was inspired to that magnificent sonnet which is the most splendid of all the tributes ever paid to Oxford the enchantress:

> "Ye sacred nurseries of blooming youth!
> In whose collegiate shelter England's flowers
> Expand, enjoying through their vernal hours
> The air of liberty, the light of truth;
> Much have ye suffered from Time's gnawing tooth;
> Yet, O ye spires of Oxford! domes and towers!
> Gardens and groves! your presence overpowers
> The soberness of reason; till, in sooth,
> Transformed, and rushing on a bold exchange,
> I slight my own beloved Cam, to range
> Where silver Isis leads my stripling feet;
> Pace the long avenue, or glide adown
> The stream-like windings of that glorious street—
> An eager novice robed in fluttering gown!"

He was for the moment carried completely out of

himself: in a second sonnet he makes a sort of shamefaced apology.

> "Shame on this faithless heart, that could allow
> Such transport, though but for a moment's space:
> Not while, to aid the spirit of the place,
> The crescent moon cleaves with its glittering prow
> The clouds, or nightbird sings from shady bough,
> But in plain daylight!"

The spirit of the place, now fully realised, and perhaps now fully realised for the first time, as an incarnation of poetry, had intoxicated him. Just five years later, on such another May day in 1825, the same intoxication, in its still more potent effect on a poet who was in his first youth, and who was not only in Oxford but of it, inspired Beddoes to a lyrical outburst that sets him for a moment by the side of Keats. It is the poetry of Oxford in one of its loveliest phases, the spirit of the summer term incarnate.

> "In every tower that Oxford has is swung
> Quick, loud, or solemn, the monotonous tongue
> Which speaks Time's language, the universal one
> After the countenance of moon or sun,
> Translating their still motions to the earth.
> I cannot read: the reeling belfry's mirth
> Troubles my senses; therefore, Greek, shut up
> Your dazzling pages; covered be the cup
> Which Homer has beneath his mantle old
> Steamy with boiling life; your petals fold,
> You fat, square blossoms of the yet young tree
> Of Britain-grafted, flourishing Germany.
> Hush, Latin, to your grave; and with the chime
> My pen shall turn the minutes into rhyme . . .
> So come, shake London from thy skirts away:
> So come, forget not it is England's May.
> For Oxford, ho! Here thou at morn shalt see
> Spring's dryad-wakening whisper call the tree
> And move it to green answers: and beneath,
> Each side the river which the fishes breathe,

THE POETRY OF OXFORD 241

> Daisies and grass, whose lips were never stirred
> Or dews made tremulous but by foot of bird:
> And here a primrose pale beneath a tree,
> And here a cowslip longing for its bee,
> And violets and lilies every one
> Grazing in the great pasture of the sun."

Just at that point came a check. The Oxford Movement is formally dated as having been born on the 14th of July 1833: it formally came to its conclusion on the 8th of October 1845. During these twelve years, and for a period extending both before and after them for some years more, Oxford, and with it the poetry of Oxford in so far as it was a vital function of the place, was deflected violently from its course.

Anglicanism has produced vast quantities of verse, mostly bad, but often refined and melodious. Oxford itself, as one would expect, figures in the poems of Keble. It figures still more largely in the poems of those others who are already almost forgotten names, or retain a precarious and ghostly life in anthologies where the collector has cast his net widely. In the *Minstrelsy of Isis* may be found ten or a dozen specimens of Faber, at once the most prolific and the most graceful of the school. In these poems he embodied the spirit of Oxford as he felt it—a combination of religious and antiquarian sentiment with a real and keen sense of natural beauty. While he and the other Anglican poets were still writing and still held the field, the revolution overtook them. In the year 1853 the volume of poems appeared which included the *Scholar Gipsy*.

When we speak of the poetry of Oxford, it is of the *Scholar Gipsy* and of *Thyrsis* that we immediately and instinctively think. These two poems seem to include or to blot out nearly everything else. It would be idle to analyse them; it would be useless to praise them. If I were to begin quoting from them now it would be impossible to stop. After more than half a century they preserve their radiance and magic unimpaired. Description more exquisite than the city and her lovely surroundings had ever received before is fused in them with a faultless power of imaginative interpretation. The only way in which it is possible to criticise them is simply to read them, pausing in every verse over some new felicity of phrase or epithet— —" the warm green-muffled Cumnor hills "—" those wide fields of breezy grass where black-winged swallows haunt the glittering Thames "—" the causeway chill where home through flooded fields foot-travellers go "— " bluebells trembling by the forest ways "—" threshers in the mossy barns "—" boys who in lone wheatfields scare the rooks," and in the centre of all, felt rather than described, " that sweet city with her dreaming spires," Oxford herself like the soul of poetry.

Words would be wasted on these poems; and the more so, because whatever can be said of them, and of the spirit or personality of Oxford which they embody, has been excellently said in another form. Mr. Reginald Fanshawe's *Corydon*, an elegiac and reflective poem of great skill and beauty, has done this. If I deny myself the pleasure of quoting from it, it is only because the limits of space forbid. Those who do not know it already will I am sure be grateful to me if I cause them to make its acquaintance.

The *Scholar Gipsy* has sunk into the common consciousness; it is inseparable from Oxford; it is the poetry of Oxford made, in some sense, complete. But it would be curious to find out—and it could be more or less found out—whether its effect was at all immediate. I fancy it was not. Arnold used to complain half humorously of being an unpopular author, and he was certainly for a long time not a popular poet. The Oxford poem of 1853 which had vogue and fame was of a very different quality; it was the Installation Ode to the Earl of Derby. It is amazing to read the Ode and think that its glittering mechanical rhetoric could have ever been accepted, then or at any time, as expressing the poetry of Oxford. It is like a stained-glass window of the same period. Isis keeps a silver requiescat all night long; the moon walks up and down among the starry fires; dying pleasure sings with sweet and swanlike tone. The climax is where Oxford herself, in whose mouth the main part of the poem is placed, bethinks herself that she has said enough in her own glorification, and breaks off with this happy turn:

> "But night is fading—I must deck my hair
> For the high pageant of the gladsome morn.
> I would not meet my chosen Stanley there
> In sorrow or in scorn."

It was the epoch of mid-Victorianism triumphant; a period to which time is beginning now to lend the enchantment of distance, but which artists who lived in it found hard to bear.

In these two poems of Arnold's it might seem that the poetry of Oxford had reached not merely completion, but finality. But in poetry there is no finality. Progress is the essence of its being. And the spirit of Oxford, though it is persistent and continuous, also changes, shifts, develops, revealing fresh depths to new eyes, or expanding to fresh embodiments under a new touch. We may say that in Arnold the poetry of Oxford at last became fully articulate. It might be better to put it that the poetry of Oxford before him and the poetry of Oxford after him are different things. The book did not close with him; there are pages of it since opened, there are pages still unwritten.

In such matters prose is more definite than poetry, or at least, it lends itself to a clearer definition. What the spirit of Oxford is to different minds, all of them approaching it at a high imaginative tension, may be illustrated by a few quotations, all very brief, and all highly charged with meaning.

Keats writes in 1817: "This Oxford, I have no doubt, is the finest city in the world—it is full of old Gothic buildings, spires, towers, quadrangles, cloisters, groves, &c., and is surrounded with more clear streams than ever I saw together."

The words are singularly like those I quoted already from an Elizabethan poet; they have the same clean definition, the same primitive directness of vision. In sharp contrast to them is this passage by Hazlitt written a little later:

"There is an air about it resonant of joy and hope: it speaks with a thousand tongues to the heart: it waves its mighty shadow over the imagination: it stands in lovely sublimity on the hill of ages, and points with prophetic fingers to the sky: it greets the eager gaze from afar, with glistening spires and pinnacles adorned, that shine with an eternal light as with the lustre of setting suns; and a dream and a glory hover round its head, as the spirits of former times, a throng of intellectual shapes, are seen retreating or advancing to the eye of Memory: its streets are paved with the names of learning that can never wear out: its green quadrangles breathe the silence of thought, conscious of the weight of yearnings innumerable after the past, of loftiest aspirations

THE POETRY OF OXFORD 245

for the future: Isis babbles of the Muse, its waters are from the springs of Helicon, its Christ Church meadows classic Elysian fields."

The substance of this passage (which, for all its splutter of redundant rhetoric, is perfectly sincere) is the common theme of the lesser, the uninspired, Oxford poets. They are often feeling after something else, and something better worth saying; but this, in one form of words or another, is all they can manage to say.

Next to it let me put the famous sentence from the Preface to Arnold's *Essays in Criticism*, with its unequalled combination of beauty and satire. It is the magnificently ironic answer of Oxford herself to those who approach her in the spirit of Hazlitt. Even Heine never excelled this picture of a queen of romance, grown a little elderly, but unravaged by intellectual life.

"Beautiful city! so venerable, so lovely, so serene! steeped in sentiment as she lies, spreading her gardens to the moonlight, and whispering from her towers the last enchantments of the Middle Age: adorable dreamer, whose heart has been so romantic, home of lost causes, and forsaken beliefs, and unpopular names, and impossible loyalties! what example could ever so inspire us, what teacher could ever so save us?"

The next passage I quote is but a single phrase, leaping out at high imaginative tension, and extraordinary in the way in which it reveals and fixes an image like something seen by a lightning flash. It comes, apropos of nothing, in the middle of the talk between Will Green and the man from Essex in the *Dream of John Ball*.

"'Hast thou seen Oxford, scholar?'

"A vision of grey-roofed houses and a long winding

street and the sound of many bells came over me at that word as I nodded 'yes' to him."

Now once more, pass away from all these to another appreciation of Oxford, perhaps the most remarkable of all in its dark passion and haunting significance. It is by the only survivor now left of the great Victorian writers; and Mr. Hardy, although it is in the art of prose that he is pre-eminent, has also the instinct and the accomplishment of a poet. Here there is no vivid single objective impression; the effect is got by subtle accumulation and suggestion. It is the voice of a new world: or rather of a world infinitely old, but become newly and appallingly articulate.

"It was a windy, whispering, moonless night. After many turnings he came up to the first ancient mediæval pile that he had encountered. It was a college, as he could see by the gateway. Close to this college was another; and a little further on another; and then he began to be encircled as it were with the breath and sentiment of the city. A bell began clanging, and he listened till a hundred and one strokes had sounded. He must have made a mistake, he thought; it was meant for a hundred. High against the black sky the flash of a lamp would show crocketed pinnacles and indented battlements. Down obscure alleys, apparently never trodden now by the foot of man, and whose very existence seemed to be forgotten, there would jut out into the path porticoes, oriels, doorways of enriched and florid middle-age design. He began to be impressed with the isolation of his own personality. Seeming almost his own ghost, he gave his thoughts to the other ghostly presences with which the nooks were haunted. He saw that his destiny lay not with these, but among the manual toilers in the shabby purlieu which he himself occupied, unrecognised as part of the city at all by its visitors and panegyrists, yet without whose denizens the hard readers could not read nor the high thinkers live."

Arnold was of the transition. Wandering, in his own melancholy words, between two worlds, one dead, the other powerless to be born, he had the genius to fix the portraiture of the older Oxford as it was just before it began to pass away. Since then both the outward aspect and the inner life and spirit of Oxford have been in the course of a continuous and vast revolution, a revolution whose vastness only fails to impress us because it is masked by its continuity. The first distinct new note after him in the poetry of Oxford is the note of distress and pain at the effects of that revolution when they began to manifest themselves. Thirty years ago, that note was beautifully struck in a sonnet, the form and spirit of which are alike characteristic of the period, and are not, in my judgment, unworthy of the subject. I hope I shall not alarm the modesty of Mr. Bowyer Nichols by quoting his lines; but indeed it is a regret shared by all his friends that he has let the world see so little of his fine insight and delicate craftsmanship. "Here in these walks," he wrote then,—in the walks of Magdalen—

> "Here in these walks where May brings June to birth
> Peace reigns and rest: these leafy aisles are free
> From harm of axe and hammer; every tree
> Dense-clad with summer and shrill-tongued with mirth.
> Spirit of beauty, very God on earth,
> Earth loves thee ever and is loved of thee.
> Is it by man alone that thou must see
> Wrong done thee, thankless change and waste and dearth?
> Nay, but thou lovedst us too in days gone by.

> Wilt thou not turn and visit us in pity,
> Here, where thou once wast wont to show thy face
> To those whose sons forget thee or deny,
> Before they have destroyed thy holy city
> And quite laid waste what was thy dwelling place?"

That is almost the last note of the romantic revival, of the movement which vainly strove to recreate the past and lay an arresting hand on the present. But poetry, like life, had to move on.

The main effort of art since then, not of the art of poetry only, has been to find a new language. Descriptive poetry and descriptive painting had both done all they could. To continue on the same lines meant that art was becoming academic once more, that it was being given over to secondary emotions and an increasing imaginative unreality. Like the new painting, the new poetry set itself to the task of reproducing life not as something solid and outlined, but as fluid, impalpable, cognisable only as a complex of impressions: even these impressions only existing, for the purposes of art, in the emotion which they evoke. The older art had mastered a language in which it could express form and action; the language sought by the newer art was one which should express atmosphere. The two kinds of art are not hostile to one another, though their followers often are; they deal with the same matter; but they approach it in a different way.

Of this impressionist poetry, where atmosphere and emotion are everything, the poetry of Oxford offers one remarkable example. There are those among us who, like myself, have grown up in and stand by the more ancient tradition; but we too can recognise, with hope and gratitude, that this new language in poetry can do things which the other could not; and that it can do them so as to create beauty, so as to reincarnate and reinterpret life. There are many methods of art: there are only two kinds of art, good and bad: and if two pieces of art fret and clash, it is only because, and in so far as, one or the other, or both, are bad art.

About fifteen years ago, a series of tiny volumes of poetry came out, in paper covers, under the name of the Shilling Garland. It went on, I think, for a dozen numbers or so before it gently disappeared. The greater number of the authors were Oxford poets. The late Canon Dixon contributed a selection of his austere and refined lyrics. There was a volume of short poems by Mr. Bridges—who is not only an Oxford poet but also, in more than one ode or elegy of exquisite finish and high temper, an interpreter of the poetry of Oxford. There was the first, or all but the first, flower of the Muse of Mr. Binyon, distinguished even then by a singular gravity and sweetness. But among all the rest there is a single poet and a single poem outstanding; and these were the creator and the creation of a new Oxford poetry. The poet was Mrs. Woods; the poem, which gave its name to the little volume, was called *Aëromancy*.

"All art," Pater said, "constantly aspires towards the condition of music: and the perfection of poetry seems to depend in part on a certain suppression of mere subject, so that the meaning reaches us through ways not distinctly traceable by the understanding." Just at present music itself is perhaps the most living and most interpretative of the arts as actually practised: however this may be, the new quality in poetry which came of its greater approximation towards the condition of music has the effect of giving to poetry a fresh medium of expression.

This poem, by virtue of the new method in fine and capable hands, captures and embodies the inmost spirit of Oxford. The opening lines of *Aëromancy* bear a singular verbal likeness to those I have already quoted from Beddoes, that wayward and ineffectual genius who felt poetry so keenly and did so little with it. But the likeness is external; the contrast is vital.

> "The watchers on the everlasting towers,
> Blind watchers of bright heaven, the bells who own
> No changing years, but the unchanging hours—
>
> Listen! they strike; a sinister monotone
> Deep as all time. The same sound, and who hears
> Could be the same, did she not hear alone.
>
> Those iron tongues have portioned out our years
> Indifferently, with fateful rumours blown
> About the solemn spires and aery tiers
>
> Of clustered pinnacles, and far unknown
> Utterance that communes with the void. It fills
> The valley broadening round their ancient throne
> Out to the edges of the violet hills."

This is the new method in art, used by a strong and delicate hand. Without any disastrous loss of either form or colour, the artist, working in a medium where language approximately reaches the effect of music, is able to give a new expression to atmosphere and emotion. The poet, piercing further inward below the surface, draws the spirit of poetry from deeper recesses. It is what Wordsworth had done a century before; it is what poetry is perpetually doing, perpetually has to do, that it may keep itself alive by getting afresh at the sources of life. The poetry of Oxford has here become transmuted and essentialised into the poetry of a secret garden—*hortus conclusus,*

THE POETRY OF OXFORD

fons signatus—such as that garden and fountain whose image it goes on to create in a passage that follows:

> "How in yon high-walled garden has mine ear
> Hung on their imminent voices, where the yew
> Darkens above each grey majestic pier
>
> Of the antique gate. 'Tis closed: none passes through.
> But in the unfooted mimic theatre
> A fountain springs, scattering a lonely dew.
>
> Time was this formal garden seemed our own,
> So world-forgot and beautiful: the glow
> Of its great flowers, the birds that as alone
>
> Made sparkling sport upon the fountain's rim,
> Its diamond drip into the pool, o'ergrown
> With iris and pale reed, the skyey, slim
>
> Poplar that still October turns to flame,
> All was our own—the couchant monsters grim
> Remember it: and the bells sound the same."

That garden is Oxford. It is indeed an actual garden, one we pass by, or even may enter, any day; but for the poet it is only the point at which Oxford is made imaginatively visible. The music of the poetry calls out, attaches, gathers up about that point, the spirit of Oxford, and makes it speak.

It speaks again, retracing the process through which it formed itself. *O what is this that knows the road I came?* that single line of Rossetti, by a sort of triumphant magic, had already said the thing once for all.

> "Hour after hour most ignorantly I heard.
> A certain night, a warm and obscure night,
> On a dim lawn I found the master-word.
>
> Dawn and high day, wan visitings of light
> Out of the haunting moon, come to the bells:
> Heaven's horologe turns in their darkling sight.

Blind aëromancers, from their hollow cells
Float forth the eyeless ghosts of all hours dead
With voices hidden as the sigh in shells.

The living hour leaps clangorous overhead
To living ears. A thin ethereal
Long sound pursues, the sweep of pinions spread,

Rushing they knew not whither, and the call
Of the oblivious ghosts wild-whispering
To dust of unremembered burial.

. . . That Hour forbore

To come again and whisper all she knew.
Young was she yet, and taught me first her own
Young secret. Hark! the ancient hours renew

Their solemn solitary undertone;
And I do hear them, yet as one who hears
A talk confused in a tongue half-known,

With hints of roaring battle, hopes and fears,
And festival and music and shrill play,
Of loves forgotten and forgotten tears,

And one grey murmur under arches grey—
The sigh of cloistral hours that fain would tell
Of how they stole and stole long lives away,
Issueless, void, alike, innumerable."

Is poetry trying here to do more than poetry can do? To this question, of whatever poem it is asked, there is but one answer: nothing is more than poetry can do; for poetry, as Shelley said of it in words not less true than noble, is the very image of life expressed in its eternal truth. But even if we vary the question and ask whether it is trying here to do something different from what it can do, trying to pass beyond itself and become another art, the answer must still I think be the same. To determine whether it can do anything or not, there is but one criterion; does it do it? The progress of poetry, as I have over and over again insisted, is traceable from now backward to the remotest part, but is incalculable from now forward to the nearest future. Any day it may effect, to all seeming with effortless ease, what it has never done yet. It may master the new language of atmosphere and emotion as completely as it mastered, long ago, the language of description and reflection.

In stanzas added as an epilogue to this poem, the author returns to more familiar ways. Perhaps this is the most beautiful passage in the whole poem. It also concentrates and presents the poetry of Oxford, with a fresh delicacy and sweetness. But it does so now through the old and known methods (though enriched, I think, by the influence of the new language); through description, through visual images quickened by imagination. The poetry of Oxford here is all crowded, as though in a magic convex mirror, into one corner of it, a house and garden in Holywell—as Holywell was then.

> "There was a summer silence in the street
> Where half the shouldering gables caught the sun,
> Your bloomy window fragrant in the heat.
>
> Methought 'twas but a little way to run
> To cross your threshold; then a shadowy space;
> Reach the gay garden and yourself and one
>
> Standing amid her flowers. In many a place
> Does this white moon of May find multitude
> Of flowers more beautiful than her own face:
>
> What long glades pale with hawthorn, what bedewed
> Soft slopes o'erspangled with the cowslips' sheen
> And nested primroses, a late lone brood.
>
> Through nets of delicate shadow she hath seen
> The sea-blue splendour of wild hyacinths spread
> Up Wytham woods, under the first fresh green:

O'er foamy orchards her young light is shed
And flash of wilding blossom and the pride
Of country gardens richly tapestried

With royal tulips sumptuously dyed
Purple and gold and sanguine, striped and smeared,
Or pure in their keen colour as a bride

Is in her whiteness. Yet as oft she peered
Over the black tower, smiling silverly,
In yonder strip of city earth appeared

As crowded wealth of flowers as she might see
By ample lawns o'erflowed with ministrant air,
Or hollow coverts none explore save she."

This is the poetry of Oxford speaking still in the same language as that of the *Scholar Gipsy*, though in a different manner and with a different accent; and also, I may add, with a new grace.

For this is a woman's poetry, and may be the beginning of more. To Oxford men Oxford is, or at least has been, so much a part of themselves that they are in some ways almost unconscious of it. To see a thing as it is, one must be a little outside it. It is part of the relation of Oxford men to Oxford (and part of Oxford's special charm), that they never get quite outside of Oxford; or if they do, it is either through indifference or through hostility—neither of them keys to unlock the springs of poetry. Here we have a poet who with a knowledge of Oxford as nearly as may be complete, yet not absorbed into its machinery, and not having merged her own personality into its corporate life, has been able to express, with an intimacy and suggestiveness not attained by other poets, the Oxford atmosphere, the Oxford emotion.

Genius is individual. But the adjustment now in

process between the differentiated complexes of sensibility, interpretative faculty and discursive intelligence —I apologise for using such long words—otherwise known as men and women, suggests and already shows, not in this instance or in this sphere alone, further possibilities. A little volume of poems, *Leaves in the Wind*, was recently published in Oxford by a new author, who chooses to be known under the name of Elsa Lorraine. She is, as Mr. Armstrong tells us in a prefatory note, in the strictest sense a daughter of the University, though not of course a member of it, and not even of British blood on either side. In these poems we find, as Mr. Armstrong goes on to say with exact and admirable truth, " the Oxford atmosphere tempered or transmuted by an imagination which is not of Oxford." The workmanship in these poems is still tentative; the imagination has not yet found its wings. But in some of them which are specifically poems of Oxford there is, very distinct, the new note of which I have been speaking. A sonnet on the Radcliffe Square, overcharged with imperfectly fused thought and imperfectly refined expression, is nevertheless entirely original and very remarkable: and the same praise may be given with even less reservation to another on St. Mary's Church—a subject which a hundred artists have tried to translate into language and which will still tempt a hundred others. Arnold, as it happened, never touched it. The passage which of all I know comes nearest to putting its poetry into words is not even by a poet at all; it is a casual sentence in Henry Kingsley's *Ravenshoe*. Or again, we may compare with the subtle technique and insight of *Aëromancy* a fragment in Elsa Lorraine's volume on the vision of the entrance into Oxford from the east— still incomparably lovely in spite of all that modern changes have done to spoil it since Mr. Nichols wrote the sonnet I quoted already—the verses beginning:

> "The curtain wrought in green and gold
> Of the twelve poplars by the bridge
> Autumn-day after autumn-day
> More slender and transparent grows."

The lines are imaginatively symbolic. For the inner movement of poetry now is towards making description or narrative more and more translucent, towards making external things the veil or atmosphere through which the soul is seen, out of which the soul takes form and substance.

Oxford is in transition; no one needs to be told of this. Poetry is in transition, as it always is and always will be. And the poetry of Oxford is in transition likewise. I have indicated one side of the new development which we may conjecture it to be taking. Others, not less important, are more distant and as yet more obscure. The enormous expansion which Oxford is undergoing on every side and in every aspect of her life involves changes equally great in what may be called the spirit or personality of Oxford, in her impact on the poetic imagination, her vivifying power upon art. And if art is seeking a new language, this "ancient Oxford, noble nurse of skill," may do much towards developing that language; the more so now that she draws into herself, and enriches herself with, the youth, the enthusiasm, the inherited or acquired aptitudes of a larger world: while she still retains her own high intellectual tradition, and much of her own distinctive, perennial, and incommunicable charm.

Unpoetical periods are periods of poetical germination. The spirit of poetry, like sap in winter, withdraws into its central springs, to pass there in silence through secret changes and prepare itself for a new resurgence. Meanwhile the visible life of art runs low; belief wavers, aims fluctuate; creative imagination disappears behind piled outworks of research, criticism, and experiment. The poet, in every age, is under the impression that he has been born too late; and that cry is generally most audible just at the times when poetry is on the verge of its greatest movements and its most splendid achievements.

One thing at least is certain; and that is, that just as Oxford herself is passing through a process of expansion and modernisation, the poetry of Oxford, the imaginative pattern and interpretation of Oxford life, must undergo a corresponding change. It will not go on indefinitely re-weaving the pattern of a fading past, sentimentalising over an academic tradition.

> "The elms are bare, the creepers die
> In scarlet on the wall:
> It is a place of ghosts, and I
> Am ghostlier than all "—

this verse, from a recent poem by one of the most graceful of the modern Oxford poets, Mr. St. John Lucas, expresses a mood which merely leads poetry up a blind alley. Oxford is a place of ghosts only to those who have become ghosts themselves.

My colleague Professor Holmes in his recent volume, *Notes on the Science of Picture Making*,—a book which may be read with great interest and profit by others as well as by painters—just touches on the future of painting. He indicates or suggests that the future of that art may lie in the development of what may be called socialist painting. This is so with poetry also. Oxford has opened not only her gates, but her eyes; she is realising the world. And no poetry in future will be the poetry of Oxford in any full sense which does not take account of more than Oxford poetry has hitherto taken account of; which does not take account of those other lives whose destiny is included with ours, those without whom the readers could not read, nor the artists live. The seven seals of the book which this University bears on her arms have been one by one opened. At the opening of the last there is silence; but it is in that silence that the seven angels take their trumpets and prepare themselves to sound.

IMAGINATION

THE word imagination, like most of the terms used to express vital and organic functions, is vague and ambiguous. Of those who have, whether of set purpose or incidentally, dealt with imagination as a quality or essence in poetry, the greater number have either not defined the term at all, or have given some definition of it which has not satisfied any one except themselves. Both courses are open to exception. But the former of them, the absence of any definition, is the source of much confusion; for there are fallacies which the existence of some definition, even if it were only approximate and provisional, would at once render obvious, but which in the absence of anything of the sort may elude observation and must in any case perplex argument. The defence made for avoiding definition would probably be the same as is made for refusing to define poetry; namely, that in a general way, the import of the term is a matter of common knowledge, and that any attempt to define it more closely only leads to wrangling over abstractions without adding anything to real knowledge, or even to real clearness of thought.

It is true that a strict definition of any vital process, just as of life itself, is theoretically unattainable. Life cannot be subsumed under any larger concept, nor can it be expressed in terms of anything which is not itself alive. Poetry, as a function of life, is subject to the same law: and to carry the matter one step further, imagination as a function of poetry—for of poetry in the real and not merely the formal sense it will be agreed that imagination is a function and not an accident—likewise eludes definition. But in all these cases something short of a strict definition is discoverable—something that might rather be called, in the term with which modern criticism was enriched by Cardinal Newman, a note, or if that word be regarded as having slipped through over-use into meaninglessness, something that may be called, and is, a central guiding clue. It is discoverable, and it is not only discoverable, but is necessary. It will at the least keep critics from mutually chasing one another's shadows and never getting face to face, like Lysander and Demetrius in the wood. I wish in this lecture to discuss the matter so far as may enable us to clear our minds on certain points. So much is necessary towards any distinct appreciation of what is implied, when we speak, as we all do, of imagination as being in some sense the essence or principle of poetry; and so much is useful for practical guidance in the pursuit, not merely in the criticism, of poetry as an art. For like all arts, poetry is a matter very largely of sound craftsmanship; and sound craftsmanship is not an instinct, it is an acquisition. It can even, to a greater degree than is always recognised, be taught; it does not come without learning, without practice; and the learning will be more substantial, the practice more fruitful, if they are guided from first to last by clear thinking. The poet must know what he would be at; he must be conscious, whether through direct instruction or not, of certain things to be aimed at and of certain things to be avoided. Above all, he must know good art when he sees it; and this knowledge, while it largely comes, of itself as one might say, through habituation to good work, is made more solid and more certain if he is able to apply to any work, his own or that of others, a few very simple and practical criteria such as distinguish good work from bad.

The canons of art when stated seem very simple: but that is just their value; it is their simplicity which makes them applicable. The simpler they are, the more practical they are likewise: and they cannot be so simple that they may not be ignored or forgotten unless, by habit and training, we apply them uniformly and continuously. We may make mistakes in their application at first; but by continuing to apply them, the mistakes will tend to correct themselves; the judgment will become swifter and truer, until at last it will work without effort like an acquired instinct. It was one of the most fertile doctrines of William Morris that the appreciation of art is natural; that normal human beings are potential artists, and that in order to make this potentiality actual only two things are required: first, a little guidance at the beginning, such guidance as can be, and must be, given not in this only but in every field of life, by the master to the scholar, by the skilled craftsman to the apprentice, by experience to inexperience; and secondly, the clearing away of the mass of purely artificial obstacles created by false conventions, conventions false because they are, when looked at closely, meaningless.

Any definition, or quasi-definition, of imagination which I may incidentally propose in this discussion will then be personal and provisional; it will merely crystallise, or summarise, for a particular purpose, a particular way of regarding poetry. And the particular purpose in question is this: to connect it with a similarly provisional definition of poetry which I have already given, and to indicate how the two things play into one another and throw light upon one another.

The use of the word imagination as a term of art—I am using the phrase "term of art" in the lawyer's sense—is a comparatively modern thing: and modern usage, broadly speaking, all goes back to and starts from the doctrine struck out by Wordsworth and Coleridge in combination. This was first expounded at any length in Wordsworth's famous Supplementary Preface of 1815; it was worked out with great eloquence and brilliance, though as usual fragmentarily and incompletely, by Coleridge in the *Biographia Literaria* a couple of years later; and it was in fact the staple of the poetical criticism of both poets. Before that period there had been no attempt to fix the word down to a precise and technical meaning: and in particular, the terms imagination and fancy, on the distinction between which both Wordsworth and Coleridge laid such immense stress, had normally been used as interchangeable. "A faculty called imagination or fancy" was part of the accepted nomenclature of eighteenth-century psychology. It has indeed remained so in much modern usage, even that of authors who have employed language most carefully. A striking instance occurs in Darwin's *Descent of Man*. "By this faculty," he writes there, "man unites, independently of the will, former images and ideas, and thus creates brilliant and novel results." This singular statement, however we may turn it, is certainly not true of imagination in the Wordsworthian sense, whether or not it be true of the faculty which Wordsworth separates and distinguishes from imagination under the name of fancy. Imagination, in this usage, is a term indicating something capricious, inconsequent, and unreal. So we often speak of a description or account as being "imaginative" when we mean to say that it has no connexion, or only a slight connexion, with reality; that it is fanciful, and either untrue from the point of view of intelligence, or misleading from the point of view of conduct, or both.

It is interesting however to notice that if we go back much earlier, to a time before our language had been formalised and when Latin words were used more sparingly and more choicely, we shall find the term imagination often coupled with the term wisdom, with an implied sense of an affinity between the two things. Thus the author of *Piers Plowman* assigns both to the operative sphere of the *Spiritus prudentiae* and opposes them to "weening," or as we might say after Wordsworth, to fancy:

"Wenynge is no wysdome ne wyse ymagynacioun."

Similarly, "sage and imaginative" is a conjunction of words used by Berners in his *Froissart*, and elsewhere by other authors of the same period. Imagination was regarded as a quality of poetry in the sense in which the "sage poet" was the only worthy wearer of the laurel. It was the *alta fantasia* of Dante; a faculty so high that it only lost its power in face of the central splendour of Paradise. But we shall perhaps gain more insight into the power and scope of the word by looking at Shakespeare's use of it. For it is the central quality of Shakespeare's work that he uses language, not more closely or accurately, but more vitally, at a higher power and tension, than any other English writer. His use of a word does not help us directly towards its definition; but it gives us a new insight into its range and scope, its vital potency.

The *locus classicus* here is of course the famous speech of Theseus in Act v. of the *Midsummer Night's Dream*, and the comment made on it by Hippolyta. It is worth while quoting these in full:

> "More strange than true: I never may believe
> These antique fables, nor these fairy toys.
> Lovers and madmen have such seething brains,
> Such shaping fantasies, that apprehend
> More than cool reason ever comprehends.
> The lunatic, the lover and the poet
> Are of imagination all compact:
> One sees more devils than vast hell can hold,
> That is, the madman: the lover, all as frantic,
> Sees Helen's beauty in a brow of Egypt:
> The poet's eye, in a fine frenzy rolling,
> Doth glance from heaven to earth, from earth to heaven;
> And as imagination bodies forth
> The forms of things unknown, the poet's pen
> Turns them to shapes and gives to airy nothing
> A local habitation and a name.
> Such tricks hath strong imagination,
> That if it would but apprehend some joy
> It comprehends some bringer of that joy:
> Or in the night, imagining some fear,
> How easy is a bush supposed a bear!"

So Theseus discourses; and Hippolyta answers:

> "But all the story of the night told over,
> And all their minds transfigured so together,
> More witnesseth than fancy's images,
> And grows to something of great constancy:
> But howsoever, strange and admirable."

In this passage, which we are accustomed to quote fragmentarily and so to miss a great deal of its meaning, there are several things to notice. In the first place, we must carefully observe its dramatic quality. The speech is put into the mouth of Theseus: into the mouth, that is, of one of the most prosaic and unimaginative of Shakespeare's characters: the consummate type of what Arnold called the barbarian, and yet with a strong dash in him of the Philistine. The type is fully seized, and drawn with masterly accuracy. In this speech Theseus gives his notion of poetry, which is that of his class: he couples it with love and lunacy as a thing rejected by cool reason, abnormal and even morbid; something that his own superior common sense looks on with a sort of indulgent censure. Poetry is to him partly a frenzy—a fine frenzy, to be sure—and partly a trick. The poet is something between a child and a savage, whose imagination makes a bear out of a bush: the ponderous witticism is almost in the manner of a "beef-witted lord" like the Ajax of *Troilus and Cressida*.

But while the discourse is that of Theseus, the language is that of Shakespeare: his own swift insight and luminousness shape the phrases which Theseus uses, and the mind of Shakespeare glitters through them. The "seething brains" of which Theseus speaks with placid contempt are the human soul working at its highest power. The particular phraseology is, more than once, significant in the highest degree. He speaks of "shaping fantasies," of "strong imagination." The epithets are carefully chosen: they enforce the doctrine that imagination is not a weakness, but a strength, not a disintegrating, but a constructive force. Not only does it apprehend more than comes within the scope of "cool reason," of the mind working at low temperature; but it has the power of turning its apprehensions into comprehensions, of making them real, making them organic. It "bodies forth forms," it makes the unknown into the known by turning it to shapes. Hippolyta, already in training to become an ideal wife, feels that the account given of the matter by Theseus is confused and unintelligent, but does not say so; she merely, in a few gentle words, enters an implied protest against the acceptance of Theseus' views. Very characteristically, he does not even listen to what she says, but turns to another subject: for Bottom and his company are just filing on to the stage.

There are other passages in Shakespeare which reinforce the thought implied by him here, the view of imagination as something strong, large, and constructive. We can see this view in phrases like the "strong imagination" of Antonio in the *Tempest*, the "big imagination" of the Poet in *Timon*—one of the most brilliantly conceived and subtly modelled among Shakespeare's minor characters—or where Miranda speaks of imagination "forming a shape," and Hamlet of imagination "giving shape" to offences. Or again, where the Friar in *Much Ado* says:

"The idea of her life shall sweetly creep
Into his study of imagination,"

and where Hamlet once more says that imagination may trace the dust of Alexander, what is implied in the terms "study" and "trace" is nothing casual, erratic or irresponsible, but a process of the higher intelligence involving solid application and consequential reasoning. To this aspect of imagination as, in the full sense, a rational faculty, we shall have occasion to return. But for the present let us pass on to the doctrine set forth by Wordsworth and Coleridge.

That doctrine was slowly evolved by Wordsworth, according to his wont, through hard thinking and intense brooding over the depths of his own mind. In the Preface to the second edition of the *Lyrical Ballads* (1800), he still uses the word imagination in a customary and imperfectly defined sense. "The principal object proposed in these Poems," he writes there, " was to choose incidents and situations from common life and to relate or describe them throughout, as far as was possible, in a selection of language really used by men, and at the same time to throw over them a certain colouring of imagination whereby ordinary things should be presented to the mind in an unusual aspect." I have quoted these words in full, in order to avoid any possibility of misconception; what in them is relevant to the immediate point may now be repeated in an abridged form, and generalised, so as to apply the statement to poetry generally. "Poetry," the sentence would then run, " relates or describes chosen incidents and situations, at the same time throwing over them a colouring of imagination." Imagination here is something which gives a particular colour to the things which poetry presents; it is not something which gives them shape and structure, it only sets them in a new light. This may be called the normal and popular content of the term: the faculty, in its essence and effect, is not creative and organic, it is only illuminative; and this illumination, so far as the definition goes, may be either true or false, its specific "difference" being that it is unusual.

It is instructive to compare this with what Coleridge says in the *Biographia*, where he notes as the excellence of Wordsworth's poems their "balance of truth in observing with the imaginative faculty in modifying the objects observed, and above all, the original gift of spreading the tone and atmosphere of the ideal world around . . . incidents and situations." The toning or colouring power is here sharply distinguished from the imaginative faculty; and the latter is cursorily described as a modifying power.

This is Wordsworth's later doctrine, though it is hinted at rather than fully stated.

This doctrine is set out in the Preface of 1815, in the course of an enumeration of what Wordsworth calls the powers requisite for the production of poetry. These he sets down as observation and description, sensibility, reflection, invention, judgment, and together with these, "Imagination and Fancy to modify, to create, and to associate." Poems, he adds, may be arranged according to the power among all these which is predominant in their production. He attempted a classification of his own poems in this way, not to his own satisfaction, nor to the enlightenment of his readers. What he says about Fancy is acute, interesting and suggestive; yet it may be doubted whether it does not, through too strained and mechanical an antithesis, actually obscure the distinction which it is meant to illustrate; one is not without an uneasy feeling that he is apt to be guided, in assigning certain poems or passages to the heading of imagination and certain others to the heading of fancy, by no other criterion than that of a personal preference for the one poem or passage over the other. It is always to be borne in mind, in studying Wordsworth's criticism, that while on general principles he is sound and thorough, his application of them to particular instances is often bungling and occasionally even fantastic. He was so habituated to moving among the recesses of his own mind, among the deep springs of life, that when he emerges from them he is sometimes like an owl in the daylight. It is better, for the present purpose at least, to ignore what he says about fancy as something contrasted with imagination, and to stick to what he says about imagination itself; the more so that the antithesis, whatever value it may have as barely stated, is overlaid by him with so many incidental qualifications and reservations as to lose much of its significance. He speaks of fancy aiming at a rivalship with imagination, and imagination stooping to work with the materials of fancy. Fancy is also, he says, under her own laws a creative faculty; but he has just said that the law under which the processes of fancy are carried on is capricious, and its influence unstable or transitory. This comes dangerously near being a contradiction in terms; and when he adds that "fancy is given to beguile the temporal part of our nature, imagination to incite and to support the eternal," he is writing like Coleridge rather than like himself, evading the point in a luminous haze of sentiment and rhetoric. The preface, as you may remember, breaks off abruptly; the reason which he himself assigns for this is that while it was his intention, when he sat down to write, to have made it more comprehensive, he fears he has already detained the reader too long. It may be suspected that he was aided towards the decision of coming to a conclusion by a feeling that the distinction on which he has been laying stress as fundamental is turning out to be not of kind at all, but only of degree.

What he says about imagination itself is this. "Imagination is a word denoting operations of the mind upon external objects, and processes of creation or of composition, governed by certain fixed laws." "The processes of imagination are carried on by conferring properties upon an object or abstracting them from it," in either case enabling the object to react, as though it were a new existence, on the mind which has performed the process. Finally—and this is the most important statement of all—"Imagination also shapes and creates."

In the *Biographia Literaria* Coleridge, according to his wont, extends and refines or embroiders upon these bare and concise statements. I need perhaps hardly recall the fact that the chapter on imagination which Coleridge had written, or says he had written, for that work, does not appear in it. "I shall content myself," he says, "for the present with stating the main result of the chapter, which I have reserved for future publication." That publication never took place. Our loss is great. But our gain is also not inconsiderable; for the "main result" or summing up of his doctrine which he gives is, for him, unusually compact, and also unusually lucid. By drawing, with a firm hand, an arbitrary distinction between fancy and imagination, he is able to avoid Wordsworth's confusion and give each of the terms a quite definite meaning. Fancy and imagination, according to this delimitation, are distinct and different faculties, not higher and lower degrees of one and the same power. Fancy is a mode of memory, emancipated from the order of space and time, and receiving all its material ready made from the law of Association. Imagination is primarily "a repetition, in the finite mind, of the eternal act of creation." There is also, he goes on, a secondary imagination, identical with the primary in kind, and differing only in degree and in mode of action, "an echo of the former." It dissolves in order to re-create, or at the least, to idealise and unify. It is essentially vital.

This definition, alike profound and luminous, requires hardly any expansion or comment. Two terms in it however may be made clearer by a word of explanation. To idealise—a word which Coleridge, though he did not actually introduce it into English, was the first to bring into general currency—bears with him its proper meaning, to give form, in the Platonic sense. And when he speaks of imagination as vital, he conveys the same sense in other words; the form, or idea, is vital, because it is through it that the matter which it informs is vitalised, or indeed, in any intelligible meaning, exists. Coleridge here follows the doctrine and language of the English Platonists of the seventeenth century. A definition given by one of that school, Norris of Bemerton, puts the matter pretty clearly. "By the ideal state of things," he writes, "I mean that state of them which is necessary, permanent, and immutable, not only antecedent and pre-existing to this, but also exemplary and representative of it." The wording here deserves close attention, particularly that of the last clause.

Imagination then is the power or faculty which creates, in so far as creation is within human power. It is the likeness or echo of the divine creative power; like it, according to its measure, it gives shape and substance to what had neither, what was without form and void; it puts into shape what was shapeless, it fills out into substance what was void. It dissolves in order to re-create, or if the word create be too strong, to unify and idealise; to bring, that is, the material with which it deals within the compass of a single pattern. That pattern is in some sense pre-existent—for nothing can be made out of nothing—but is also, in Norris' phrase, "exemplary and representative," or, in the more modern words which I have already quoted, an image of perfection condensed out of the flying vapours of the world.

Here, as in other instances, we have the great advantage of being able to check Coleridge's prose by his poetry. For his prose criticism, even when most luminous, is apt to be clouded by rhetoric, and its outlines lost in an iridescent mist of words. Language intoxicates him, and the thought, swathed in gorgeous rhetoric and ramifying into subtle dialectic, becomes dark with excess of light. When he theorises, he is apt to lose touch of reality. In the passage from the *Biographia Literaria* from which I have been citing, he is, for once, comparatively clear and precise. But in the very next chapter of the same work he throws us back into confusion again by re-defining imagination as a magical power. Magical, in a sense, it may be: but it is clear that when we call a thing magical we are deliberately giving up the attempt to give a rational account of it, or to explain what it actually is.

But in his poetry—and when I speak of Coleridge's poetry I mean the poetry of those six wonderful years in which he was one of the immortals—his touch is certain, his power of definition impeccable. The last great poem of that great period is the *Dejection* Ode of 4th April 1802. In that Ode—his swan-song over what he felt to be his own approaching extinction as a poet—he defines or substantialises imagination by a single masterly touch, at the end of a passage where every word is loaded with meaning.

> "O Lady! we receive but what we give,
> And in our life alone does nature live.
> Ah! from the soul itself must issue forth
> A light, a glory, a fair luminous cloud
> Enveloping the earth:
> And from the soul itself must there be sent
> A sweet and potent voice, of its own birth,
> Of all sweet sounds the life and element.
>
> O pure of heart! thou needst not ask of me
> What this strong music in the soul may be,
> This beautiful and beauty-making power. . . .
> Joy, Lady, is the spirit and the power,

Joy is the sweet voice, joy the luminous cloud ;
And thence flows all that charms or ear or sight,
All melodies the echoes of that voice,
All colours a suffusion from that light.

There was a time when though my path was rough,
This joy within me dallied with distress,
And all misfortunes were but as the stuff
Whence Fancy made me dreams of happiness.
But now afflictions bow me down to earth.
Nor care I that they rob me of my mirth,
But oh ! each visitation
Suspends what Nature gave me at my birth,
My shaping spirit of imagination."

Imagination, in this wonderful passage, is brought before us as a "potent voice," like the voice which said "Be," and the world was: a "strong music," which compels and marshals into its rhythm the fragmentary evanescent sounds of life: a "shaping spirit," which creates, out of formlessness and incoherence, images of perfection. It is the music-making power, in the sense in which the universe is built out of music ; its character and essence are in its shaping potency. As Browning finely says of music that out of three sounds it can fashion, "not a fourth sound but a star," so Coleridge tells us that imagination fashions out of what are called real things, out of "incidents and situations" as Wordsworth said, not other incidents and situations, but something archetypal and eternal, something, in the Platonist's phrase, "exemplary and representative," a pattern or rhythm according to which and by means of which these so-called realities intelligibly and essentially exist. And this shaping power is not only human, but so essentially and vitally human that the happiness of life consists in it. Without imagination life is joyless; nay more, the two things are the same: imagination is joy. Even

S

when warped and distorted, even when exercising itself viciously, it is still joy of a sort—one of those *mala mentis gaudia* which Virgil in his vision of the underworld saw couching, side by side with Anguish and Death, in the gateway of Hell. In its right exercise it is the substance and consummation of human felicity—that εὐδαιμονία which Aristotle agrees with the Christian theologians in naming as the chief end of man.

I would ask you to observe then how this definition of imagination given by Coleridge incidentally and as it were involuntarily in two words, the "shaping spirit," coheres with the definition which in a previous lecture I have given, or suggested, of poetry. On its formal and technical side, according to that definition, poetry is patterned language. But as there is no such thing as art in the abstract, as poetry consists of form and substance, whether we choose to speak of it as form which has embodied itself in substance or as substance which has taken form, the substantial and vital quality of poetry must be analogous to its formal quality. And this is the case. For just as the technical art of poetry consists in making patterns out of language, so the vital function of poetry consists in making patterns out of life. These patterns are latent and implicit; poetry reveals, and in a quite real sense, creates them. It "lifts the veil," in Shelley's words, "from the hidden beauty of the world, and makes familiar objects be as if they were not familiar." This it does by virtue of imagination, by the potency of the shaping spirit.

These definitions constitute a single doctrine; or we need not call them definitions; we may be content to consider them as a central clue, to guide us through materials and processes which are in the highest degree subtle and complex. But if we hold by this clue it

will give coherence to our whole view of poetry; and
not only to our whole view, but our whole appreciation
of it, and our whole attitude towards it. It will even
provide us with a test by which, if we will only apply
it sincerely, we may distinguish, not one kind of poetry
from another, but true poetry from its counterfeit. It
will free us, or at least go a long way towards freeing
us, from one of the great dangers of poetical criticism,
the practice of classifying poets and putting poems in
competition with one another. More important still, it
will help us towards reading poetry as it ought to be
read; may I even say here in a nursery of potential
poets, towards writing it as it ought to be written?
It may save us from what befalls so many, the falling
away from poetry, the getting out of touch with it, in
advancing years. There are several reasons why this
happens, most of them well enough known; but one of
them is not so well known as it should be. It is this:
that in youth we take to poetry unreasoningly, and
love it for its accidents more than for its essence.
We do not then—or few of us do—know how to read
poetry; our appreciation of it, sincere so far as it
goes, is superficial. As time goes on, the superficial
attraction loses its hold, and there has been no deeper
and more vital attraction growing up to take its place.
We cease to care for bad poetry; good and well.
We cease to care for the things in poetry that once
attracted us, but that were not the poetry, though
we could not distinguish then between them and
the poetry with which they were bound up; there
would be no harm in that. But unhappily we had
never taught ourselves to care for the poetry itself, for
its own sake; and when the shadow passes, we are
without the substance. The care of this world and
the deceitfulness of riches are responsible for much;

but it is still more common that the love of poetry is not devoured up nor choked, but simply fades, because it was never really part of our life. "Forthwith they sprung up, because they had no deepness of earth: and when the sun was up, they were scorched, and because they had no root, they withered away." If poetry has ever become a shaping spirit in us, an organic and constructive element in our life, it never ceases to be so. Something which men call their imagination, said Rossetti, may decline as the animal spirits lessen, but the genuine thing grows with age.

The poetic imagination is not confined to poets, though it is only in poets that it works fully. It makes poets create patterns of life. But the same faculty, at a feebler power and lower tension, is present in the readers of poetry, enabling them, in a greater or less measure, to realise or appreciate the patterns created by the poets. It is by virtue of this fainter power of imagination that poetry, in some sense, lives anew, is created anew, in the mind of each of its readers. Any poetry that we read is vital to us just to the degree in which we thus create it anew for ourselves by some imaginative faculty of our own. This inchoate faculty, present to some degree in all normal human beings, can like any other faculty be developed by study and exercise. The "study of imagination," to recur to Shakespeare's phrase, is neither futile nor negligible; it is part, and a most important part, of education, of the realisation and conquest of life.

This is the doctrine of imagination, expressed in what, broadly speaking, are the terms of Platonism. But before leaving the subject it is worth while to point out, very briefly, how the Aristotelian doctrine set forth in the *Poetics*, coming at the thing from a different direction and using a completely different set of terms, reaches the same conclusion.

Poetry is, according to Aristotle, imitation in the material of language. Imitation, μίμησις, has two notes or characteristics; the first is that it is innate in, or connate with, mankind, σύμφυτον τοῖς ἀνθρώποις: the second is that it is a natural and universal source of pleasure. It takes its place in the general scheme of life as follows.

Human activity has three spheres or methods of operation, distinguishable by analysis, though interfused and incorporate in actual life. First, thought, or the energy of intellect. Secondly, action, or the energy of will and character. Thirdly, production, or the energy of creation, of making things exist which did not, in the same sense, exist before. This last faculty again has a double sphere, distinguishable both in logic and in fact. Man creates in order to satisfy external wants. He also creates for the pleasure of creating. This latter kind of creation is art. And art working in the material of language is poetry.

In a life such as it ought to be, all the faculties, with the natural pleasure attached to their exercise, must work and be developed. Creation with pleasure and for the sake of creating is the only kind of creation in which the specific creative energy—an energy essential in human nature and co-ordinate with the energies of thought and action—is fully and harmoniously exercised. That is to say, imagination is an integral part of life; and poetry, which is the product of imagination working in language, is a necessary element in any life which is not defective, which does not fall gravely short of fulfilling its meaning.

In both these views alike then—and between them they sum up the profoundest thought of mankind—poetry is something not external to life, but immanent in life and interpretative of it, giving life its meaning or pattern. In both alike imagination is something not external to poetry, but its constituent and vitalising spirit. Poetry shapes life; imagination is the shaping spirit in poetry.

May I add one more word, addressed not to those who read poetry, but to those who write it? On these I would impress, with all the strength I can, to keep in mind that of all the poetical faculties and in all the poetical methods—and of both there are many—this strong shaping power imagination, is most central and most essential. Turn back to Wordsworth's list of the powers, as he calls them, requisite for the production of poetry. First he names observation and description; the open eye which sees life not blurred and featureless, but everywhere filled with form and colour, and the command of language which can translate life as thus seen into words, can put down a clear record of clear impressions. Next, there is sensibility; delicacy of perception added to clearness, the power of responsiveness to slight touches: so that the "finely touched spirit" (in Shakespeare's admirable phrase) is sensitive to subtleties of form, to play of colour, to the latent harmonic relations which vibrate throughout life and make the finer texture of experience. Then there is reflection; the faculty of weighing and plumbing experience, of penetrating below the surface aspect of things and brooding over them in the still darkness, far down among the central springs of thought and emotion. In addition to these, there is invention, the active intelligence which puts forth on voyages

IMAGINATION

of discovery, and passing beyond the material of observation as responded to by sensibility and rehandled by reflection, creates for itself new incidents and situations, new combinations of language, new cadences and harmonies. Finally, there is judgment, the presiding power which moves among all the rest, ordering them and setting them in their place, determining what shall be chosen and what rejected, testing them and passing sentence on them.

But over and above all there is imagination, the shaping spirit; and without imagination there is not poetry. The observation may be clear and the description true; the sensibility to impressions may be delicate, and the reflection over the content of experience, whether experience from without given by life, or experience from within given by living, may be careful and even profound. These only bring one to the point where the process of the poet begins. In that process, as in all human processes, success will imply skill of invention, and soundness of judgment, But these things are all external to the process itself. which is the work of imagination; the shaping, the composition into patterned language conveying a pattern of life, of the matter observed and described, apprehended by sensibility and worked over by reflection, set out by invention and weighed by judgment.

Without this shaping spirit poetry remains uncreated. There is such a thing, no doubt, as impressionist poetry: but its impressionism, if it is really poetry and not merely a phantom or counterfeit of poetry, is not the imaginative substance of the poetry; it is only one particular method among others of setting that substance forth. Nor is that substance a matter of intellect, though it involves intellectual processes carried on at a high power, what Rossetti called, in an apt phrase, fundamental brainwork. It is a thing which, dealing with impressions through intelligence, creates out of them an organic pattern, a vital structure. Much of what is brought before one as poetry is merely the inorganic material for poetry, not yet in any fully effective way passed through the shaping process and become alive. Much is merely the ornament of poetry; ornament, it may be, gracefully and delicately wrought, but with little meaning or value, because it is not ornament designed for, and taking its organic place in, a structural composition. I would not undervalue these things or say that the labour spent on them is wasted. But they are preparations for poetry; they are not poetry itself.

KEATS

In our time, Keats has come by his own. There is no need to insist on what is universally recognised, that he stands in the first rank of the English poets. There is little, if any, need to refute, or even to notice, the obloquy that he suffered under in his lifetime, nor to comment upon the tardy and tepid appreciation which he won for many years after his death. His light goes on burning clearer and larger. Even the criticisms which are still made on certain qualities and certain imperfections in his poetry are made—with but few exceptions, and these of little importance—in no spirit of detraction, but rather with the view of distinguishing what is best in it from what is faulty through youth, through inexperience, through the influence of bad models on one who was little more than a boy; and towards the end, through illness and a fever of the heart. Such criticism is not only just but necessary. What is neither necessary nor just, and what is now less and less done, is to adopt, in making it, a tone either of fault-finding or of apology. They who level at my offences, he might say like Shakespeare, reckon up their own. And the patronage which in his life was the one thing that he could not bear, even from the greatest of his contemporaries, is equally ill-bestowed upon his poetry now. It requires no apology; it requires understanding. Love and admiration we may and must give to it: it hardly needs praise, except the praise of admiring thankfulness: such praise as Landor speaks of when he says:

> "There is delight
> In praising, though the praiser sit alone
> And see the praised far off him, far above."

To no one else, perhaps, among the English poets, do the words of Odysseus to Diomede in the Iliad so fully apply: "Praise me not much, neither find fault with me at all."

It is specially gratifying to remember here that so much of the best and finest appreciation of Keats has come from Oxford. It was not so at first. It was a Cambridge man, the late Lord Houghton, who was the first to redeem England from the reproach of neglecting him, who really made him known. And in continuing this work, it is another Cambridge man, Sir Sidney Colvin, who has done most to elucidate and fill in Lord Houghton's sketch by giving us Keats' fascinating letters and by his biographical and critical study of Keats in the *English Men of Letters*—a book which I may without presumption call a masterpiece, for in doing so I am only mentioning an acknowledged fact, not passing any judgment of my own. But the tribute paid by Oxford to Keats, the work done for him by Oxford, has in recent years been but little less. I need hardly mention, and I may assume that they are already familiar, the editions of Keats' poems by the late William Arnold, an accomplished scholar, a fine critic and a patriotic citizen, whose premature death was a grave loss to his country and to letters, and more recently by Mr. de Sélincourt, who did so much for the School of English Literature in Oxford before he left it for another University. Of this last edition it may be said that in virtue of its thoroughness and its critical insight, it took its place at once as definitive and classic. I need hardly mention the brilliant Essay on Keats by Mr. Bridges, who brings such a fresh eye and mind to whatever he touches. Nor need I recall how Keats has been handled, how his poetry has been interpreted and communicated to the University and to the world at large by three occupants of the Chair of Poetry; for I may assume likewise the general knowledge of Arnold's masterly appreciation in the Second Series of *Essays in Criticism*; of Francis Palgrave's edition, in the introduction to which Palgrave's own fine taste and judgment were reinforced by the judgment and taste of Tennyson; and more recently, of Mr. Bradley's study of Keats in special relation to the Letters, first given from this Chair and now accessible in his volume of *Oxford Lectures on Poetry*.

Indeed the question may at once arise, when one casts one's eye over these names, what occasion there is for adding to the list, and whether for the present at least the last word on Keats has not been said. To this question, or objection, there are two answers. One is, that at no time can the last word be said on any great poet; to each of his lovers he means something different, and each has his own word to say about him; for the appeal of all great art is direct and individual, and it calls for individual interpretation. The other is simply this, that I should not like to quit this Chair without having said something from it about a poet whom I read year by year with increasing love and deepening admiration, and who seems to me to go, in some respects, straighter than almost any other English poet to the heart of poetry.

When critics, as they all rightly do, lay stress on the fact that Keats died at the age of twenty-five, in order to emphasise the swiftness of his achievement and the marvellousness of his genius, they really understate the case. For even in that short life, the body of poetry which makes him immortal, which sets him, as Arnold says, with Shakespeare, was all produced within two astonishing years—or to be accurate, not even years, but two periods of eight or nine months each. *Endymion* was begun in April 1817 and finished in the following November. That is one of the two periods. The other, the *annus mirabilis* in the fullest sense, begins, after an interval of a little more than a year, in December 1818 or the beginning of January 1819. In it were written—is there such a constellation of blazing jewels in nine months of the life of any other poet?—*Hyperion, The Eve of St. Agnes, Lamia, La Belle Dame Sans Merci, The Eve of St. Mark*, and the six great Odes. The last of these, the *Ode to Autumn*, written at Winchester on the 19th of September 1819, was also Keats' last great poem. He was already fatally ill. A few months later he had his death-sentence; and he lingered on for another year only as a doomed man. "I have a habitual feeling," so he wrote pathetically in one of his last letters, "of my real life having passed and that I am leading a posthumous existence."

He wrote, to be sure, fine poetry, both before and after these two periods, and also in the interval between them. The sonnet *On first looking into Chapman's Homer*, the first poem in which he shows himself not only a pupil, a poet in the making, but a poet of actual accomplishment and mastery, dates as far back as the spring of 1815, two years before *Endymion* was begun. The equally famous and equally magnificent sonnet, *Bright Star! would I were steadfast as thou art*, was written on the blank leaf in his Shakespeare on the 28th of September 1820, just a year after the *Ode to Autumn*. It was literally his last poem, as the other may in a sense be called his first. These two sonnets alone would give him a place among the English poets; and so would other poems which do not fall within the two miraculous periods. But speaking largely we may say that it is the work of these two periods—the latter of the two pre-eminently, though the former alone would be sufficient—which gives him not only a place among the poets, but a place not inferior to the highest.

The priceless letters of Keats enable us to form in our minds something like a solid image of him in this brief period of his culminating achievement as a poet: at the time when, in his own burning words, " Poetry has conquered ; I have relapsed into those abstractions which are my only life—and I am thankful for it. There is an awful warmth about my heart like a load of Immortality." One of these letters, above all, gives by itself this image—not a picture, but more, something in the round, something that places him before us, as one might say, on all his sides, in all three dimensions. This is the famous journal-letter, written at intervals in the spring of 1819 to George and Georgiana Keats, his brother and sister-in-law, while he was waiting to get the first news from them of their arrival at the settlement on the Ohio, at what is now Louisville, to which they had emigrated the year before. We know little or nothing of Georgiana Keats—to whom in the main this and the other joint-letters were really written—beyond what is told us by the letters themselves and by one charming sonnet addressed to her. But it is certain that she was a great dear; Keats was very fond of her; and the way in which he writes, or rather talks on paper, to her, with its affection and absolute unrestraint, brings us very close to Keats himself. His own sister Fanny was only a schoolgirl. Between Georgiana and him, just as if she had been his sister by birth, there was that unique relation which except between brother and sister can hardly exist, and which even so is somewhat rare and very precious. In a famous passage of his Autobiography, Gibbon has described it in one of his august sentences: " It is a familiar and tender friendship with a female much about our own age; an affection perhaps softened by the secret influence of sex, but pure from any mixture of sensual desire, the sole species of Platonic love that can be indulged with truth and without danger."

From this journal-letter I will quote, not making many comments but leaving it in the main to produce its own impression.

" I have not been to see your Mother since my return from Chichester—I believe I told you I was going thither. I was nearly a fortnight at Mr. John Snook's and a few days at old Mr. Dilke's. Nothing worth speaking of happened at either place. I took down some thin paper, and wrote on it a little poem called St. Agnes' Eve.

" In my next packet, as this is one by the way, I shall send you the Pot of Basil, St. Agnes' Eve, and if I should have finished it, a little thing called the Eve of St. Mark. You see what fine Mother Radcliff names I have—it is not my fault—I do not search for them. I have not gone on with Hyperion, for to tell the truth I have not been in great cue for writing lately; I must wait for the spring to rouse me up a little."

He had not been in great cue for writing lately, and he had written *St. Agnes' Eve* in the last three weeks!

"The only time I went out from Bedhampton was to see a Chapel consecrated—Brown, I, and John Snook the boy, went in a chaise behind a leaden horse. Brown drove, but the horse did not mind him. This chapel is built by a Mr. Way, a great Jew converter, who in that line has spent one hundred thousand pounds. He maintains a great number of poor Jews. Of course his Communion plate was stolen. He spoke to the Clerk about it—The Clerk said he was very sorry, adding, ' I dare shay, your honour, it's among ush.'

"The chapel is built in Mr. Way's park. The Consecration was not amusing. There were numbers of carriages, and his house crammed with clergy. They sanctified the chapel, and it being a wet day, consecrated the burial ground through the vestry window.

" Neither Poetry, nor Ambition, nor Love have any alertness of countenance as they pass by me; they seem rather like figures on a Greek vase.

" I am, however, young, writing at random, straining at particles of light in the midst of a great darkness. Give me this credit—do you not think I strive to know myself? with no Agony but that of ignorance, with no thirst of anything but Knowledge.

" When you have nothing else to do for a whole day I tell you how you may employ it. First get up, and when you are dressed, as it would be pretty early with a high wind in the woods, give George a cold Pig with my Compliments. When you are both set down to breakfast, I advise you to eat your full share, but leave off immediately on feeling yourself inclined to anything on the other side of the puffy—avoid that, for it does not become young women. After you have eaten your breakfast keep your eye upon dinner—it is the safest way. You should keep a Hawk's eye

over your dinner and keep hovering over it till due
time, then pounce, taking care not to break any plates.
While you are hovering with your dinner in prospect
you may do a thousand things—put a hedgehog into
George's hat—pour a little water into his rifle—soak
his boots in a pail of water—cut his jacket round into
shreds like a Roman kilt or the back of my grand-
mother's stays—sew *off* his buttons.

" ' O what can ail thee Knight at arms
    Alone and palely loitering?
The sedge has withered from the Lake
    And no birds sing!

' O what can ail thee Knight at arms
    So haggard, and so woe-begone?
The squirrel's granary is full
    And the harvest's done.

I see a lily on thy brow,
    With anguish moist and fever dew,
And on thy cheek a fading rose
    Fast withereth too.'

' I met a Lady in the Meads
    Full beautiful, a faery's child.
Her hair was long, her foot was light
    And her eyes were wild.

' I made a Garland for her head
    And bracelets too, and fragrant Zone.
She looked at me as she did love
    And made sweet moan.

' I set her on my pacing steed
    And nothing else saw all day long,
For sidelong would she bend and sing
    A faery's song.

' She found me roots of relish sweet
    And honey wild and manna dew,
And sure in language strange she said,
    I love thee true.

'She took me to her elfin grot
   And there she wept and sighed full sore,
And there I shut her wild, wild eyes
   With kisses four.

'And there she lulled me asleep,
   And there I dream'd Ah Woe betide!
The latest dream I ever dreamt
   On the cold hill side.

'I saw pale Kings and Princes too,
   Pale warriors death-pale were they all,
They cried, La belle dame sans merci
   Thee hath in thrall.

'I saw their starv'd lips in the gloam
   With horrid warning gaped wide,
And I awoke, and found me here
   On the cold hill's side.

'And this is why I sojourn here
   Alone and palely loitering;
Though the sedge is withered from the Lake
   And no birds sing.'

"Why four kisses, you will say—why four, because I wish to restrain the headlong impetuosity of my Muse—she would fain have said 'score' without hurting the rhyme—but we must temper the Imagination, as the Critics say, with Judgment."

That is Keats: and I do not know that any critical introduction will give one a clearer or more solid image of him. Of course one should read the whole letter; but what I have read gives its essence, and the essence of Keats himself. Distilled into poetry, concentrated and illuminated by the genius of one who understood and appreciated him, it is given again in the stately lines of Rossetti:

"Around the vase of Life at your slow pace
   He has not crept, but turned it with his hands,
   And all its sides already understands.

> There, girt, one breathes alert for some great race,
> Whose road runs far by sands and fruitful space,
> Who laughs, yet through the jolly throng has passed;
> Who weeps, nor stays for weeping; who at last,
> A youth, stands somewhere crowned, with silent face."

We may compare with this nobly imagined and nobly executed passage what Keats himself wrote to Woodhouse a little earlier than the letter from which I have just been quoting: " I will speak of my views, and of the life I purpose to myself. I am ambitious of doing the world some good: if I should be spared, that may be the work of maturer years—in the interval I will assay to reach to as high a summit in poetry as the nerve bestowed on me will suffer. All I hope is, that I may not lose all interest in human affairs; that the solitary Indifference I feel for applause, even from the finest Spirits, will not blunt any acuteness of vision I may have. I do not think it will."

This independence of judgment, this solitary indifference to applause, is central to Keats. It is the more remarkable in him because he was so fine-strung, so acutely and tremulously sensitive, so hungry for affection and so lavish of it. Wordsworth seems to have cared for nobody, outside of his own family circle; even there he exacted service rather than gave it; everything had to give way to what he for the moment required: he wrote an Ode to Duty, as his friends said, and then considered he was done with that subject. Of Milton this could not have been said; but duty was for him a part of self-culture; his real life was, like his art, alone. Yet Keats, when it comes to a matter of his art, is as proud and independent as Wordsworth or Milton. Even to Shelley, when Shelley gave him advice about poetry—and one cannot doubt that it was given not only with the insight of a great poet, but with Shelley's invariable sweetness and courtesy—he bristles up and becomes for once quite disagreeable.

One might say indeed hastily, when Keats speaks of his indifference to applause, that there was little or no applause for him to be indifferent to. But this would be a mistake; there was plenty of it waiting if he would consent to be false to his art, and to swerve from his high purpose. There were voices to left and right, luring him from his path; but almost from the first, and almost to the last, he shut his ears and walked straight forward. The concessions he made in his last year of illness must not be counted against a dying man. In his pupilage, Leigh Hunt was always pressing him, by precept and example, to be silly; the orthodox critics, blind as owls to his excellencies, brutal to any weakness in him that they could pounce on, were ready to praise him if ever he went really wrong. A well-known story illustrates this. One of his early sonnets, the one beginning, *How many bards gild the lapses of time*, was read to Horace Smith. It is a poor sonnet; no worse than what many great poets have written in youth before they found themselves, but only interesting because it is by Keats, and has glimmerings in it of the real Keats of two or three years later. But it contains one perfectly abominable line,

"That distance of recognisance bereaves."

Smith went straight for it with unerring accuracy. "He was specially struck with it," is the record, "and observed, 'What a well-condensed expression for one so young!'" It was fortunate for Keats that he was indifferent to such applause as that.

What made him indifferent to it was partly temperament, partly his extraordinary critical insight. Just think of what he said, in 1817, about Wordsworth's *Gipsies* and Hazlitt's criticism on it. "It is a bold thing to say, and I would not say it in print, but it seems to me that if Wordsworth had thought a little deeper at that moment, he would not have written the poem at all." Then he goes on, "Nor is it fair to attack him: for it is with the critic as with the poet; had Hazlitt thought a little deeper and been in a good temper, he would never have spied out imaginary faults." Over such insight as this the enchantments of the Sirens have no power.

I do not propose to attempt any general appreciation of Keats' poetry. That has been done, and done as well as I could do it. What I wish to do now is to consider some particular features and elements in his poetry and in his poetical development that do not seem to have been quite fully brought out. Unless they are brought out, appreciation of Keats, though perfectly sound and right, and even in its main substance complete, will have some gaps in it.

The solid greatness of *Endymion* is now recognised. Even by its admirers it used to be thought of as a sort of wilderness of capricious or fantastic beauties: it was a romance as incoherent in structure as it was rich in ornament. We can see now, by the help of abler and more appreciative criticism, that it is not that. So far from being without thought, it suffers from being overloaded with thought beyond what Keats was able to express clearly or articulately. So far from being a fantasy or series of fantasies, it is a spiritual allegory, confused indeed, or rather perplexed, but serious, even profound. When Keats told Shelley to "be more of an artist, and load every rift of your subject with ore," he was speaking of what he had done himself. To Shelley indeed he goes on to say, "Is not this extraordinary talk for the writer of *Endymion*, whose mind was like a pack of scattered cards?" But we must supplement this by what he had said elsewhere and before he had lost his nerve: "That which is creative must create itself. In Endymion I leaped headlong into the sea, and thereby have become better acquainted with the soundings, the quicksands, and the rocks, than if I had stayed upon the green shore and piped a silly pipe." He could afford, a year or two after he had written *Endymion*, to look back on it as a slight thing, even as a failure. But no one else can afford to do so.

Nor again does it lead to the clearest view of *Endymion* to regard it as revolutionary in art. Revolutionary no doubt it was, as all new movements in art are. But it was so in its effect rather than in its purpose and essence. It was simply Keats writing as well as he could—"as good as I had power to make it" is his own phrase. Then he published it in order to get rid of it; in order to begin again and do better. He would not waste time over altering it and making it better. Other tasks for other worlds; this task was done, and done with. "Had I been nervous about its being a perfect piece, and with that view asked advice, and trembled over every page, it would not have been written; for it is not in my nature to fumble." When we criticise *Endymion*, when we discriminate in it between what is good and what is not so good, or what is frankly bad, we run the risk of falling into just the mistake that Keats himself had the genius and the insight to avoid. It could not have been written otherwise; it is a living organism, which only exists, and can only be dealt with, as a single thing.

Thus it is that our appreciation of *Endymion* normally passes through three stages. There is the first intoxication, when it comes with its full impact on us in youth, producing its effect as a whole in some sense, but still confusedly:

> "A wilderness of sweets, for Nature here
> Wantoned as in her prime, and played at will
> Her virgin fancies, pouring forth more sweet,
> Wild above rule or art, enormous bliss."

Then there is an intermediate period—many readers, not a few genuine lovers of poetry, never get beyond it—when we see the faults, the immaturities, the lapses of taste; and of course the poem is full of all these if we look for them. The "enormous bliss" turns at this stage into a series of enormities that set our teeth on edge. It is a disillusionment like that of Endymion's own waking.

> "Lo! the poppies hung
> Dew-dabbled on their stalks, the ouzel sung
> A heavy ditty, and the sullen day
> Had chidden herald Hesperus away,
> With leaden looks: the solitary breeze
> Blustered and slept."

But if we have patience, there comes a time when the faults cease to matter, when we do not trouble about them; when we do not even desire that the poem should be other than what it is, realising at last, as Keats did from the first, that it could not be other than what it is. And then, if I may judge from my own experience, it resumes all its fascination, and now permanently; it becomes what Keats meant, a joy for ever.

> "Its loveliness increases; it will never
> Pass into nothingness: but still will keep
> A bower quiet for us, and a sleep

Full of sweet dreams, and health, and quiet breathing.
Therefore, on every morrow, are we wreathing
A flowery band to bind us to the earth,
Spite of despondence, of the inhuman dearth
Of noble natures, of the gloomy days,
Of all the unhealthy and o'erdarkened ways
Made for our searching: yes, in spite of all,
Some shape of beauty moves away the pall
From our dark spirits. Such the sun, the moon,
Trees old and young, sprouting a shady boon
For simple sheep; and such are daffodils
With the green world they live in "—

and such is *Endymion*. To quote again from it:

"Its influence,
Thrown in our eyes, genders a novel sense,
At which we start and fret; till in the end,
Melting into its radiance, we blend,
Mingle, and so become a part of it."

Looked at in this way, *Endymion* is simply the incarnation of poetry in Keats in the year 1817. There is plenty in it to criticise; but we shall be inclined to feel that the time is in some sense wasted in criticising it, which we might spend in reading it. Otherwise we shall be apt to fall into the mistake of regarding the faults as substantive things. They are not that, any more than the beauties are. Both are merely qualities of the thing itself.

Endymion is the palmary instance of what is more clearly marked in Keats than in almost any other poet, the progress of poetry in the poet himself. The progress is so swift, the medium in which it takes place so transparent, that one can see the movement, one might almost say, from page to page. In his short poetical life, it is as though he were rapidly shedding skin after skin, and throwing the cast skin away from him, pushed out and falling away under the pressure of the swift central growth. It is as though the seven-years' change that insensibly replaces the human body by wholly new tissues were going on visibly, at seven-fold speed. This early poetry of his is never static: it is what is just caught for a moment in the very act of transformation. Even, for instance, at the points where *Endymion* is likest Leigh Hunt, the likeness is superficial and transitory. There are lines and passages in the *Story of Rimini* which give a momentary impression of being like Keats.

"April with his white hands wet with flowers"—

some one who came suddenly on the line might very well say, or think, "Surely that is Keats"; and similarly with the line about the fountain that

"Shakes its loosening silver in the sun":

or with a passage, once or twice, running into several lines. Take one instance:

"Roses in heaps were there, both red and white,
Lilies angelical, and gorgeous glooms
Of wall-flowers, and blue hyacinths, and blooms
Hanging thick clusters from light boughs; in short,
All the sweet cups to which the bees resort."

It would be possible to mix up, for a moment, that garden in the wood at Rimini with the bower of Adonis in *Endymion*. But as soon as one looks at it with a steadied eye, the difference becomes clear. To feel it, one has not to go to Keats where he is absolutely miraculous, to lines like—

"As does the nightingale up-perched high,
And cloister'd among cool and bunched leaves—
She sings but to her love, nor e'er conceives
How tiptoe Night holds back her dark-grey hood":

or the couplet, with its dark splendour and wild piercing sweetness:

> "And here is manna pick'd from Syrian trees,
> In starlight, by the three Hesperides."

It is sufficient to take a passage where he is only, so to speak, at his normal, not at his best:

> "Above his head
> Four lily stalks did their white honours wed
> To make a coronal; and round him grew
> All tendrils green, of every bloom and hue;
> Convolvulus in streaked vases flush,
> The creeper, mellowing for an autumn blush,
> And virgin's bower, trailing airily."

That is not so good, technically, as the passage from the *Story of Rimini* which I have just quoted. The metre straggles and trails. It is impossible to say that "Four lily stalks did their white honours wed" is even a passably good line: still less that it is a line with the quality of Hunt's "lilies angelical and gorgeous glooms." But the vital difference is this, and it transcends or ignores all merely technical points: the Hunt is static, inert, finished; the Keats thrills and is alive. The growth and progress of poetry pulsate in it. Then Keats passes forward and leaves it behind.

This process of perpetual transformation and reincarnation may be traced most plainly if we look at it going on in a single separable group of Keats' poems, in his Odes. Let us look at them.

I omit, as of little importance for this purpose, like the rest of his early and only inchoate work, the two Odes written before *Endymion*, the *Ode to Apollo*, and the *Ode on a Lock of Milton's Hair*: and also the two pieces included as Odes by Mr. de Sélincourt, but hardly belonging to this type of poetry under any ordinary definition, the lines *To Fanny*, and the piece beginning *What can I do to drive away Remembrance from my eyes?* I omit likewise the four lovely lyrics in the volume of 1820, *Ever let the Fancy roam*, *Bards of Passion and of Mirth*, *Souls of Poets dead and gone*, and, *No, these Hours are gone away*. These four are sometimes called Odes, and in fact Keats calls one of them an Ode himself; but if one has to give them a technical name, they are not Odes, but rondels. Apart from these, there are ten or eleven Odes to consider: the precise number is arguable, as I will explain directly. Three, or four, of these occur in *Endymion*; one, the *Ode to Maia*, is of the intermediate year; the other six all belong to the *annus mirabilis*, and are justly singled out as standing apart in literature. "Had Keats left us only these," Mr. Bridges says, and one can hardly disagree, "his rank among the poets would not be lower than it is."

The Odes in *Endymion* are, like *Endymion* itself, not yet poetry consummate, but poetry in the very act and process of full creation. Two of them are mere fragments—the Hymn to Neptune in Book III. and the Ode of Diana in Book IV.; both of these break off, dramatically for the purposes of the poem, in the middle of a line and of a sentence. Another, the exquisite song of the Indian Maid in Book IV., can perhaps be called an Ode, but doubtfully. It is a unique and extraordinary experiment in what we may alternatively call the treatment of an Ode in the manner of a rondel, or the expansion of a rondel into the scope and movement of an Ode. Keats himself, it is worth noting, calls it a rondel, or, in the form of the word that he uses, a roundelay. The fourth, or the third if we exclude this one, is the Hymn to Pan in the first book.

In all these, we see Keats getting at the Ode, both in form and in substance. The metrical form in the two fragmentary Odes is irregular, the movement uncertain. The Ode has not yet fully realised itself and taken shape. In the Hymn to Pan it has almost done so; it is shaping beautifully, but is not quite shaped. Keats has got hold of the strophic form and is playing on it, fingering the strings and seeing what it will do. He never perhaps wrote anything in a way more beautiful, but its beauty comes in and through what is imperfection. He and poetry will shed this off them, throw it behind them, and pass on.

The "immortal fragment of inimitable beauty"—I quote Mr. Bridges again, for I cannot better his words—the *Ode to Maia*, belongs, as I said, to the intermediate year, the year of pause and concentration. I do not call it the year of growth, though it was that too, and very remarkably; but the growth in and throughout the two great years was equally swift and equally remarkable. This is the first poem of Keats in which we feel, without any doubt or qualification, his complete mastery of the instrument. The fragment has only fourteen lines: it is even uncertain whether these were meant to be a complete strophe, and how either the theme or the rhythmical movement would have been developed by him. What we do know when we come to it, and what we know at once, is that the poet who wrote it had the Ode, as a form of poetry, fully between his hands. And so it was: for when we pass on to the six Odes of 1819, we find his mastery of the instrument complete. The Ode is now an attained thing. He has settled its structure and movement; he has compassed its form: so sure of it, and of himself, is he now, that he can play with it, can make the subtlest variations upon a perfect pattern, can even in one case leave the pattern altogether with triumphant success. For Keats never stands still, never repeats himself. "Rounded by thee, my song should die away," he wrote in the *Maia* Ode. But that round had no limit to its expansion.

When he wrote the six Odes, Keats had, so far as concerned his own use, created and defined the form of the Ode. In the *Ode to Psyche* he cast that aside and created something quite new, a design so beautiful that we do not miss the pattern. But in the other five, the pattern on which he settled down is of their essence. It is the pattern of a ten-line stanza consisting of a quatrain followed by a sestet. And when I say settled down, I mean settled down on it as a central pattern or motive, round which he kept moving, varying the detail, never making it exactly the same twice. Not only does the metrical form of these five Odes vary slightly between each and the others, but all except one have internal variations also. The *Ode to Indolence*—and this is a touch which is extraordinarily fine, whether it be calculated or instinctive—is precisely regular throughout. The Odes *To Autumn, To Melancholy,* and *On a Grecian Urn* vary the rhyming system between stanza and stanza. In the *Ode to the Nightingale,* not only is there the exquisite device of the shortened eighth line, which changes the poise and movement of the whole stanza, but the second stanza ends on a hypermetric line, " And with thee fade away into the forest dim "—with an instinct so wholly right, with an effect so perfect, that one may know the poem by heart and never notice the variation, but only feel the magic of the cadence. In the *Ode to Autumn,* the latest and the most absolutely faultless of them all, it would be curious to ask how many of the thousands by whom it is read and loved

and known have even noticed that the ten-line has
become an eleven-line stanza, and that the whole tone
and colour of the Ode are thus, by a device as simple
as it is masterly, carried into the metrical form itself.
The added line gives, as it is difficult to say how
anything else could have given, the richness, the lin-
geringness, the superflux, which are of the imaginative essence of the subject. Form and substance are
wholly fused, and the body of the poem cannot be
distinguished from its soul.

When we pass from the Odes to *Hyperion*, here too
we see poetry in the act of growth, and now the growth
is so rapid that the execution could not keep pace with
it. Keats dropped it; took it up again—the one instance in which he did such a thing—and began,
with dying hands, to remodel it; and left it, a superb
and wonderful fragment, like the Transfiguration left
half-painted on the easel of Raffaele. The distance
between it and *Endymion*, when we remember that there
are only thirteen or fourteen months of time between
them, is incredible. Let us take one concrete instance,
which will serve as well as another for an illustration,
and set beside one another two passages from the two
poems which deal with the same motive of stillness.
First, that from Book I. of *Endymion*:

> " And as a willow keeps
> A patient watch over the stream that creeps
> Windingly by it, so the quiet maid
> Held her in peace ; so that a whispering blade
> Of grass, a wailful gnat, a bee bustling
> Down in the bluebells, or a wren light rustling
> Among sere leaves and twigs, might all be heard."

Now, that from the beginning of *Hyperion*:

> " No stir of air was there,
> Not so much life as on a summer's day

> Robs not one light seed from the feather'd grass,
> But where the dead leaf fell, there did it rest.
> A stream went voiceless by, still deadened more
> By reason of his fallen divinity
> Spreading a shade : the Naiad 'mid her reeds
> Press'd her cold finger closer to her lips."

Between these two passages, each perfect of its kind, poetry in Keats has undergone an enormous expansion. It has become at once larger and deeper. This immense growth in range and power had all been made in the year's interval.

Poetical growth, like all other functions of life, is secret; it cannot be analysed and accounted for. But we can trace, and mark definitely in it, certain factors; and there is one factor here of great importance, which has not yet, I think, been singled out and weighed. Stress has been laid, and rightly, on the Miltonic influence and its effects. But there was another influence almost as potent, but more indirect and thus less obvious. It is that of Dante.

In the revised *Hyperion* of a few months later, this influence is still more marked. Curiously, it was almost ignored until recently : Mr. Bridges was the first to name it and bring it out clearly. But when he says that it appears in the revised *Hyperion* for the first time, I think he fails to notice that in the original *Hyperion* it is already present. Unless I misunderstand him, he thinks that between the two versions Keats had been reading Dante in the original, and thus got at qualities in Dante's poetry which he could not get at through a translation. It is worth while looking into this.

We know that Cary's Dante was the one book that Keats took with him on his Scottish tour in the summer of 1818. We also know that he was studying Italian, in order to read the Italian poets, in the summer and autumn of 1819—that is, between the composition of the earlier and the later versions of *Hyperion*. To this there are a number of allusions in his letters. But he never speaks of reading Dante in the Italian. In September he writes from Winchester, three days after he had composed the *Ode to Autumn*, that he is reading Ariosto, not managing more than six or eight stanzas at a time. He was still, that is, a beginner, who found Ariosto difficult; and this does not look like reading Dante. But there is more than this presumptive evidence; for in the same letter he goes on to speak of the reading of Dante as something to come, and as part of his reason for learning Italian: it is, he says, well worth while. The conclusion seems certain, that when he wrote the revised *Hyperion* he still knew Dante only through Cary, and that the heightened Dantesque influence in the revision (which, as Mr. Bridges well says, is shown not merely in the gravity of the vision, but in echoes of the Italian balance, and in a mastery here and there, both in thought and style, of Dante's especial grace) is only the deepened working of what was already there, and what he had got through Cary. The instinct which enabled Keats to divine Greek poetry from what he found in Tooke's Pantheon and in Spence and Lempriere would find no difficulty in seeing Dante through a translation. And Cary, we must recollect, gives much of Dante's poetry; he still remains, after all the modern versions, the classical and in some respects the unreplaceable English translation. Only there is this to remember: that Cary's Dante is not only Dante imperfectly given (as all translations of poetry must be), but Dante, one might say, a little Miltonised: and the result is that the Dantesque influence in

Hyperion—which also I think exists, though it is less clearly traceable, in others of Keats' poems of that year—was mixed up with, and has not been discriminated from, the Miltonic influence itself, which is so patent, and which was so powerful that Keats himself rebelled against it and deliberately resolved to break away from it.

This Dantesque influence is strongest in Book I. of *Hyperion*. The whole *mise-en-scène* there has clear traces of Dante's Inferno—the City of Dis, the Centaurs, Malebolge, the Giant-rimmed embankment between the eighth and ninth Circles. But the influence is not only general, it is now and then specific; there are at least a dozen passages where it may be clearly discerned, in points of substance and style.

A few may be named as instances. When Keats makes Oceanus say to Hyperion,

"Seize the arrow's barb,
Before the tense string murmur,"

there is a reminiscence, hardly uncertain, of Virgil's words to Dante:

"Disse: Scocca
L'arco del dir, che infino al ferro hai tratto."

Or take these lines:

"By her in stature the tall Amazon
Had stood a pigmy's height: she would have ta'en
Achilles by the hair and bent his neck."

That is exactly Dante's manner of pictorial exemplification, and his manner of using the classical mythology for imaginative purposes. Or again, take this passage:

"She went
With backward footing through the shade a space:
He follow'd, and she turn'd to lead the way
Through aged boughs, that yielded like the mist
Which eagles cleave upmounting from their nest,"

That is Dante's manner of visualisation, reinforced by a characteristically Dantesque simile. Only two poets have written in just this manner; and they are Dante and Keats.

Here too we may again clearly recognise the Dantesque simile:

> "As with us mortal men, the laden heart
> Is persecuted more, and fever'd more,
> When it is nighing to the mournful house
> Where other hearts are sick of the same bruise;
> So Saturn . . ."

Another instance of striking affinity, combined with and partly due to actual suggestion, occurs at the beginning of Book II. of *Hyperion*, in the description of Saturn's arrival at the "sad place" (this phrase itself is Dante's and is very characteristic of him), when the fallen Titans are huddled together:

> "Where their own groans
> They felt, but heard not, for the solid roar
> Of thunderous waterfalls and torrents hoarse
> Pouring a constant bulk, uncertain where:
> Crag jutting forth to crag."

This cannot fail to remind us of the description of the central chasm in the last canto of the *Inferno*:

> "Che non per vista, ma per suono è noto
> D' un ruscelletto, che quivi discende
> Per la buca d' un sasso, ch' egli ha roso
> Col corso ch' egli avvolge : e poco pende."

Even in single lines there is now and then an accent, new in Keats, but in no way Miltonic, indeed essentially un-Miltonic, which bears the closest affinity to Dante's. Take lines like these:

> "There was a listening fear in her regard."

> "To the level of his ear
> Leaning with parted lips."

U

"While still the dazzling globe maintained eclipse."

"And plunged all noiseless into the deep night."

The manner is so exactly Dante's that one finds one's self as it were involuntarily trying to remember what the Italian of them is. It is a more intimate and subtler link between Keats and Dante than that which the Miltonic inversions and Latinisms of *Hyperion* create between Keats and Milton. For that is a likeness of manner, and sometimes only of mannerisms; this is something deeper, a likeness of mind. The two poets have a subtle kinship in manner of visualisation, in evolution of thought and in use of ornament; but also, and even more vitally, in the way in which their imagination works. The resemblance is not imitative; it comes naturally and unconsciously from a spiritual affinity; from a similar height and outlook having been reached on the mountain of poetry.

Not in *Hyperion* only, but throughout the work of this year, we have this increased height, this widened outlook. There is a firmer and larger handling, as we see in the Odes, and also very remarkably in *Lamia* and the *Eve of St. Agnes* as compared with the *Isabella* of the year before. And as Keats ascends, his horizons expand: they begin to give large prospect into new worlds of poetry. In the remodelled *Hyperion* he is moving towards that final height of poetry which transcends both romance and epic by transforming and merging both into direct vision. In the *Belle Dame Sans Merci* he goes straight, without apparent effort and by pure instinct of genius, to the centre of romanticism. In the lovely fragment of the *Eve of St. Mark* he divines and anticipates the later movement which, originated by Rossetti and Morris forty years

THE PROGRESS OF POETRY

The lectures I have given during the last five years have all dealt in one way or another, and in one or another of its many complex aspects, with the progress of poetry; and I may now be allowed to recapitulate.

Poetry is a function of life; and life being the continuous operation of a force or a complex system of forces, poetry must like all other vital functions share this quality of movement, of existing in and manifesting itself through movement. Poetry is an interpretation of life; and the interpretation must, like the thing interpreted, be organic and in continual progress, taking form from point to point, from moment to moment.

But poetry is also a pattern of life; in a phrase which I have already more than once quoted, and to which I would once more return, it condenses out of the flying vapours of the world an image of human perfection. In all its shapes, in the hands of all the poets, it has for a moment caught some such image of perfection. And it has not only caught the image, but fixed it. This is its quality as art. For that is the function which art alone can perform: not only to apprehend a pattern which subsists behind life, out of which life is created and towards which life moves; but also to make that apprehended pattern permanently visible, to fix and record the momentary image as it flashes and disappears.

Thus the movement of poetry, while in one aspect, and that the more obvious, it is irregular, interrupted, seemingly unaccountable, is, if we regard it in another aspect, continuous and organic. The pattern with which it is concerned, which it seeks, finds and records, manifests itself here and there, now and then; glimpses of it are caught and withdrawn. The poets appear irregularly, now in groups and again singly, sometimes clearly following some development, some line or current of imaginative advance, sometimes seemingly in isolation or in opposition. They come before or behind their age, or dropped into their age, as it were, out of another. Poetry brightens and dwindles: now it burns with a wide steady glow, now it concentrates into a brilliant point. Sometimes for a whole age, and in a whole area or period of civilisation, it seems to disappear: only after it has rekindled elsewhere can men, looking back, realise that its life was in fact continuous; that the unpoetical periods were those in which the life of poetry was undergoing a change, and that in that change the movement, which is its life, then consisted. But while fragments of the pattern are successively made visible by the poets, the pattern itself is one; it is the single perfection attainable by the single thing to which we give the name of life. Only the pattern itself is not a fixed and imposed pattern; it also, no less than life, is alive. To put it into words is like drawing a flame; it can never be drawn alike twice, because it never looks the same twice, although it is the same flame.

Poetry, on its formal and technical side, is patterned language; and language likewise, being one of the ways of giving expression to life, is alive and perpetually in movement. Each race has its own language; and within a single race the language alters, changes colour, shifts its outline, with each generation. Even this is understating the case; for within the same country and the same period, the language of no two people is quite the same, if they each use language imaginatively, if, that is to say, it is alive in their hands and a function of their own live personality. All poets use language thus; and so it is, that alike in its substantial and its formal character, poetry presents this double aspect. On the one hand, it is a single continuous vital movement, being the pattern and expressive function of a single thing, life; and its form is similarly a single continuous creation of pattern in a single material, language. On the other hand, it is in substance, the aggregate of an infinite number of luminous spaces, as one might say, in which for a moment some point or aspect of life is caught, takes shape and is thus fixed for record and in some sense made permanent; and in form, an endless tissue of patterned language, in which, as it flows off the loom, the pattern is perpetually varying, not only from country to country and from age to age, but in the same age and country from poet to poet, and in the same poet from moment to moment.

To the historian, it is the movement, the progress and flux of poetry, that is most prominent, that most engages attention and invites appreciation; and thus we have histories of poetry, in which the poetical product of some country or period is methodically arranged, enumerated, and criticised; in which the growth, culmination, and decay of some particular form of poetry are traced and examined; in which, for the space under survey, we are given a reasoned catalogue of poets and their works.

The theorist or analyst approaches poetry in a different spirit. Working on the material arranged for him by the historian, he classifies the extant product of poetry under heads, assigning to each its particular mark and quality; he collects and disposes metrical forms, methods of handling, styles of composition; he makes those generalisations which are afterwards erected into laws, and rule, or are thought to rule, the practice of poets, until it is found that they are not laws at all, but merely provisional theories or convenient summaries of facts; that they have become obsolete or useless, that poetry has moved away from them, and that the laws of poetry are like the laws of life, a secret.

To a larger and more profound view, however, poetry appears not only as a movement, but as a substance, solid, continuous, and in a sense unchangeable. We may be reminded of the majestic passage of Lucretius[1] in which he sets forth, with unsurpassed force and impressiveness, the double doctrine of the perpetual movement, the racing speed, of the atoms and the worlds, and the eternal balance and peace of the whole universe, and illustrates it by one of his noblest similes, that of the great army filling a whole plain with the glitter and thunder of its movement; " Yet there is some place on the mountain heights from which they seem to stand still, a steady brightness upon the plains."

> " Et tamen est quidam locus altis montibus unde
> Stare videntur, et in campis consistere fulgor."

That steady brightness, the sum total of a complex, multitudinous and ceaseless movement, also belongs to poetry. Subtle and ethereal as it is, fragile and fleeting as its incarnations appear to be, poetry is nevertheless more real, more substantial than those flying

[1] *De Rerum Natura*, ii. 308–332.

vapours which constitute what we call the real world, and which in poetry are condensed and acquire permanence; which in poetry, and in poetry alone, become real in the highest sense. Though it is perpetually in movement, though indeed it *is* movement, one might say of it, as of the ether of the physicists, that—I quote Clerk Maxwell's words—it "is certainly the largest, and probably the most uniform body of which we have any knowledge." The analogy is fertile; it becomes still more impressive if we turn to the statement of the most recent physical doctrine. "I am now," Sir Oliver Lodge writes in his treatise on the Ether of Space, " able to advocate a view of the ether which makes it not only uniformly present and all-pervading, but also massive and substantial beyond conception. It is turning out to be by far the most substantial thing—perhaps the only substantial thing —in the material universe. Compared to ether the densest matter, such as lead or gold, is a filmy gossamer structure, like a comet's tail." More than that; matter is composed of ether; what we call solids are composed of the one fluid. Anything which we call material, be it an atom or a world, is a specifically modified portion of ether: it is the ether doing something. And the ether, so far as we can define it, is itself an energy, a movement; and yet that movement is, in its sum, rest. " Matter seems to have no grip of it," Sir Oliver Lodge goes on to say : " all potential energy exists in it. It may vibrate and it may rotate, but it is stationary— the most stationary body we know; our standard of rest." In some such way we may regard poetry likewise ; and it will add a new force and meaning to what has been said about poetry by great thinkers, and by the poets themselves, when they have assigned to poetry a greater permanence, a more solid reality, than can be claimed for anything else made or handled by mankind.

This is the transcendental aspect of poetry, regarded as a permanent essence, an universal energy. But poetry in that sense is, like the universal ether, incognisable to our senses; we can only see and feel it, we can only know of it, through the matter which it creates, and in which it manifests itself. Poetry as materialised in poems, in the actual product of poets, is what we can actually see and handle. This matter, this embodiment of poetry in poems, is always changing, and we can realise that in its changes it follows certain lines of force, certain streams of vital progress. The idea of progress involves the ideas of space and time; in the sense in which poetry is a spiritual ether, an all-pervading energy, it is independent of space and time; but poetry as we know it is the progressive manifestation or materialisation, in poets and their poems, of part after part of the total perfection. The images in which poetry consists are always being woven and unwoven, condensing and disappearing. The work of the poets is only to be realised and appreciated in the light of this movement; and conversely, the movement itself, the progress of poetry which has throughout and from first to last been the subject of our consideration, is only to be realised through acquaintance with the work of the poets. To understand what poetry in itself is, we must understand the actual poems—or some of them at least—in which poetry has found progressive expression.

Such understanding is not a merely intellectual process; it is imaginative, and as such creative. It is the interpretation of poetry, to ourselves or to others, in some such way as poetry itself is the interpretation of life. Poetry does not merely interpret, it effectually creates the world: and so by a strict and real analogy, the reading of poetry, to be effective, must re-create the poetry read, must re-poetise it. The image of perfection, once materialised in words by the imaginative force of the poet, has to be relit or rekindled by the sympathetic imagination of the lover of poetry.

This process can be perpetually repeated; it has to be perpetually repeated. And though repeated, it is always with a difference. The new mind brings with it to the recorded image a new imaginative quality, new associations, new experience. Thus it is, that while the stimulus, the quickening power, of the poet is potentially permanent, is capable, even in a distant age, and to people speaking a different language, of renewing its effective power as an interpretation of life, the interpretation of poetry is equally endless, and the next word always remains to be said about any poet and any poem.

Whether we regard poetry transcendentally as an universal essence, or historically as a progress manifested in the extant work of poets, from Homer or the predecessors of Homer down to the present moment, it is alike true that poetry is one thing, just as life itself is one thing. Wherever we touch it, we find it, at that point, in that concrete instance or manifestation, organically connected with all other poetry. Our study of its progress may be taken up at any point; for, at any point, it is in the line of historical descent and ascent, and connected vitally with other poetry, not merely that of the same poet or the same school, or the same nation and language, but with all poetry from first to last. We cannot stop anywhere, and separate any poet from his environment, both the more immediate environment of his own time, and the larger environment of the times which together with his own constitute one single movement, one pattern endlessly woven.

It is useful, however, in studying poetry either as an essence or as a movement, to concentrate upon the great poets. We may thus escape being bewildered by multiplicity of detail; we shall be dealing with poetry at its highest power and in its clearest manifestation; in them we shall find centres of force in relation to which the streams of tendency group themselves, fixed points which signal to one another.

In dealing with our own poetry, I have attempted to deal with it in this spirit. In my opening lecture, I went back to Gray's Ode, as the classical text of a doctrine and practice which are still applicable. The actual progress of poetry, regarded from our point of view, as it falls into perspective when seen from the place we occupy, followed certain main historical lines.

The statement of the progress of poetry given by Gray, "from Greece to Italy, and from Italy to England," is almost baldly simple. It is true, and we shall always find occasion to go back to it for guidance. But it is not the whole truth, as he himself knew, and as we, with an immensely widened range of knowledge, cannot for a moment fail to realise. On all sides, at every point, it must be enlarged and amplified. Even of the progress of poetry in Europe it gives a very incomplete account; and Europe is not, and never was, separate from the other continents which reach down upon the Mediterranean basin. Extra-European influences have gone largely towards determining the progress even of strictly European poetry; and of much poetry written in Europe it would be either untrue, or all but meaningless, to say that it is strictly European. This applies to Greek poetry itself, although Greek poetry approximates more nearly than most others to being a native and indigenous growth. Ionia was in direct touch with that Asiatic East to which it geographically belongs. The Iliad is not without significant traces of a non-European element. The Greek lyric, the Greek drama, both incorporate Asiatic factors, and represent an outgrowth of poetry quickened by foreign fertilisation. The later Alexandrian schools of Greek poetry, as their very name implies, sprang up in an environment where East and West interacted upon one another: Egypt and Syria, even when under Greek rule and even where most largely Hellenised, remained essentially what they had been, provinces of an Asiatic Empire. After the central life of poetry had passed to Italy, the African poets of the fourth century had an important, possibly a decisive share in effecting the movement of transformation by which the germs of Romance poetry, as distinguished from Latin poetry, were created, and in thus initiating the Middle Ages. In the Middle Ages themselves, a wholly foreign influence, that of Arab and Arabo-Persian poetry, acting through Provence and Sicily as well as more directly, infused new blood, new forms, a new imaginative interpretation of life, into both the earlier French and the later and more centrally classic Italian poetry. As we approach nearer modern times, we can see the movement of poetry widening, its progress becoming more multiplex. It passed from Italy to England as Gray says: but that passage took place very largely through France; and the affiliation of English to French poetry is now recognised as a fact on which full stress must be laid alongside of the direct main movement of poetry from Italy to England. It is so with Chaucer; with whom indeed the risk is of over-stressing the French and under-stressing the Italian parentage. It is so with the whole Elizabethan age: it is so with Dryden and the Augustans. The eighteenth and nineteenth centuries have gone on further towards the merging of separate streams of progress into an œcumenical movement. It has been becoming more and more the case that all poetry is in touch with all other poetry. Any new poetical movement now, through the diffusion of knowledge and the intercommunication of ideas, almost at once affects the whole movement of poetry as a common art and a common inheritance throughout the world.

This integrating process in poetry itself as a human art, and a function of human life, has been reflected in a corresponding integration of criticism. The great poets still remain, as they always have been and always will be, unique, apart, and individual. But the art of poetry is felt as one art and not many; its progress is the progress, through many poets, each in his own time and manner sharing a single inspiration, of an impulse and an achievement belonging to the whole human race.

The integration of criticism is the task which any exponent of poetry must now keep before him as a guiding and controlling motive. In fuller terms the matter may be expressed thus. Any poem, or more largely, any work of art, is the projection and materialisation, upon a particular point and in a particular manner, of the vital and universal imagination, which is the essence or soul of art: the making visible, in a recorded and thus in some sense a permanent shape, of some part of that pattern of life towards which all

THE PROGRESS OF POETRY 319

art is directed. In all art there is a common element, for all life, the whole vital process and progress of existence, bears to some extent the same interpretation, though in variable perspective, in a multiplicity of colours and tones. Yet the interpretation is always different, because it is always personal and individual. Poetry can be regarded either as a process of historic evolution, or, apart from the forms of time and space, as the invisible movement—visible, that is to say, not in itself but only in the matter which it creates—which one can only define by saying that it underlies all else, that it is substance, energy, life.

We stand now at a point following the end of a century of extraordinary poetical production. That century includes great names in the poetry of other countries and languages; but the main life, the central current of poetry, has throughout it been in England and the English-speaking world. The wonderful outburst of poetry which began with the *Lyrical Ballads* of 1798 opened a period during which the progress of poetry was as visible as it was splendid. The last of the great Victorian poets have now passed away. There is a feeling that the progress of poetry has come to a pause, that poetry is for a time exhausted by its own fertility. But more than that there is a feeling, in some quarters at least, that poetry itself is exhausted, that it has said its word, given its interpretation, fulfilled its progress.

This at least is a mere fallacy. Poetry, as the imaginative interpretation of life, is a function of life which must continue its movement so long as the movement of life itself continues. The world cannot live on the art of the past. That art is indeed not of the past only; it is an existing and living force. It has become, in a sense, part of life. But just as the patterns of life which it created call for continually fresh interpretations, so life calls to be rewoven in continually fresh patterns.

Criticism, in the highest sense of that ambiguous word, that is to say, the interpretation and re-creation of extant and inherited poetry, new or old, can never exhaust itself so long as poetry exists. Poetry, the interpretation and re-creation of life, can never exhaust itself so long as life exists. Both, each in its own sphere, are a perpetual progress, an endless integration. And there is, as I have elsewhere indicated, another reason why there must always be new poetry. It is this; that poetry will always be, somewhere and by some minds, neglected or misunderstood; and it is just this neglect or this misunderstanding which new poetry is needed in order to correct. For the same imaginative effort and impulse which enter anew into past poetry and thrill to it vitally, likewise, and as part of the same process, create poetry afresh. If at any time past poetry fails from the living virtue which it once had, a new poetical instinct must arise to redeem the failure: and that instinct not only vivifies the old poetry, but creates new. The two movements are theoretically distinct, but actually inseparable.

A time in which poetry as a creative vital process should cease, and a future age find all its wants in that direction satisfied by continuing to read Wordsworth, is only thinkable if the creative instinct were to cease likewise. It can hardly be made more grotesque by being put in different language: that the affairs of the Muses should be wound up, and the shareholders live on the capital realised by the liquidation as long as it lasted. That could not be long; it would very soon be used up, would dissolve and disappear. But indeed it is not thinkable even thus: for if the creative instinct ceased, the appreciative instinct, which is the same thing working on a different plane, would cease likewise, at the same time, by one and the same movement. Poetry would be dead in both senses. Poetry is not a thing, it is an energy: as Aristotle defined it, a productive energy: and when a productive energy ceases to produce, it ceases to exist at all. If the art of the living poet became extinct, the poetry of past ages would become dead art. The dead praise thee not, neither any that go down into silence.

Nor is it true that criticism and poetry are in some way hostile to one another. Criticism in its true sense is simply appreciation, and it would be plainly absurd to say that art cannot live or thrive when it is appreciated. The progress of poetry has its periodic movement, as all vital functions have. So has the progress of criticism; and the two periods do not coincide: but neither do they alternate. It is nearer the truth to say that, when poetry is at a low vitality, poetical criticism also tends to lower its lights, to stiffen and become mechanical. But it is just at that period of its declension that it turns from its higher function to another which, though useful and even necessary, is lower, that of analysing and classifying, of accumulating and assorting facts. It spreads itself out over this occupation; and thus its bulk may be largest, and its seeming importance greatest, when it is doing its work least powerfully and least effectually.

The feeling, so often expressed, that the present time is in the sphere of poetry a critical and not a creative age, is partly the expression of the fact that we have behind us, extending over the first three quarters of the nineteenth century, a period of immense and brilliant poetic production which makes the periods both before and after it pale by comparison; partly the result of another fact which perhaps receives insufficient notice, that the appreciation of poetry, poetical criticism in its higher and truer sense, has in the last generation enormously increased, both in width and in depth. Neither of these facts is in the least to be lamented; both on the contrary are grounds for gratitude and satisfaction. We are too apt to forget that nearly all the great poets of the past reached, in their own time, but a small audience, and often met with neglect where they did not meet with abuse. The decay of poetry, like the degeneration of mankind, is one of those illusions which seem eternal and unconquerable. Despondency over the actual case of poetry, gloomy apprehensions for its future, are no peculiar feature of this age. The golden past merely means the luminous haze over a horizon which shifts with our advance. 'Tis distance lends enchantment to the view. Our own dull foreground will in time take on the same enchantment.

Again and again, as we shall find if we take the pains to look, the cry over the decay of poetry has been raised most piercingly when poetry was in point of fact taking a new advance, achieving a new perfection, opening out a new world; not in times of decay, but in times of germination, or even of full flower. Τίς δέ κεν ἄλλου ἀκούσαι; "What new poetry is worth listening to?" is the murmur of Theocritus when he was creating, and bringing to perfection, a new and far-ranging type of poetry, of extraordinary beauty, and of no less extraordinary influence: for the Theocritean pastoral at once became, and has ever since remained, one important mode of the poetical interpretation of life. *Omnia iam volgata*, " poetry is used up," is the echoing complaint of Virgil, when, at the point of junction between the old and the new world, he was consummating the one, looking forward into and opening out the other. Spenser's *Tears of the Muses* is one long wail over the degradation and dissolution of poetry in England.

> " Heaps of huge words uphoarded hideously,
> With horrid sound though having little sense,
> They think to be chief praise of poetry,
> And thereby wanting due intelligence
> Have marred the face of goodly Poesy
> And made a monster of their fantasy."

So he wrote just at the time when, in his own hands and those of his followers or colleagues, poetry was creating itself anew and breaking out into the full splendours of the Elizabethan age. Milton never failed in his own sublime arrogance; yet even he, when *Paradise Lost* was more than half written, doubted whether " an age too late " might not have damped his wing and be fatal to his ascent. Blake's lovely lines on the disappearance of the Muses not only contradict what they purport to convey, but are one of the early preludes to a chorus which soon began to swell and deepen.

> " Whether on Ida's shady brow,
> Or in the chambers of the East,
> The chambers of the Sun, that now
> From ancient melody have ceased:
>
> Whether in Heaven ye wander fair,
> Or the green corners of the earth,
> Or the blue regions of the air
> Where the melodious winds have birth:

324   THE PROGRESS OF POETRY

> Whether on crystal rocks ye rove,
> Beneath the bosom of the sea,
> Wandering in many a coral grove,
> Fair Nine, forsaking Poetry!
>
> How have you left the ancient love
> That bards of old enjoyed in you!
> The languid strings do scarcely move,
> The sound is forced, the notes are few."

Nothing of languor here at least; no scantness of notes, no forcing of the sound. And before Blake died, there had been added to English poetry all Byron, all Shelley, all Keats, all that is most precious of Coleridge and Wordsworth. Among modern poets we can see that the complaint has almost become common form, much as the invocation of the Muse used to be. It is recurrent in Tennyson from first to last, from the time when as a boy he thought Byron's death meant the extinction of poetry, to the old age in which he gracefully and half humorously complained that we were made poor by the mass of our own riches, that the love of letters, overdone, had swamped the sacred poets with themselves. It is most marked of all in our own Oxford poet, Arnold. His volume of 1867 includes pieces which are among the permanent treasures of English poetry—*Thyrsis, Dover Beach,* the *Stanzas from the Grande Chartreuse.* But it also contains those verses entitled *The Progress of Poesy* which may claim to be the most dismal of English lyrics; and he prefixed as a motto to the whole volume the less dismal but almost as melancholy quatrain:

> "Though the Muse be gone away,
> Though she move not earth to-day,
> Souls, erewhile who caught her word,
> Ah! still harp on what they heard."

Coming still closer, M. Maeterlinck, in the days, now

receding into distance, when he was a poet, of small production indeed but of strange newness and intangible charm, uttered his musical wail over the imagined disappearance of poetry:

> "J'ai cherché trente ans, mes sœurs,
> Et mes pieds sont las:
> Il était partout, mes sœurs,
> Et n'existe pas."

But there is another source likewise of this pathetic fallacy: it arises from this, that poetry, like the life of which it is a function, moves in a different orbit from the life of the individual. It is rare, if it ever happens at all, that any one preserves into mature and declining years the receptiveness of youth—or more than receptiveness, for it is an active quality, the instinct which leaps to meet new poetry half-way. With many, the sensibility to poetry dwindles, dries up, almost if not wholly disappears. With many more, probably with nearly every one, it can only move along channels already familiar. We return to our first loves, but we cannot take up with new ones. The language of the new poetry is strange to us, and we cannot or will not learn it. Our own poetry, the poetry which we have known and to which we have responded, retains or reassumes much of its old power to move and thrill us. We appreciate it in many ways better. We enter into it more deeply because we bring to it an added depth of experience; and it brings with it a new and perhaps a still more precious power, to uplift, to calm, to console. But upon the newer poetry the older generation is apt to look with a mixture of bewilderment and prejudice. You may remember a striking passage in a letter of Horace Walpole when he was retiring from Parliament in 1768. Public affairs, he writes to

George Montague, have ceased to interest him, and can never again have the charm or the dignity that they once had: "Could I hear oratory beyond my Lord Chatham's? Will there ever be parts equal to Charles Townshend's?" In poetry the complaint is as old as Simonides: κούρων ἐξελέγχει νέος οἶνος οὐ τὸ πέρυσι δῶρον ἀμπέλου, "the new wine of boys cannot rival last year's gift of the vine": the new poetry, like the new wine, οὐκ ἐξελέγχει, "is not convincing."

This is the more so with poetry, because the earlier-known poetry stirred in us not only intelligence and admiration, but passion. Youth looked on it like a lover. Mr. Bradley, in a lecture given from this Chair and now published, on Shelley's view of poetry, summed up that view in a single phrase: "Love talking musically is poetry." And to the lover his own love is the love of beauty at its culmination, of a perfection from which all variations must be for the worse. In all love there is a tinge of jealousy: the personal note tends to become exclusive. "Say, how has thy beloved surpassed so much all others?—*She was mine*." For the lover, in all ages, the object of his love seems, and indeed is, something unique and incomparable.

"O me, what eyes hath love put in my head,
    Which have no correspondence with true sight?"

Love's eyes see the beloved, but to other beauties are blind.

"When she and I shall be lying
    Dust at your feet,
Hours such as these shall be flying,
    Life be as sweet,
Women as lovely hereafter,
    Tender and wise,
Born with her bloom and her laughter—
    Not with her eyes."

The progress of poetry passes away from us, and we fancy that poetry itself is passing away. Poetry indeed, as I have insisted, has a periodical movement of its own; its visible progress is intermittent, not continuous; looking back on its past course, we can see easily how it has here and there, now and then, blazed out in a great poet, and has grown languid and thin in times when there has been no poet of the first order. But looking forward we can see nothing; and even looking on what is immediately about us, after the quick receptiveness of youth is gone and the weariness of weakening life has set in, we must recognise that our eyesight has become imperfect, and that the power of appreciating a new art is a power which has passed, or is passing, from us to a new generation.

For this as well as for other reasons, I have not in the lectures which I have given from this Chair set myself to deal with the poetry which is being produced at the present day, and still less to offer any conjecture as to the line which the central progress of poetry is now taking, or as to its future development. It will not be expected of me, and if it were, it would be idle, to say whether or not we have among us, here in England now, any one who is, actually or potentially, a great poet, one whom a later age will look back upon as belonging to the choir of Helicon and will place on the shining roll which holds the names of five centuries, from Chaucer's to Swinburne's. Time will show that; and "so to him we leave it." But some general considerations may be offered, which rise naturally out of the central view of poetry as a movement, expressing itself in patterns of language which are also moving and alive. And these considerations do not lead to discouragement.

When people speak, as they do, of the increasing

complexity of modern life, the phrase bears two senses, both of them justified by facts. Modern life has, in the first place, a larger bulk of realised past behind it. All that past in some way lives in, is integrated into, the present. Life thus necessarily becomes more complex by the mere efflux of time.

But its realised complexity—the complexity of which we are conscious, and which acts directly on the intellect and imagination—has been increasing with multiplied speed owing to the enormous expansion of knowledge. Apart from the fact that there is more of the past for us to know, we know more of it at any given point than was ever known before. In poetry alone, whole provinces have been added to our knowledge; the stream has widened into a flood.

And again, life is more complex in the sense that we apply to it a larger and more intricate machinery. Our armament for dealing with it—our calculus, in the phrase of the mathematicians—has expanded almost as fast as the material with which it deals. The aggregate complexity over the whole of life is enormous, just as it is in a particular art like that of poetry, or a particular science like that of astronomy.

Again, when they speak of the increasing stress of life, and of its increasing haste, this is only the same thing from another aspect. The increased stress means that more and more of latent force is released and converted into actual energy. The increased haste means that the progress and evolution of life is going on at a quicker pace. Now if poetry be, as it is, a function of life, life at great complexity means poetry of great range; life at high stress means poetry at high tension: life at great speed means poetry in rapid movement. All three together mean that the task set before poetry is larger and higher than ever.

Will poetry prove unequal to it? Will it be evermore a life behind? Rather may we believe that the day's work will be done in the day; that the progress of poetry will follow and sustain the progress of life. Browning, the most keen-sighted and deep-minded, when at his best, of modern poets, has taught us this: indeed it may be called the sum and substance of his teaching. In a well-known passage of *One Word More* he enforces it by an image of unsurpassed splendour, that of the moon turning a new side to her chosen mortal:

"Side unseen of herdsman, huntsman, steersman,
Blank to Zoroaster on his terrace,
Blind to Galileo on his turret,
Dumb to Homer, dumb to Keats—him, even!

There will always be the one word more.

Can there then be poets, now or in the future, so consummate and satisfying, so high in the sphere of poetry, as the great poets of the past, as Homer and Virgil, as Shakespeare and Milton? Rossetti, in a graver mood and with a truer insight than when he spoke of Keats having done everything, gave the real answer in his Sonnets on Old and New Art.

" Were thine eyes set backwards in thine head,
Such words were well; but they see on, and far.
Unto the lights of the great Past, new-lit
Fair for the Future's track, look thou instead."

We can never go beyond perfection; but a new perfection is always before us.

" Though God hath since found none such as these were
To do their work like them, because of this
Stand not ye idle in the market-place.
Which of ye knoweth he is not that last
Who may be first by faith and will? yea, his
The hand which after the appointed days
And hours shall give a Future to their Past?"

To this great end the interpretation of poetry, which is the office of this Chair, is ancillary. It helps, after its measure, to light anew the lights of the great past, to brush away dimness that has crept between, to turn clearer eyes towards them.

Whatever reason there may be for doubt as to the present position of poetry, there are two things to be noted which are encouraging.

The first of these is a notable and widespread advance, both in mastery over the formal technique of patterned language, and in the apprehension of what great poetry really is, and of what all poetry ought to be. Βούλεται ποιεῖν πολλάκις, ἀλλ' οὐ δύναται, says Aristotle of Nature: "She often wishes to make"— yes, or to make poetry, for the word may bear that meaning also—"but cannot." And so too we may say of the poetical instinct, the shaping power of imagination working in patterns of language. But if with the will to make is coupled the knowledge of how to make, the trained skill and sound instinct of the craftsman, the power to make becomes nearer to realisation.

The second encouraging thing is the advance, also widespread and notable, in the standard and quality of poetical criticism in its highest sense, that is to say, in the appreciation of poetry. Increased technical skill and increased appreciation are preparing a way before the feet of poetry. Amid whatever confusion and distraction, beneath whatever apparent languor or decay, this is a time of manifold and rapid germination: the ferment is not that of dissolution, but of quickening. For the flowering and fruitage, for the actual creation of a new and great poetry, it awaits, as it did before Homer, before Virgil, before Milton, the incalculable and unprevisible individual genius. But a future age may look back to the clouded lights which we are apt to regard as a Dusk of the Gods, as the coming of darkness over poetry, and see in them the first flushings of a splendid dawn.

Above all, no inference, and least of all any inference of discouragement, can be drawn from the enormous masses of minor poetry, or what purports to be poetry, which are now being produced; and the greater part of which is, as artistic product, as poetical achievement, worthless. This is no new thing; it is common to all times, and at the times of the greatest poets the output of inferior or bad poetry has very probably been the largest. The uses of minor poetry would make an interesting subject for discussion; but this is not the time and place to enter upon it. It is one of the many tasks I must leave to some successor: *spatiis exclusus iniquis praetereo atque aliis post me memoranda relinquo.* It is one of the doubtful joys of a Professor of Poetry that he is called upon to read, and often asked to give an opinion upon, a great deal of minor poetry. One thing however I may mention as interesting. Here in Oxford, among the "younger gown," the compositions sent in for the Newdigate Prize during my tenure of office have been on a much higher level, both of technical skill and of imaginative value, than they used to be when I acted as an examiner between twenty and thirty years ago. This seems to indicate —I think it does—a larger and better appreciation of poetry among the newer generation. A better appreciation means, economically, a larger demand. But demand creates supply. Artistically, it means a truer and deeper instinct for poetry. But the instinct for poetry is the same instinct which makes poets.

In any case, the production of minor poetry, however excessive we may think it, whatever disadvantages may attach to it, is, in a larger view, only one instance of the enormous wastefulness of Nature. " Of fifty seeds she often brings but one to bear " : the rest she casts as rubbish to the void; or rather, resumes them into herself to be used again. She has the inexhaustible patience of one who has all time and all material at her disposal; to her failures as to her successes she comes with the one inflexible order; *materies opus est, ut crescant postera secla*. And to the minor poets also, Poetry herself comes by glimpses.

> "We have gone by many lands and many grievous ways,
> And yet have we not found this Pleasure all these days.
> Sometimes a lightening all about her have we seen,
> A glittering of her garments among the fieldes green,
> Sometimes the waving of her hair that is right sweet,
> A lifting of her eyelids or a shining of her feet,
> Or either in sleeping or in waking have we heard
> A rustling of raiment or a whispering of a word,
> Or a noise of pleasant water running over a waste place,
> Yet have I not beheld her nor known her very face."

To any among my audience who feel in them an instinct for poetry I have only one word to say. Do not spend life indefinitely on school exercises. Remember that to be an art-student is no life in itself, but only as it leads to being an artist, a creator. Do not sink into the barren work of copying or inventing or elaborating ornament, which is not poetry, but only material for poetry, only has meaning or value in relation to constructive and imaginative design. Study, but produce. Design, create, execute. And when you have done this, it will not be amiss to remember Horace's advice about suppression until the ninth year.

And for the rest, for those who are not actual or potential poets, but who love poetry, I would say this; if we fix our minds firmly on the Progress of Poetry, on poetry as a thing perpetually moving, living, reincarnating, we shall not only hold the central clue to its meaning, but be assured of its immortality, and of our own.

> "That one face, far from vanish, rather grows,
> And decomposes but to recompose,
> Become my universe that feels and knows."

This is the last lecture which I give as Professor of Poetry. I cannot quit the office to which the favour of the University appointed me five years ago without some word of farewell. He that putteth off his harness is seldom, if ever, under any temptation to boast; and it is in no boastful spirit, but in humility and gratitude, that I may speak to-day of the honour and the responsibility of the position from which I now retire. The quinquennate seems, at the end of it, a mere swallow-flight through a lighted hall from darkness into darkness. A son of Oxford must needs feel towards that elderly but irrepressible enchantress an affection which he hardly asks or expects her to reciprocate. He murmurs to her with his last breath,

> "But thou, O mother,
> The dreamer of dreams,
> Wilt thou bring forth another
> To feel the sun's beams,
> When I move among shadows a shadow, and wail by impassable streams?"

The reply of Oxford to this agonised question is a quiet but emphatic affirmative. A generation ago, or less, there was indeed, or so the rumour has reached me, some project or suggestion—a vapour which floated on the skirts of more massive schemes of reform—for extinguishing the Poetry Professorship, and devoting its modest endowments to scientific purposes. Certainly it would be ground for a sharper pain than that of regret if I thought that any such project were likely to be revived, and that colour might be given to it by the ineffectiveness or inadequacy of the Professor who is now laying down his office. But I hope and believe that the University will show herself, as ever, generous to the weakness of her children and servants, and constant to the ideals which they, as well as she, try to the best of their ability to inculcate and to pursue. The exponents of letters pass away; the Republic of Letters is immortal. It is in this belief that I make way for a twenty-fifth occupant of the Chair which the University of Oxford, for its own honour and for that of poetry, has maintained for two hundred years.

Date Due